# Imperative of Economic Growth in the Eurozone

## Competitiveness, Capital Flows and Structural Reforms

**Lubor Lacina**
Mednel University in Brno, Czech Republic

**Antonin Rusek**
Susquehanna University, Pennsylvania

(Editors)

**Vernon Series in Economics**

VERNON PRESS

www.vernonpress.com

*In the Americas:*
Vernon Press
1000 N West Street,
Suite 1200, Wilmington,
Delaware 19801
United States

*In the rest of the world:*
Vernon Press
C/Sancti Espiritu 17,
Malaga, 29006
Spain

Vernon Series in Economics

Library of Congress Control Number: 2017948007

ISBN: 978-1-62273-263-0

# Table of Contents

# List of Authors

**István Benczes**, Institute of World Economy, Corvinus University, Budapest, Hungary

**Carsten Colombier**, Federal Finance Department, Bern, Switzerland and Institute for Public Economics, University of Cologne, Germany

**Zdenek Kudrna**, University of Salzburg, Austria

**Gabor Kutasi,** Corvinus University, Budapest, Hungary

**Stanisław Kasiewicz, Lech Kurkliński,** ALTERUM Centre for Research and Analysis of Financial System, Warsaw School of Economics, Warsaw, Poland

**Jarosław Kundera,** Institute of Economics, University of Wroclaw, Wroclaw, Poland

**Lubor Lacina,** Mednel University in Brno, Czech Republic

**Rajmund Mirdala,** Faculty of Economics, Technical University of Kosice, Kosice, Slovakia

**Antonín Rusek**, Susquehanna University, Pennsylvania, USA

**Roman Stöllinger**, The Vienna Institute for International Economic Studies, Vienna, Austria

**Václav Šmejkal, Stanislav Šaroch,** ŠKODA AUTO University o.p.s., Mlada Boleslav, Czech Republic

# List of Abbreviations

| | |
|---|---|
| ADF | Augmented Dickey-Fuller |
| AG | Advocates General |
| AGS | Annual Growth Survey |
| AIC | Akaike Information Criterion |
| AMECO | Annual Macro-economic Database |
| AMR | Alert Mechanism Report |
| ARDL | Autoregressive Distributed Lag |
| CABP | Cyclically Adjusted Primary Balance |
| CIT | Corporate Income Tax |
| CJEU | Court of Justice of European Union |
| CMU | Capital Markets Union |
| COFOG | Classification of the Functions of Government |
| CSR | Country-specific Recommendations |
| CT | Constitutional Treaty |
| DG Employment | Directorate-General for Employment |
| ECB | European Central Bank |
| ECI | Export Complexity Index |
| ECJ | European Court of Justice |
| ECOFIN | Economic and Financial Affairs Council |
| EDP | Excessive Deficit Procedure |
| EFSF | European Financial Stability Facility |
| EFSI | European Fund for Strategic Investments |
| EIP | Excessive Imbalance Procedure |
| EMU | Economic and Monetary Union |
| ESCB | European System of Central Banks |
| ESF | European Social Fund |
| ETUC | European Trade Union Confederation |
| EU | European Union |
| EU-15 | First 15 Member States of the EU |
| EU-19 | 19 Current Members of the Eurozone |
| EU-28 | 28 Current Member States |

| | |
|---|---|
| FE | Fixed Effects |
| FR | Fiscal Rule |
| FTT | Financial Transaction Tax |
| GDP | Gross Domestic Product |
| GNI | Gross National Income |
| HC | Heteroscedasticity-consistent |
| HICP | Harmonised Index of Consumer Prices |
| IMF | International Monetary Fund |
| IR | Interest Rate |
| IRR | Interest Rate Shock |
| IV | Instrumental Variables |
| LSE | Least Qquares Estimators |
| LTR | Long-term Interest Rates |
| MIP | Macroeconomic Imbalance Procedure |
| MT | Maastricht Dummy |
| MTO | Medium-term Budgetary Objectives |
| NATO | North Atlantic Treaty Organization |
| NPE | New Political Economy |
| OCA | Optimum Currency Area |
| OECD | Organisation for Economic Co-operation and Development |
| OG | Output Gap |
| OLS | Ordinary Least Qquares |
| OMT | Outright Monetary Transactions |
| OPP | Observance of the Principle of Proportionality |
| PIGS | States of Portugal, Italy, Ireland, Greece and Spain |
| PIT | Personal Income Tax |
| PP | Phillips-Perron |
| RQMV | Reverse Qualified Majority Voting Procedure in the Council |
| SE | Standart Errors |
| SGP | Stability and Growth Pact |
| SIC | Schwarz Information Criterion |
| SME | Small and Medium-sized Enterprises |
| SNA | System of National Accounts |
| SVAR | Structural Vector Autoregression |
| TEU | Treaty on European Union |

| | |
|---|---|
| TFEU | Treaty on Functioning of the European Union |
| TFP | Total Factor Productivity |
| TI | Tradability Index |
| TS | Tradability Scores |
| TSCG | Treaty on Stability, Coordination and Governance |
| UK | United Kingdom |
| US | United States [of America] |
| VAT | Value Added Tax |
| VAX | Value Added Export |
| WIOD | World Input-Output Database |

# List of Tables

# List of figures

# Abstract

## Ch.1, Growth and the Real Convergence in the Eurozone

## (Lacina, Rusek)

**Abstract**: The mixture of the recent EU policies – mainly the "fiscal compact" and the OMT approach by the ECB – restored the nominal stability for the Eurozone and therefore preserved the common currency. However, the same steps resulted in a widening gap between the Northern tier and the Mediterranean countries. To address this issue – which is potentially a mortal threat to the Eurozone in its present configuration – the three policy options are available: A restoration of a real convergence, the Eurozone's restructuring or a "muddling through". The first two require radical policy steps which in the present political and economic climate are commonly considered unlikely. That leaves "muddling through" as the likeliest future approach. However, its inherent ad hoc nature breeds uncertainty, which, combined with a complacency stemming from the recent "successes" increases the possibility of a destructive future dynamics.

## Ch.2, Does Baumol's Cost Disease Produce Adverse Growth?

## (Colombier)

**Abstract:** Based on a panel of 23 OECD countries this chapter shows that the government sector is partly contracted by Baumol's cost disease. We provide empirical evidence that not only total government expenditure but also public expenditure on health, education and general administration are affected by Baumol's cost disease. As we show, Baumol's cost disease produces adverse consequences under a balanced budget rule such as a debt brake. Governments face a serious dilemma. Breaching the rule would certainly cause reputational losses for governments, which might affect their borrowing costs and therefore, the sustainability of public finances. Adhering to the balanced-budget rule means risking budget-crowding out of cost-disease affected public expenditure with an ensuing long-run deterioration of these services and/ or foregoing growth opportunities. Governments of the EU member states and EU policy makers should therefore revise the EU Fiscal

Compact to reconcile it with Baumol's cost disease. Additionally, we apply outlier-robust estimation methods, which are particularly suited to deal with the distinct heterogeneity of panel datasets.

## Ch.3, Fiscal Union under Unsustainability of Public Debt (Kutasi)

**Abstract:** Some EU members faced years of crisis in the first half of the 2010s with an excessive initial public debt, but several others had broad room for fiscal stimulus. However, the prolonged duration of the European economic depression expended public budgets, while exhausting stimulus policies and sovereign solvency. Meanwhile, one of the ways out of depression is a proposed centralization of the EU through fiscal union. Are the eurozone countries ready to participate in a risk pool in public finances? The study seeks to answer this question. The chapter presents the hypothesis that the sustainability of public finances deteriorated during the global and euro crisis in the majority of eurozone member countries and in the EU, and this phenomenon is discouraging the core countries from seeking the fiscal union. The analysis uses the Blanchard indicators of fiscal sustainability and the sovereign risk rating of the EURO-18 and EU-28 countries. The analysis presents as results a theoretical summary of fiscal sustainability, the development of fiscal sustainability in the EU member states, indicators of convergence or divergence of fiscal sustainability in the Community, and conclusions based on the indicators of the likelihood of a fiscal union.

## Ch.4, The Principle of Proportionality (Kasiewicz, Kurkliński)

**Abstract:** This is an attempt to assess regulatory impact with reference to a popular principle of proportionality. It undergoes large modifications; its interpretation is broadened and it gets adapted to the factual assessment of legislative processes. The principle of proportionality includes three significant elements: adequacy, necessity and proportionality sensu stricto. The proposed method in the law-making process comes down to three stages. The first one is interpretation of the subjective scope of at least three abovementioned components. The second stage consists in transformation of the adopted scope into clear and quite simple criteria. The third stage is attributing relevant measures to particular criteria. The proposed approach to regulatory impact assessment has been termed as the model of the

Observance of the Principle of Proportionality. The authors present the model assumptions, identify and particularize the criteria of main areas of the principle of proportionality and then determine its scoring methods. The final result of the chapter is a synthetic calculation: an ordered measure of the observance of the principle of proportionality for a specific regulation.

## Ch.5, Fiscal Policy of the EU Countries in the Time of Crisis

## (Kundera)

**Abstract:** In a situation as deep a crisis as 2008 the EU countries have carried out policy to restore macroeconomic equilibrium comprising various fiscal instruments. They have not opted for the classic methods of fight against the crisis by increasing public expenditure, but favored rather austerity programs to restore budgetary balance by increase taxes and reduce budgetary expenditure. Taking into consideration the economic consequences of these fiscal policy the main objective of this chapter is to examine the evolution of the budgetary revenue and expenditure in the EU member states during the economic crisis. On the basis of the statistical data the analysis shows the EU members significantly reshaped the tax structure during the crisis with noticeable shift from direct taxes to indirect taxes as a less harmful for economic growth. Increasing the consumption taxes in the EU members was accompanied by "fiscal devaluation" in direct taxation due to CIT rates reduction. Furthermore the economic crisis has influenced not only budgetary revenue in member countries, but also budgetary expenditure, where their share in GDP after a short-lived increase finally has been reduced. Empirical estimates for Euro Area have revealed that taxes changes appeared to imply lower multiplier than public spending, so tax increase usually entail lower effects on GDP and unemployment than austerity policy.

## Ch.6, Inflation Expectations and Long-term Interest Rates

## (Mirdala)

**Abstract:** Recent deflationary pressures and ultra-low interest rate environment in the Euro Area revealed fundamentally specific implications for the evaluation of monetary policy effectiveness. Redefinition of traditional views on price stability and the role of inflation expectations under near zero level inflation environment draws attention of increasing number of empirical studies. Changing contribution of inflation expectations and expected real interest rates to the long-term interest rates determination represent one of the most important implications of the recent deflationary periods in the Euro Area. In the chapter we employ SVAR methodology to identify inflation expectations and expected real interest rates shocks and calculate variance decomposition and impulse-response functions of long-term nominal interest rates. Our research revealed considerable differences in the role of inflation expectations and expected real interest rates shocks in determining long-term interest rates between core and periphery countries of the Euro Area. The crisis period even intensified this trend.

## Ch.7, Social Market Economy Leading the EU out of the Gridlock?

## (Šmejkal, Šaroch)

**Abstract:** From the entry into force of the Lisbon Treaty, the EU has, among its constitutional objectives, the goal of achieving a highly competitive social market economy. At the same time, however, the EU has not been given any specific powers to actively develop its social policy, and having to cope in parallel with the economic and fiscal crisis, it has given preference rather to austerity than to social welfare. After more than seven years of legal force of the Lisbon Treaty there is still no clarity on how should the EU interpret the legacy of German post-war *Sozialmarktwirtschaft;* whether it should strive for its own economic and social "Constitution", or whether it can try to fulfil the objective of social market economy through the existing instruments of EU law and policy measures. The chapter argues that some, rather partial, measures enacted by the EU would be desirable and feasible without creating a danger of over-regulation that would threaten the freedoms of the internal market or distort the existing division of powers between the EU and the Member States in the social field. The social market economy concept, being itself a compromise between the free markets and social welfare requirements, can act there as a guarantee that neither unbounded market freedoms nor socializing policies would dominate the EU.

## Ch. 8, Revisiting Baumol's "Growth Disease"

## (Stöllinger)

**Abstract:** This chapter integrates the tradability index into a growth framework. This newly developed index captures the extent to which an economy specialises in the production of tradable output. It can equally be interpreted as the predicted openness of a country given its economic structure. I embed the tradability index into a cross-country growth model to test a tradability-based variant of Baumol's growth disease. According to this hypothesis, countries that specialise in the production of tradable goods grow faster due to (i) higher productivity growth in tradable-goods producing sectors and (ii) the lack of demand constraints given the Abstract.opportunities to sell on the world market. The prediction is confirmed for a sample of mainly European OECD and non-OECD countries though the impacts depend on countries' stage of development.

## Ch. 9, Are Fiscal Rules Really Omnipotent? The Case of the EU

## (Benczes)

**Abstract:** The reform of economic governance in the European Union has recently targeted four major areas: (1) strengthening fiscal discipline by tough fiscal rules; (2) establishing solid institutional mechanisms for an effective crisis management and resolution; (3) creating joint guarantee for national government debt; and (4) laying down the foundations of a fiscal union. The strengthening of fiscal rules has been the aim of both the so-called six-pack and the fiscal compact. As far as crisis resolution is concerned, the EU has created the European Stability Mechanism. Issuing joint guarantees on national debts did provoke harsh debates in the EU, but no real deal has been achieved yet on euro-bonds. The idea of a fiscal union, however, does not seem to be a short or medium term priority for most of European policy makers. In fact, there is no consensus on the very meaning of a fiscal union in the EU. In turn, this study critically evaluates the consequences of adopting stricter fiscal rules and it also reflects on the main concepts and ideas concerning a European fiscal union. In harmony with the literature, the chapter argues that rules could significantly contribute to the effectiveness of fiscal adjustments. More importantly, however, it can be also demonstrated that the most successful episodes were the ones where fiscal rules were adopted only *after* the start of the deceleration of the gross public debt-to-GDP ratios. In consequence, domestic rules were hardly the sole triggering factors of maintaining fiscal discipline; rather, they served as the key elements of a comprehensive consolidation package. It can be safely argued, therefore, that the most successful countries decided to adopt fiscal rules not because they wished to stop fiscal profligacy at some time in the future (as the most recently adopted fiscal compact envisions it), but because these countries wanted to explicitly signal their strong commitment to fiscal discipline in the present. In other words, it is not fiscal rules (or a fiscal compact) *per se* what matters in delivering fiscal stability, but a strong political commitment and national ownership in particular. As far as the prospect of a fiscal union is concerned, the study provides a detailed analysis of both the expenditure and the revenue sides of national general governments and makes it clear that a fiscal union might not be a realistic scenario even in the longer future.

## Ch. 10, Reforming the Eurozone: at Mercy of Politics (Kudrna)

**Abstract:** The Eurozone was stabilized by the non-orthodox monetary policy of the European Central Bank as well as the set of reforms including the European Stability Mechanism and the Banking Union. At the same time, the institutional architecture of the Eurozone remains incomplete and requires introduction of some elements of fiscal and political union. While there is no shortage of recommendations for economic reforms, the most binding constraint is political. The Eurozone member states seem unable to agree on further reforms, even though they all agree that these are necessary. The result is a "muddling through", when the minimalist reforms are agreed upon at the latest possible moment and only under pressure of acute crisis. This chapter briefly outlines political economy constraints on alternative reform scenarios as well as some low-probability high-impact factors that could alter the Eurozone reform path. However, it concludes that the muddling through strategy is likely to remain dominant.

# Introduction

Contributions in this volume explore the economic performance of the European Union, the underlying trends, and economic policies. Emphasis is placed on the post-2008 period – e.g. the "Euro Crisis" and its aftermath period. The experiences and the functioning of the European Economic and Monetary Union will be explored in the environment of twofold challenges of EU expansion (post-2004) and the increasingly globalized world economy.

European economic recovery appears to be taking hold. So is European crisis over? The acute phase of the crisis passed, however, the medium and the long-term issues remain to be answered. The current fiscal stabilization has been achieved, restoring the stability of the Euro. The policies of the "internal devaluations" are working, albeit slowly, to restore the competitiveness of countries most affected by the crisis. However, the growth remains at best sluggish. The medium and long-term outlooks remain highly uncertain, fomenting the social tensions and endangering the political stability.

The restoration of economic dynamism is increasingly perceived as the answer for the "European" future – economically, politically and socially. There is a broad consensus that dynamic structural reforms and the restoration of competitiveness on the scale of the global economy are the key answers to current European challenges. However, there are no answers yet to deeper questions: What do mean the structural reforms in particular? What is the role of capital flows? And what constitutes the improvement in global competitiveness?

However, the one thing appears to be obvious. Whatever the form of the fiscal and banking union(s), the transfer of resources is implicit (and seemingly necessary) for those unions if they are to provide the underpinnings for the current structure of the monetary union. This indeed raises the question of the governance of these unions – both fiscal and monetary. After all, the provision of resources implies an allocation – and it is hard to imagine that resources will be provided to the common pool (e.g. to the fiscal and banking union) unless the provider has some say with respect to the allocation of those resources. And that requires some form of common (e.g. centralized) decision-making procedures, in all likelihood exceeding the common understanding of Acquis communautaire as it exists today – e.g. some form of the effective political union.

Given the significant political content in deciding about taxes, expenditures and resource transfers (e.g. the fiscal and banking unions), some mechanism of the political governance involving the democratic processes appears to be necessary for these unions.

Contributors to this volume were selected to analyze various aspects of the processes of the Eurozone governance reform and (desirable) the growth. They provide a balanced and multifaceted look at the Eurozone's dynamics since its inception in general and in the last five years in particular. The issues analyzed include the discussion of the Eurozone dynamics, growth and reform, dilemmas associated with fiscal and banking unions and the interplays between the economic, legal and political. (More details are in the list of contents with abstracts bellow.)

The basic idea which connects all contributions is the analysis of the problems which affected the Eurozone in the past decade and the challenges and dilemmas the Eurozone will face in the coming years. The analytical approach which connects the arguments pointing out to the need for reforms in EU governance and policies with the discussions of the nature and feasibility of possible reform directions permeates all contributions. The research techniques vary, from the political economy approach of Rusek and Lacina (chapter 1) to the sophisticated economic analysis by several other contributors. And, indeed, authors in this volume cover a wide variety of the EU performance subjects, which they cover with a broad methodological flexibility.

The publication is the compilation of contributions of 11 authors from 7 countries – Austria, Switzerland, USA, Poland, Slovakia, Czech Republic and Hungary. The chapters are stylistically and content-wise independent, so that the reader may start with any one, according to an interest and preferences. To facilitate readers flexibility, the remainder of this introduction provides the short synopsis of each individual chapter.

In Chapter 1, Lubor Lacina, and Antonin Rusek explore the challenges, both internal and external the EU in general and the Eurozone, in particular, will face in the next decade or so. Most important of those will be a continuing rise of the emerging markets, with its asymmetric impact on the Eurozone member economies. This will only be exacerbated the increasing divergences between the countries on the Mediterranean littoral and the countries North of Alps (referred to subsequently as South and North respectively). (The essence of the problem is that the rise of emerging markets increases the competition on the consumer goods markets worldwide – e.g. in the area where southern European countries historically have – and still have – a strong, but weakening presence. However, the same phenomenon – the rise of the emerging markets – increases their demand for capital goods, historically the strong area for the countries North of Alps, centered on Germany.) Finally, the demographic dynamics will exert influence over both the productivity and the fiscal positions.

To confront these challenges successfully, the restoration of growth is the imperative for the EU and the Eurozone's future. However, not any growth will do. The emerging markets challenge requires a growth based on the innovation and creativity (e.g. the increases in productivity), especially in the South. This type of growth improves competitiveness and should arrest and hopefully reverse the divergence tendencies. Moreover, its fiscal implications would help to address the looming demographic challenges – especially the rising expenditures on pensions and healthcare across the EU.

Based on a panel of 23 OECD countries Carsten Colombier shows that the government sector is partly contracted by Baumol's cost disease in chapter 2. He provides empirical evidence that not only total government expenditure but also public expenditure on health, education and general administration are affected by Baumol's cost disease. He points out that Baumol's cost disease produces adverse consequences under a balanced budget rule such as a debt brake. Governments face a serious dilemma. Breaching the rule would certainly cause reputational losses for governments, which might affect their borrowing costs and therefore, the sustainability of public finances. Adhering to the balanced-budget rule means risking budget-crowding out of cost-disease affected public expenditure with an ensuing long-run deterioration of these services and/ or foregoing growth opportunities. Governments of the EU member states and EU policymakers should, therefore, revise the EU Fiscal Compact to reconcile it with Baumol's cost disease.

In Chapter 3 Gabor Kutasi points out that some EU members faced years of crisis in the first half of the 2010s with an excessive initial public debt, but several others had broad room for fiscal stimulus. However, the prolonged duration of the European economic depression expanded public budgets, while exhausting stimulus policies and sovereign solvency. Meanwhile, one of the ways out of depression is a proposed centralization of the EU through the fiscal union. He asks whether the eurozone countries are ready to participate in a risk pool in public finances and seeks to answer this question. His argument presents the hypothesis that the sustainability of public finances deteriorated during the global and euro crisis in the majority of eurozone member countries and the EU, and this phenomenon is discouraging the core countries from seeking the fiscal union. His analysis uses the Blanchard indicators of fiscal sustainability and the sovereign risk rating of the EURO-18 and EU-28 countries. The analysis presents as results a theoretical summary of fiscal sustainability, the development of fiscal sustainability in the EU member states, indicators of convergence or divergence of fiscal sustainability in the Community, and conclusions based on the indicators of the likelihood of a fiscal union.

The principle of proportionality as a new concept for the regulatory impact assessment is discussed by Stanisław Kasiewicz, Lech Kurkliński in chapter 4. There is an attempt to assess regulatory impact concerning a popular principle of proportionality. It undergoes large modifications; its interpretation is broadened, and it gets adapted to the factual assessment of legislative processes. The principle of proportionality includes three significant elements: adequacy, necessity and proportionality sensu stricto. The proposed method in the law-making process comes down to three stages. The first one is an interpretation of the subjective scope of at least three abovementioned components. The second stage consists in the transformation of the adopted scope into clear and quite simple criteria. The third stage is attributing relevant measures to particular criteria. The proposed approach to regulatory impact assessment has been termed as the model of the Observance of the Principle of Proportionality. The authors present the model assumptions, identify and particularize the criteria of main areas of the principle of proportionality and then determine its scoring methods. The final result of the chapter is a synthetic calculation: an ordered measure of the observance of the principle of proportionality for a specific regulation.

Jaroslaw Kundera then analyzes the reform of economic policy coordination between the Euro Area member countries in chapter 5. He points out that Since 2008 the Euro Area has brought about the most severe crises, and the current situation in the Euro Area is far from stability. The crisis of the Euro Area turned out to be a crisis not only economies of member countries (Greece, Ireland, Spain, and Portugal) but also the crisis of mechanism of integration. To develop effective methods to combat the crisis and prevent future breakdowns present reform must cover not only the changes in the economic policy of the individual member states but also a mechanism for European integration. It is especially about the economic policy carried out at the level of the EU institutions that affects the economic policies of individual member countries. Hence the main goal of this chapter is to find an answer to the question, what changes should make the EU and its member countries to overcome the present crisis and prevent their occurrence in the future. Lessons are drawn from the current euro crisis to be such institutional changes within the EU, to ensure better coordination of economic policies between member partners.

In chapter 6, Rajmund Mirdala discusses the Inflation Expectations and Long-term Interest Rates in the Euro Area. He points out that recent deflationary pressures and ultra-low interest rate environment in the Euro

Area revealed fundamentally specific implications for the evaluation of monetary policy effectiveness. Redefinition of traditional views on price stability and the role of inflation expectations under near zero level inflation environment draws the attention of increasing number of empirical studies. Changing contribution of inflation expectations and expected real interest rates to the long-term interest rates determination are one of the most important implications of the recent deflationary periods in the Euro Area. In the chapter, the author employs SVAR methodology to identify inflation expectations and expected real interest rates shocks and calculate variance decomposition and impulse-response functions of long-term nominal interest rates. Research revealed considerable differences in the role of inflation expectations and expected real interest rates shocks in determining long-term interest rates between core and periphery countries of the Euro Area. The crisis period even intensified this trend.

Václav Šmejkal and Stanislav Šaroch ask whether the social market economy approach can lead the EU out of the gridlock in chapter 7. They point out that from the entry into force of the Lisbon Treaty, the EU has, among its constitutional objectives, the goal of achieving a highly competitive social market economy. At the same time, however, the EU has not been given any specific powers to actively develop its social policy and having to cope in parallel with the economic and fiscal crisis, it has given preference rather to austerity than to social welfare. After six years of legal force of the Lisbon Treaty there is still no clarity on how should the EU interpret the legacy of German post-war Sozialmarktwirtschaft; whether it should strive for its own economic and social "Constitution", or whether it can try to fulfil the objective of social market economy through the instruments of EU law and policy measures. Authors argue that some, rather partial, measures enacted by the EU would be desirable and feasible without creating a danger of over-regulation that would threaten the freedoms of the internal market or distort the existing division of powers between the EU and the Member States in the social field. The social market economy concept, being itself a compromise between the free markets and social welfare requirements, can act there as a guarantee that neither unbounded market freedoms nor socializing policies would dominate the EU.

The empirical investigation of the tradability of output and the current account in the European context is the subject of inquiry of Roman Stöllinger in chapter 8. He put forward the hypothesis that increasing specialisation in the production of non-tradable output has a negative impact on the current account balance. To test this tradability hypothesis empirically, we proceed in two steps. Firstly, we develop a tradability index which captures specialisation patterns with regard to the tradability of output. Secondly, we embed the tradability index into an empirical current account model for the full sample of European countries. We find strong evidence for a positive relationship between the current account balance and the tradability index in both the short and long run. The relationship is stronger for emerging economies in Europe than for developed countries. This finding has an important policy implication: the anxieties about "de-industrialisation" in many parts of Europe seem justified because the resulting loss of export capacity increases the risk of external imbalances.

Istvan Benczes asks whether in the EU context the fiscal rules are omnipotent. He stresses that The European Economic and Monetary Union (EMU) has an unprecedented institutional set-up for several reasons. Never before in modern history – in times of peace – have countries surrendered their sovereignty on monetary policy. No regional integration has succeeded ever before in reaching such a high level of complexity, with a supranational monetary authority at the centre. And never before has monetary policy been given up without the simultaneous introduction of a federal system of spending and taxation. No one has ever debated the fact that the design of the EMU is unique. By now, however, more and more commentators claim that its design was flawed or even that it was a total failure by institutionalising an asymmetry in the conduct of economic policy.

Finally, in the last charter, Zdenek Kudrna discusses the problem of reforming the Eurozone in the light of the relationship between the economics and politics. The Eurozone was stabilized by the non-orthodox monetary policy of the European Central Bank as well as the set of reforms including the European Stability Mechanism and the Banking Union. At the same time, the institutional architecture of the Eurozone remains incomplete and requires the introduction of some elements of the fiscal and political union. While there is no shortage of recommendations for economic reforms, the most binding constraint is political. The Eurozone member states seem unable to agree on further reforms, even though they all agree that these are necessary. The result is a "muddling through", when the minimalist reforms are agreed upon at the latest possible moment and only under pressure of acute crisis. This chapter briefly outlines political constraints on alternative reform scenarios as well as some low-probability-high-impact factors (black and white swans) that could alter the Eurozone reform path. However, it concludes that the "muddling through" strategy is likely to remain dominant.

One technical note at the end of this Introduction. In discussing the dynamics of the different parts of both EU and the Eurozone, different authors in this volume use different terminology in reference to the same (or very similar) geographical entities. Editors respect authors choices. However, it may facilitate the readers better understanding if we point out the commonalities connecting the terminology used by different authors. Namely, the terms South, Mediterranean, Mediterranean littoral, PIGS and EU (or the Eurozone) periphery all indicate the group of countries on the EU southern wing: Portugal, Spain, Italy, Greece, sometimes joined by Ireland (the latter depends on the actual context in the individual contributions). Similarly, the terms North, North of The Alps and core indicate the following states: Germany, Austria, Netherlands, Belgium, Luxembourg, and France, sometimes (again, depending on the context of individual contributions) joined by Finland.

*Editors, Lubor Lacina and Antonín Rusek*

*Brno and Susquehanna, June 2017*

Chapter 1

# Growth and the Real Convergence in the Eurozone

Lubor Lacina, Antonin Rusek

## 1.1. Introduction

In the next decade or so, the EU in general and the Eurozone in particular will face a complex set of challenges, both internally and externally. Most important of those will be a continuing rise of the emerging markets, with its asymmetric impact on the Eurozone member economies. (Chen at al., 2012) This will only exacerbate the increasing divergences between the countries on the Mediterranean littoral and the countries North of Alps (referred to subsequently as South and North respectively). (The essence of the problem is that the rise of emerging markets increases the competition on the consumer goods markets worldwide – e.g. in the area where southern European countries historically have – and still have – a strong, but weakening presence. However, the same phenomenon – the rise of the emerging markets – increases their demand for capital goods, historically the strong area for the countries North of Alps, centered on Germany). Finally, the demographic dynamics will exert influence over both the productivity and the fiscal positions.

To confront these challenges successfully, the restoration of growth is the imperative for the EU and the Eurozone's future. However, not any growth will do. The emerging markets challenge requires a growth based on the innovation and creativity (e.g. the increases in productivity), especially in the South. This type of growth improves competitiveness and should arrest and hopefully reverse the divergence tendencies. Moreover, its fiscal implications would help to address the looming demographic challenges – especially the rising expenditures on pensions and healthcare across the EU.

In this context, the three issues emerge. The first and the most important one is the fact that the economic activities associated with the innovation and creativity are inherently riskier than the expansion of the existing business endeavors. That creates a funding problem. European financial sector, dominated by banks, is unsuitable to finance the new innovative but overall highly risky business ventures, especially if those are undertaken by newly created firms.

The second issue relates to labor markets. The uncertainty associated with innovative ventures will be reflected in the need for flexible labor contracts, especially if these ventures are carried by the newly established firms. Moreover, the act of an establishment of a new enterprise faces complicated procedures in many, especially southern countries. Liberalization of the entry into professions and business activities, in general, is required to facilitate the desired economy of a growing productivity, e.g. the competitive and innovative economy.

Finally, the third issue is taxation. Increased uncertainty associated with the new enterprises constituting the new productive and innovative sector can be counteracted, at least partially, by designing a simplified (and perhaps even temporarily reduced) tax liability structure which would enhance the attractiveness of this sector for both the potential entrepreneurs and employees.

To address all three issues, actions on both the EU level and national levels are required. (Only the steps including the EU will be addressed here, but including the area where the EU and member states should act together in a coordinated manner.)

Venture capital firms are the key vehicle for the creation and financing of the new innovative companies which in turn are the essence of the dynamic, productivity enhancing growth. The actual funds for the venture capital come from existing financial establishments, technically termed the "limited investors". (In the US these compose of the pension funds, university endowments, insurance companies, various investment and hedge funds, etc.) To be able to allocate a relatively small part of their funds to the high risk but high expected return venture capital, the "limited investors" need the continuous ability to diversify and hedge the rest of their portfolios – e.g. to optimize the overall portfolio's risk-return configuration. This in turn requires the financial markets which are broad (in terms of the number of instruments available to trade), deep (in terms of the large number of instruments available with different risk-return characteristics) and liquid. The large and sophisticated US financial markets provide the environment in which both venture capital firms and "limited investors" strive.

The EU economy as a whole (even without the UK) is greater than the US, so theoretically it should be able to support the non-bank financial sector comparable to the US. However, despite the advances of the last 15 years, European financial sector remains dominated by banks. Relatively small non-bank financial sector then does not provide a fertile environment for the venture capital.

Venture capital activity is the key to the creation of new firms which enhance productivity and competitiveness in the whole EU, but especially in the most negatively affected countries on the Mediterranean littoral. It would follow that the creation of a supportive environment for the venture capital activities should be one of the major goals for both the European Commission, representatives of member states and the EU as a whole.

Indeed, the new leadership of the EU recognizes the importance of the non-banking financial sector on a trans-european scale (Juncker, 2014, Hill, 2014). On the analytical side, the importance of the integrated pan-european non-banking financial sector – called the "capital markets union" (CMU) is discussed by Veron (2014). What is needed is the accelerated path of the CMU establishment, with the emphasis on its role in facilitating the activities of the venture capital in the EU in general and in its Mediterranean member countries in particular.

The creation of the CMU as a vehicle to restore the free flow of capital within the EU in general and the Eurozone in particular is the key to the political and economic stabilization of the Eurozone. It should help to restore the North to South capital flows and by facilitating the venture capital financing to help the South to promote the productivity growth and restore the competitiveness. And, indeed, the role of the European institutions is crucial in this undertaking.

However, the CMU alone is not enough to restore the Southern growth and, hopefully, the real convergence. The substantive structural changes in the Mediterranean littoral economies are needed to make these countries attractive location for the venture capital. (These are referred to below.)

Indeed, structural reforms are at the heart of changes associated with Treaty on Stability, Coordination and Governance in the Economic and Monetary Union (TSCG), the key element of the European response to the recent fiscal and financial turmoil. However, the experience of the last half a decade indicates the difficulties, opposition, and widespread resentment encountered when structural changes are implemented across the individual national economies.

To facilitate the environment which will be inviting to the venture capital endeavors – and hence providing for the start of the growth based on the innovation and productivity – perhaps a different approach should be attempted.

Individual countries should designate "economic growth and innovation areas" defined either territorially or perhaps as branches of economic activities. Within those areas, the structural reforms should be accelerated, with the aim to create a hospitable environment for the new businesses, preferably financed by a venture capital.

The creation of such areas will necessarily be country specific. Hence their establishment must be the common projects of the EU institutions and the relevant country political and economic partners. Note that the goal is to facilitate the increase in the economic activity (and hence the employment) by establishing the innovative and globally competitive economic sector in the countries on the Mediterranean littoral. When successful, this should arrest the North-South divergent tendencies within the EU and therefore to dynamically stabilize the common currency area.

The special nature of these areas and its success can be enhanced by an adjusted tax regime (the third issue mentioned above). Again, the details are specific to individual countries. Here it should be only mentioned the need for the preservation of a hardly won public finance stability and the motivational role of capital gains in the establishment and success of business endeavors financed by the venture capital.

The EU with the cooperation of the national government sets the rules governing this new reality. However, the actual activities are by and large private sector financed and operated. This by itself should contribute not only to the renewed employment dynamics but to the stabilization of public finances as well.

Currently, the European authorities are taking steps to deepen the European integration by expanding the common economic institutions. The major steps here are the Banking Union (in the process of implementation) and the Capital Markets Union (in the beginning). Furthermore the idea of a structural convergence was introduced, understood as a process of creating the similar (if not the same) legal and institutional environment in all areas of economic activity in all states sharing the common currency, provided that the autonomy of individual states and hence the existing principles underlying the European treaties are preserved. (Buti and Turrini, 2015).

The political commitment to furthering the processes of a structural convergence as a part of the deepening of European integration processes was announced in Juncker at al. (2015).

The empirical studies of the processes of the convergence or divergence of European states preferences, institutions and policies were undertaken (among others) by Fatas (2015), Bongart and Torres (2013), and Hefeker (2013). The results of these studies are mixed. Biggest problems, indeed, are the matrix and the quantification of the structural "variables".

Any discussion of the issue is conditioned on the definition of the subject. What is the "structural convergence" or for that matter the "structural divergence"? In this analysis, we accept the interpretation of the term "structural" as describing the set of preferences, political, economic, social and legal institutions and the associated policies and decision-making processes. (E.g. we exclude the interpretation of "structural" as referring to the composition of economic activities and industries.)

Given this interpretation (which we believe corresponds to the meaning of "structural" in above mentioned Buti and Torrini (2015) and Juncker at al. (2015) two types of "structural convergence" actions are possible within the boundaries of the EU and the Eurozone.

One, which could be called the "absolute" structural convergence is the transfer of institutional arrangements, policy formulations and decision-making procedures to the EU (or the Eurozone) levels. Participating member states experience the 100% loss of autonomy in such cases. The history of the European integration can be interpreted as this type of the structural convergence. It includes wide variety of actions, from the "European Treaties" (the Lisbon Treaty of 2009 is the last in the long line of those), binding decisions of the European summits (some may require ratifications by the participating countries) to the EU Commission directives and judgements of the European Court of Justice.

Institutional, policy, and decision-making structures apply uniformly across the participating countries. It can be argued that this process of absolute structural convergence in Europe was rather successful in general terms, even if the lack of a real convergence might suggest otherwise. (It is far beyond the subject of this chapter to provide a detailed discussion of the history of European integration. Moreover, the real economic convergence often fails even in the unified national states – Italy is the best-known example – where the structural convergence is absolute by definition.)

In the context of the EU and the Eurozone, the latest examples of absolute structural convergence are the ongoing projects of the Banking Union and the Capital Markets Union. High hopes are associated with these projects as far as the real convergence is concerned – but results are still in the future.

The second type of a structural convergence addresses the situation when the institutional or policy arrangements in different countries are getting closer together (becoming the "more similar"). But the jurisdiction remains on the national level, with no (or a very limited) common EU action.

The discussions (and sometimes actions) in this area are related mostly to labor markets, business creations and operations environments, and legal structures and procedures. Taxation, health care, and education are also involved. The basic idea is the identification and the subsequent emulation of the "best practice" – with the hope that this will contribute to the real convergence and the EU and the Eurozone's political and social stability.

However, several issues should be raised in this context. To start, one may ask about the determination of the "best practice". From the available literature, it appears to be a kind of arrangement which is instrumental in achieving the predetermined goal – be it the growth of the GDP per capita, productivity, competitiveness or the level of employment. But if it is so why not to adopt such an identified "best practice" as a kind of the EU standard – something which would fall under the above-discussed category of the "absolute" structural convergence. The lack of the needed political consensus may be the most likely reason – but then why should such steps be taken by individual countries independently?

Second, one may raise the question of the suitability of particular institutional or policy arrangements across the board – a precondition for the convergence. After all, there are the reasons – historical, cultural, demographic, perhaps even differences in the climate – why EU and the Eurozone member countries differ and insist on the preservation of significant political and institutional autonomies. Absent this the unified European superstate would be created long time ago.

And third, there is the question of costs – or more precisely the North – South transfers. It was pointed out that the most successful structural reforms in any European economy – the German Hartz IV package of labor markets and welfare reforms – was only made possible by Germany violating the original Stability and Growth Pact in 2003 and 2004. One would assume that similar reforms introduced in the states of the South (the approach often advocated) would be costly and would require the EU's – e.g. the North – financial support. And in the current circumstances, this is far from certain.

Hence: structural reforms – e.g. the structural convergence – are indeed useful and if designed thoughtfully they may be the key to overcoming the real divergence. However, the subject is far from simple, and it would be naive to expect the quick results.

The process of innovating and structurally modernizing the EU is extremely important and perhaps inevitable for the EU's survival. However, it is necessary to keep in mind that suggestions above are designed (and will) to produce the across the board gains in the medium and long runs, the short-run need for the resource reallocation will likely result in individuals (or groups) which may find themselves on the losing side.

To address this issue several things should be remembered. First, the impact of the reform processes will differ by a country. Hence the response (help to the affected individuals or groups) will differ by the country. This will be only exacerbated by the still preserved cultural, social and economic differences between the EU countries.

Second, the costs of the adjustment CUM help programs – as far as their necessity stems from the policies necessary to enhance and advance the EU community – should be, at least partially, financed from the common EU level. Common EU taxes on the activities as entertainment, wireless communications, etc. appear very attractive in this context.

And third, given the inevitable national specificity of the desirable adjustment CUM help programs, these should be designed together by affected nations (individually) and the EU – which indeed should carry a share of costs.

Ideas expressed in this note seek ways how to restore the growth and global competitiveness in the EU and especially in the Mediterranean Eurozone members. They seek to overcome political and institutional obstacles and via an enhanced cooperation between the EU and the national governments to reinvigorate the process of the European integration and to arrest the growing divergence between the north and South. Not the least advantage is that no changes to the existing EU treaties and governance are required.

Finally, the ideas expressed above should not be perceived as the alternative for the European Fund for Strategic Investments (EFSI – commonly referred to as Juncker's Investment plan). Rather, both ideas should be thought of as complimentary. EFSI seeks the increase in investments in the EU in general – especially in infrastructure. Ideas in this note seek the ways (and investments) aimed at the increases in productivity and global competitiveness via private sector activities, especially in South. Our conjecture is that the EU – and especially the Eurozone – need both.

To implement these ideas (including the one where preliminary steps were taken, like CMU), the following steps/actions appear desirable:

1. Political program should be formulated (along with the lines suggested above) and accepted as the EU document on the highest level (EU summit), sign by all EU leaders and the leaders of all member countries. This should be done fast as mentioned in Five predents report.
2. The "Implementation Committees" should be established, charged with defining the path and establishing the programs of defining the content of individual reform area and a tentative schedule of implementation. These committees should be established by the end of 2017, with the charge of producing the relevant program documents by the second half of 2018.

3. The membership of these committees should be composed of EU institutions and governments of member states, with the expert advisory group. It may be desirable to form subcommittees with the participation of an affected member states where a particular reforms and/or implementation issues are concerned.
4. A special "financing" commission should be established to evaluate financial requirements of reform steps and propose steps to provide such financing – by the end of 2018.
5. The goal of January 2019 (at latest) should be set to start the reform implementation. The result should be evaluated annually at the EU summit, under the overall supervision of the EU commission.

## 1.2. Mechanisms, Communications, Packaging, Institutions or Other Ways that Help Build Trust to the European Union by its Citizens

Any proposed economic, political and cultural changes are likely to encounter resentment and fail unless accepted by societies to which they are applied. Historically, the predecessors of the EU (starting from the Rome treaties in 1957) were not only accepted but often welcomed, because they represented a successful answer to challenges stemming from the inner dynamism of European nation states – as demonstrated by the two world wars. Moreover, the creation and the gradual enlargement of the European economic space provided the environment in which the challenges of the new technologies could be coped with, and the European welfare states could strive, providing both the security and general well-being to generations, something never experienced before. (Indeed, it has to be recognized that it was and remain the NATO which provides the essentials to the European external security – but this is beyond the scope of this chapter.

The success of the common European structures (which officially became European Union December 1$^{st}$, 1993) was unmistakable. However, the clouds were gathering on the horizon. Several factors are combined together.

As the memory of 1930's and WWII faded away, the war generations were replaced by people for whom the freedoms and successes of EU were part of the common environment. The attention and interests shifted to more "mundane" realities of everyday life and carriers. The perceptions of the "rising problems" were reinforced initially by rising competition (including immigration) from the new member states in the East (the key element which led to the rejection of the EU constitution in Netherland and France in 2005). Later on the impact of 2009-2014 recession (especially on the young) and restrictive fiscal policies required to restore the nominal convergence needed to preserve the common currency contributed to rising doubts about the ability to preserve the European welfare state as the economic underpinning of the EU. The recent immigration wave from the non-European countries generated a "cultural shock" and the perception that EU is not a vehicle helping to preserve the "European" identity. Finally, the continuing shift of decision-making levels to the EU level, supported by some decisions of the ECJ only reinforces the feeling in some segments of the population of EU member states that the "repatriation of powers" to the nation-state level may be preferable to the current state of affairs. (This reality, sometimes summarized under the term "democratic deficit" is certainly behind the result of the recent UK referendum.)

The reforms that restore the EU economic growth and hopefully the real economic convergence will go a long way toward the restoration of the trust in the EU and the European concept. However, somehow paradoxically, the success of the reform endeavors requires a popular support – e.g. the restoration of the belief in the desirability and success of the European program.

Some writers note and lament a limited commitment to the concept of Europe both between elites and the general electorate. They attribute this phenomenon to the failure of the past European leaderships to build a distinct European identity either to suppress existing national identities or to build the parallel one. This concept is an intriguing one and may appear attractive. However, both European integration process historically and the current EU are intergovernmental endeavors, not a pan-European movement. Such an arrangement is not instrumental to building a trans nation state identities.

(Besides, one may point out to processes of building common identities, replacing and/or suppressing the original regional ones – e.g. to the processes of German and Italian unifications in the 19$^{th}$ century. Here the social, cultural and political processes of building a common national identity took decades, despite the enormous advantage of a (more or less) common language. The common state (actual political unification) was then the final result.)

But indeed, the idea of building the common European identity together with existing national identities is an intriguing one and should be pursued. But it would be naive to expect short term positive results.

A significant body of writers (mostly academic, but some politicians as well) argue for an accelerated process of building a common European state as a tool to impose a "Europeanness" from above and facilitate more efficient and focused Europa-wide policies. Examples are proposals to create common institutional structures (European president, European government,

European finance ministry, a replacement of intergovernmental by federal governance structures, etc.) with non-trivial executive powers.

These ideas are appealing to some not only from the standpoint of political and economic efficiencies but on the social-cultural ground as well. The argument goes that the symbols of common Europeanness (president, government) are needed to focus the common European identity and to overcome the residual primary allegiance to nation states.

Perhaps, but only in a very long run. Bismarck and Cavour might be the focuses of a respective national unifications, but they would remain only regional politician without being preceded the decade's long processes of German and Italian national awakening respectively.

Besides, in the current political climate in many EU constituent state attempts to increase EU political centralization and to further reduce the role of nation states are more likely to result in the EU collapse rather than an increase pan-European identification.

Indeed, Europeans should build a relationship with the Union. This will not threaten their ties to their home country in any way. People will have multiple identities loyal to various sovereigns. A sense of togetherness must be perceived by elites as well as by the ordinary citizens of Europe and its institutions. EU through its history has become much more united and integrated, however, member countries remain different as regards their cultures, languages, political systems and economic performance. A common identity is missing.

In brief, the objective is to maintain, to the largest possible extent, the advantages stemming from the (tradition of) the nation state and interconnect them with the advantages brought by supranational settings. The system must be based, on the principle of subsidiarity and the related premise of mutual interests as a starting point.

In building trust and support for the EU, in the short (and perhaps the medium as well) term the emphasis should be placed on the following areas:

1. The principle of subsidiarity should be precisely defined in each area and each country. This would enable to precisely distinguish between the relevant responsibilities and facilitate the objective evaluation of the EU impact.

2. The educational curriculum should be developed, showing (in degrees, appropriate to different levels) the dynamism of the European integration, the history of the EU and its predecessors and showing "national achievements" which would be much diminished without the EU intellectual and financial umbrella.

3. The public relations ideas (and perhaps a permanent level organization should be established, aimed at the facilitating the positioning of the EU information in the public sphere of the each member country. (in fact, some writers, like Khanna (2011) attribute the rise of “euroscepticism” to a deficient PR.)
4. (perhaps) The EU should establish an office in the each member country, dedicated to the promotion of the EU ideas and concepts.

The proposals elucidated above may seem limited. Some may prefer more radical approach. However, the world, especially political and social world is determined by the existing culture and is path dependent. The current situation is not revolutionary. The goal now is to create enough pro-european (or, better perhaps, “anti-eurosceptic”) sentiment which will facilitate the reforms designed to restore the economic growth and the real convergence. Elucidated in the first part of this essay.

The future of EU is indeed pre-conditioned by the consent of national politicians, who are to a large extent hampered by their own interest (maintenance of power) and by voters. That is why it is important to communicate with citizens and to persuade them about the advantages of a strong Union.

Brussels must see the citizens of the Union as its partners rather than as passive recipients of information. The European bureaucracy must perceive the citizens as partners and not as passive recipients of information and should strive for dialogue. In practice, this means for example that it is not possible to repeat a Referendum until the desired results appear (e.g. Lisbon). European institutions should institutionalize relations with civil society and non-profit organizations. Experts and apolitical institutions should popularize important issues and possibly launch a public debate on these issues.

Europe should lead the dialogue with the world from a position of wisdom and economic power corresponding to her potential. The leaders of European states must learn (at least as regards the key issues) to confront each other behind closed doors but take a common and single position when they stand in front of them.

The world is changing. The memory of the past is exactly that – the memory.

## 1.3. References

BONGARDT, ANNETTE, TORRES, FRANCISCO (2013). *Forging Sustainable Growth: The Issue Of Convergence of Preferences and Institutions in EMU. Intereconomics,* #2, pp. 72-77.

BUTI, MARCO, TURRINI, ALESSANDRO (2015). *Three waves of convergence. Can Eurozone Countries start growing together again?* VOX CEPR's Policy Portal, April 17th.

CHEN, R., MILESI-FERRETTI, G-M, AND TRESSEL, T. (2012). *"External imbalances in the Euro Area."* IMF Working Paper, 12/236.

FATAS, ANTONIO (2015). *The Agenda for Structural Reform in Europe.* Presented at the Conference Growth and Reform in Europe in the wake of Economic Crisis, Bank Of Portugal, Lisbon, Portugal, May 9th.

HEFEKER, CARSTEN (2013). *The limits of Economic Policy Convergence in Europe.* Intereconomics, #2, pp. 83-87.

HILL, JONATHAN. (2014) *"Capital Markets Union: Finance Serving the Economy".* Speech at Finance and Growth Conference, Brussels, Belgium, November 6th (http://ec.europa.eu/rapid/press-releaseSPEECH-14-1460.en.htm).

JUNCKER, JEAN-CLAUDE. (2014). *"A New Start for Europe: My Agenda for Jobs, Growth, Fairness and Democratic Change."* Opening Statement at the European Parliament Plenary Session, July 15th. (http://ec.europa.eu/about/juncker-commission/docs/pg.en.pdf).

JUNCKER, JEAN-CLAUDE, TUSK, DONALD, DIJSSEELBLOEM, JEROEN, DRAGHI, MARIO (2015). *Preparing for Next Steps on Better Economic Governance in the Euro Area.* Informal European Council, Brussels, Belgium, February 12th.

KHANNA, PARAG. (2011). *How To Run the World: Charting a Course to the Next Renaissance.* Random House.

VERON, NICHOLAS. (2014). *"Defining Europe's Capital Markets Union". Bruegel Policy Contribution,* Issue 2014/12, November.

Chapter 2

# Does Baumol's Cost Disease Produce Adverse Growth?

Carsten Colombier

## 2.1. Introduction

A major drawback of balanced budget rules such as the one of the Fiscal Compact of the European Union (EU) is that the impact of exogenous determinants such as population ageing and Baumol's cost disease is not taken into account. The ageing effect and its consequences for fiscal rules are fully acknowledged (European Commission, 2015). Although many government services such as healthcare, education or the performing arts are supposed to suffer from Baumol's cost disease, apart from an early discussion, the working of Baumol's cost disease under fiscal restraints has so far been neglected in the literature (Ryan, 1992, Baumol 1985, Baumol and Oates, 1979). The absence of a discussion is even more surprising as a key issue in the EU revolves around generating economic growth in the EU crisis countries. This chapter fills this gap by analysing the impact of the cost disease under a balanced-budget rule and by providing evidence for the relevance of Baumol's cost disease for government expenditures decomposed by function. Thus, this chapter draws the attention to an important economic-policy issue pertinent to the new fiscal framework of the European Union.

Our main finding is that Baumol's cost disease produces a serious dilemma for governments who have implemented a balanced-budget rule. Governments have the choice between Scylla and Charybdis. Both governments risk reputational losses by breaching the balanced-budget rule or a budget crowding out, in particular, of cost-disease affected government expenditures and/ or missing out on growth opportunities. In the long run, cost-disease caught government services might even deteriorate. We carry out a comprehensive analysis of the impact of Baumol's cost disease on the composition of government expenditure. Our results suggest that government expenditure, in particular, those on general government, health and education and to a lesser extent on general administration, are affected by the cost disease.

The few somewhat related empirical studies focus on the impact of Baumol's cost disease on health (Hartwig, 2008; Bates and Santerre, 2013; Rossen and Farroque, 2016, Colombier, 2017), public education (Ryan, 1992; Chen and Moul, 2014; Nose, 2015) and government output (Bates and Santerre, 2015). In line with our findings, these studies provide evidence for the relevance of the cost disease in the respective sectors. Ryan (1992) gives some indication that fiscal restraints for the cost-disease-affected public education sector led to a reduction in higher education in 10 OECD countries in the 1970ies and 1980ies. A further study related to this present work by Dahan and Strawczynski (2013) analyses the impact of several types of fiscal rules such as the Stability and Growth Pact (SGP) on the composition of government expenditures. Dahan and Strawczynski (2013) decompose government expenditure by consumption, investment and social transfers. They provide evidence for a budget crowding out of social transfers by government consumption under fiscal rules. This finding, however, does not apply to countries with a strong legal commitment to social rights. Thus, budget crowding out may also occur due to factors endogenous to the political system under fiscal rules. Note that this present study takes an another stance because we analyse in which way an exogenous determinant of government expenditure, Baumol's cost disease, can affect the working of a certain type of fiscal rule, e.g. balanced-budget rules.

To estimate the impact of Baumol's cost disease on government expenditure we apply an innovative approach, developed by Hartwig (2008) and Colombier (2017), the Baumol variable. This approach avoids using deflators of government services, which are notoriously difficult to calculate (Griliches, 1992). By definition market prices are not available for government services, and it is difficult to adjust prices or deflators for quality changes (Bates and Santerre, 2015).

In the field of economics often non-high quality data are available, which can cause the widely used least squares estimators (LSE) to become inefficient and biased. Therefore, some authors propose applying robust statistical methods in economics (Temple, 2000, Zaman et al., 2001, Colombier, 2009). Since robust estimators are not as sensitive to outliers as LSE, they are able to identify the most coherent part of a data set. This ability proves very beneficial to analyse panel data due to the distinct heterogeneity of panel-data sets. Therefore, some authors strongly recommend using robust statistical methods to analyse panel-data sets (Aquaro and Cizek, 2013; Verardi and Wagner, 2011). Following this recommendation, we apply an outlier-robust estimation method to study the impact of Baumol's cost disease on government expenditure by function. We apply the robust modified M-estimator (MM) (M stands for generalised maximum likelihood estimator) which has been proposed by Yohai et al. (1991). Although, the beneficial features of robust estimators applied economists have only rarely applied robustly statistical methods. Among the few exceptions are, for example, Colombier (2009) and Sturm and De Haan (2001). According to Zaman et al. (2001), this is because applied economists are convinced that outliers are a minor problem, that large sample sizes make a systematic approach to outliers dispensable and that outliers can be detected by eyeballing them. Moreover, applied economists are often unfamiliar with estimation techniques that systematically cope with outliers.

This chapter is organised as follows. The next section sets out the concept of a balanced budget rule. In section 2.3 we show how Baumol's cost disease can impact the working of a balanced budget rule. Section 2.4 outlines the estimation approach. In section 2.5, the empirical results concerning the impact of Baumol's cost disease on government expenditure decomposed by function are presented. In section 2.9 we provide evidence for the Swiss case that balanced-budget rules exert a restrictive impact on cost-disease affected public expenditure items. Finally, section 2.10 concludes.

## 2.2. The Concept of a Balanced Budget Rule

In the wake of the Euro crisis, EU leaders have implemented several reform measures to strengthen budgetary discipline in the EU by tightening the rules of the Stability and Growth Pact (SGP) as part of the Euro-Plus-Pact and introducing a new Fiscal Compact, being the cornerstone of the Treaty on Stability, Coordination and Governance in the Economic and Monetary Union (TSCG) (see EU-Memo/11/ 647, TSCG, 2012). While the revised version of the SGP already encourages the implementation of national fiscal rules such as the German debt brake, Article 3(2) of the TSCG obliges the signatory countries to implement a debt brake, e.g. a balanced-budget rule, in national law.[1] The main elements of the Fiscal Compact can be summarised as follows:

- In accordance with the SGP the rule obliges signatory countries to define a medium-term objective for the structural budget balance that does not exceed a structural deficit of 0.5% of GDP. Only if the government debt ratio is well below 60% of GDP, governments are allowed to have a structural deficit of 1% of GDP. If a government does not meet the medium-term objective, the respective government has to

[1] Note that all EU countries signed the TSCG except for the United Kingdom and the Czech Republic.

implement measures to ensure rapid convergence towards the medium-term objective.

- Temporary deviations from the medium-term objective due to events outside the control of the respective government such as a natural disaster, global financial crisis or severe economic downturn are allowed. Moreover, an automatic correction mechanism is foreseen if a country deviates significantly from the medium-term objective or the path towards it.
- The benchmark for the government-debt-to-GDP ratio is the 60%-criterion given by the SGP. Following the rules of the SGP, a government should reduce the public-debt ratio at a velocity of one-twentieth annually, if their debt-ratio crosses the 60% limit.

To show how Baumol's cost disease can interfere with the working of a debt brake, as a reference point, we use the German debt-brake rule. The German debt brake has been serving as a blueprint for all the signatory countries of the TSCG. Debt brakes are framed against the background of the (new) neo-classical synthesis (see Colombier, 2006, 529). The debt brake aims at stabilising nominal debt over the business cycle, but budget movements due to cyclical fluctuations should be taken into account. According to neo-classical theory, fiscal policy can smooth the business cycle but is not able to enhance the long-run production possibilities of an economy. On the contrary, a too high debt-level may cause uncertainty among consumers and investors, which in turn causes interest rates to rise and as a result, crowd out private investment. Therefore, the structural government budget should be balanced over the business cycle under a debt brake. However, since the advent of endogenous growth theory, several studies show that certain kind of government spending such as educational or infrastructure expenditure can be growth-promoting (e.g. Colombier, 2009). To consider this possibility, at least to some extent, the German debt brake allows for a small structural deficit of 0.35% of GDP at the federal level. In contrast, the states (the *Länder*) are not allowed to run a structural deficit.[2] The overall limit of a structural budget deficit is in the spirit of the SGP, which foresees a close-to-balance budget over the business cycle. According to the SGP, the structural budget

---

[2] Note that the German states should have their own debt brakes implemented by 2020. Apart from the binding constraint of a balanced structural budget the states have some leeway to formulate their debt brake rules. In particular, the states can choose if their rule permits the budget to fluctuate with the business cycle. For a detailed overview see Deutsche Bundesbank (2011).

deficit must not exceed 0.5% of GDP. The German debt brake is enshrined in the German constitution (see Art. 109(1) and 115 Grundgesetz).

Moreover, according to conventional wisdom discretionary, the fiscal policy has severe shortcomings. First, due to the democratic decision process usually fiscal measure are implemented too late and may not be efficiently composed due to strong lobby groups. Second, incentives given to policy-makers or civil servants to enlarge their influence and power may lead to a deficit bias of the government sector. Nonetheless, to smooth the business cycle automatic stabilisers such as the unemployment insurance should be able to work. After a transition period that started 2011, the German debt brake has fully come into force at the federal level in 2016. At the federal level, apart from a structural component, the debt brake contains a cyclical component, which allows the automatic stabilisers to work. To give policy-makers limited flexibility the federal government can exempt from the rule under exceptional economic conditions such as a financial crisis or natural catastrophes. Along the lines of the SGP, financial transactions such as revenues for privatisation of public assets or loans to the unemployment insurance are excluded from the calculation of the deficit ceiling.[3]

In the following, a government budget identity in terms of GDP (Y) is shown.

$$gy + i\,b \equiv \tau + \Delta b \qquad (1)$$

with: $g_y$ = ratio of primary public expenditure to Y

$\tau$ = ratio of public revenues to Y with public revenues defined as: $T = \tau Y$.

b = ratio of outstanding stock of government debt to Y

$\Delta b$ = new bonds issued in the current period in terms of Y

i = nominal interest rate on government bonds

As governments in developed economies such as the EU-countries are usually not allowed to finance their deficits by printing new high-powered money, a public deficit can be financed either by tax revenues or by issuing new bonds. Under the debt brake, a limit is placed on the issuing of new bonds. This deficit ceiling can be written as follows:

---

[3] A further key component of the German debt brake is the control account, which takes forecast errors for government revenues into account. For a detailed description see Deutsche Bundesbank (2011).

$$\Delta bc \leq \sigma - \varepsilon\,(Y\text{-}Ypot)/Ypot \qquad (2a)$$

with: $Y^{pot}$ = potential GDP

$(Y\text{-}Y^{pot})/Y^{pot}$ = output gap

$\varepsilon$ = budget sensitivity with respect to a 1%-change of the output gap

$\sigma$ = structural deficit limit, for Germany: 0.35% of GDP

Under the debt-brake rule, the deficit ceiling ($\Delta b_c$) is calculated as the sum of a structural component (first term on the right-hand side (rhs) of equation (2)) and a cyclical component (second term on the rhs of equation (2)) of the government budget. Since we are interested in how Baumol's cost disease affects the working of the balanced-budget rule, we assume that the economy is in a long-term equilibrium so that the output gap vanishes e.g. $Y=Y^{pot}$. As a result, the deficit ceiling given by the debt brake reduces to:[4]

$$\Delta bc \leq \sigma \qquad (2b)$$

with: $0 < \sigma \leq 0.05$

Inserting the deficit ceiling in equation (1) and rearranging this equation leads to the following term:

$$g_y \leq \sigma + \tau - i\,b = g_c \qquad (3)$$

Unless the government is willing to increase taxes, the sum on the rhs of equation (3) is given. Consequently, a debt-brake rule imposes a limit on the ratio of the primary public expenditure to GDP in the long run. However, this can lead to adverse consequences if the government sector or a part of the government sector is contracted by Baumol's cost disease as we show in the following.

[4] The maximum structural deficit allowed under the SGP corresponds to 0.5% of GDP.

### 2.3. Baumol's Cost Disease under a Balanced-budget Rule

Baumol's cost disease is based on the assumption that an economy can be decomposed into sectors that are characterised by technologically progressive activities such as capital accumulation, innovation and economies of scale, which brings about a steady increase in labour productivity, and sectors that are characterised only by occasional productivity growth (see Baumol, 1967, 415-16). The quality (and quantity) of labour is key to the quality of products in these sectors. Labour is difficult to substitute with capital in these personal-intensive sectors so that labour-augmenting (Harrod-neutral) technical progress is hampered. Baumol (1993, 17-18) quotes healthcare, education or privately run personal services such as automotive repair or the hairdresser trade as prime examples for these non-progressive or stagnant industries (Baumol sector). Provided that the demand for the non-progressive sector is price inelastic or is subsidised by the government, the demand for labour in these sectors increases steadily.[5] In order to avoid labour shortages in the Baumol sector wages of this sector have to increase the wages in the progressive sector of the economy in the long run. The latter is usually assumed to increase with the growth of labour productivity in the progressive sector. Since the labour-productivity growth in the Baumol sector is slower than in the progressive industry, unit costs of the Baumol sector increase inevitably. This brings about higher inflation in the Baumol sector, which is dubbed *Baumol's cost disease* (e.g. Baumol, 1993).

To show the impact of Baumol's cost disease on the public budget under a debt-brake rule we decompose government services into those affected by the cost disease and other government services. Corresponding to the findings by Baumol (1967) we assume that the inflation rate of the shadow price of the cost-disease-affected government services, $\hat{p}_b$, outgrows the inflation rate of the economy, $\hat{p}$ by far.[6] The shadow price of the other government expenditure varies proportionally to the inflation rate of the economy, $\hat{p}$. The quantity of the cost-disease-affected government services is given by $G^r{}_b$, while the quantity of the other government expenditure is represented by $G^r{}_o$. Total government expenditure is decomposed by cost-disease-affected government expenditure and others (see equation (4)).

$$p_g(t)G^r(t) = p_b(t)G_b^r(t) + p(t)G_o^r(t) = \big(1 + \rho(t)\gamma(t)\big)p_b(t)G_b^r(t) \qquad (4)$$

---

[5] The same is true if the goods produced by the stagnant industries are luxury goods.

[6] The shadow price of the public sector is tantamount to unit costs of government services.

with: t = time

p(t) = GDP deflator
$p_g(t)$ = shadow price of primary public expenditure
$\rho(t) = p(t)/p_b(t)$; $\gamma(t) := G^r_o(t)/G^r_b(t)$

Equation (4) leads to the following expression for the ratio of primary public expenditure to nominal GDP:

$$g_y(t) = \frac{(1+\rho(t)\gamma(t))p_b(t)G^r_b(t)}{p(t)Y^r(t)} \tag{5}$$

with: $Y^r(t)$ = real GDP

If we transform equation (5) by natural logarithm and differentiate both sides with respect to time t, we have the growth rate of the ratio of primary public expenditure to GDP:[7]

$$\hat{g}_y = (\hat{p}_g - \hat{p}) - (\hat{Y}^r - \hat{G}^r) = (\hat{p}_b - \hat{p})\frac{1}{1+\rho\gamma} + \frac{1}{1+\rho\gamma}\hat{G}^r_b + \frac{\rho\gamma}{1+\rho\gamma}\hat{G}^r_o - \hat{Y}^r \tag{6}$$

with: $\hat{p}_g > \hat{p} \wedge \hat{p}_b \gg \hat{p}$

If the government obeys the debt-brake rule and stabilises the GDP-to-public-expenditure ratio, e.g. $\hat{g}_y = 0$, the excess of the public-sector inflation rate over the general inflation rate corresponds to the difference in the growth rates of real GDP and real primary public expenditure (see equations (6) and (7)).

$$(\hat{p}_b - \hat{p})\frac{1}{1+\rho\gamma} = \hat{Y}^r - \frac{1}{1+\rho\gamma}\hat{G}^r_b - \frac{\rho\gamma}{1+\rho\gamma}\hat{G}^r_o \tag{7}$$

---

[7] Growth rates of the respective variable are represented by the symbol "^". To keep the notation of the following equations simple, we do not include the superscripts for time t.

with: $\frac{1}{1+\rho\gamma} = \frac{p_b G_b^r}{p_g G^r} \wedge \frac{\rho\gamma}{1+\rho\gamma} = \frac{p G_o^r}{p_g G^r}$

The last two summands of the rhs of equation (7) indicate that the growth rate of real primary public expenditure consists of the weighted sum of the growth rates of real primary public expenditure affected by the cost disease, $\hat{G}_b^r$, and other real primary public expenditure, $\hat{G}_o^r$. The excess of public-sector inflation is equal to the excess of the inflation rate of the Baumol sector weighted by the share of the primary public expenditure affected by the cost disease in primary public expenditure (see the lhs of equation (7)). Naturally, a rising share of cost-disease affected public expenditure leads to an increase of the excess of public-sector inflation over general inflation.

As a consequence of Baumol's cost disease, governments have to keep the pace of real primary public expenditure increases below the growth rate of real GDP under the debt-brake rule. From equation (7) follows:

$$(\hat{p}_b - \hat{p})\frac{1}{1+\rho\gamma} = \pi <=> \hat{Y}^r - \hat{G}^r = \pi \wedge \lim_{t\to\infty}\frac{G^r}{Y^r} = \lim_{t\to\infty} e^{-\pi t} \to 0 \qquad (8)$$

with: $0 < \pi \leq (\hat{p}_b - \hat{p})$

Equation (8) shows that the ratio of real primary public expenditure to real GDP has a tendency to vanish in the long run if the government sticks to the debt brake. Therefore, the implementation of a debt-brake rule implies a continuously shrinking government sector in real terms given that Baumol's cost disease is relevant for public services. The larger the effect that is exerted by Baumol's cost disease on the government sector, e.g. the larger the value of $\pi$, the faster, the ratio of real primary public expenditure to real GDP converges towards zero.

The government has only a few options to prevent the public sector from vanishing in real terms in the long run. First, the government may opt for reducing the share of the cost-disease affected government services, e.g. $\hat{G}_o^r > \hat{G}_b^r$. As a result, the excess of government inflation over general inflation, $\pi$, converges to 0 in the long run and the shrinking of the real primary government expenditure to real GDP comes to a halt (see equations (7) and (8)). This strategy implies that the cost-disease-prone government expenditure is crowded out by the other government expenditure ('budget crowding out'). However, this option is politically unfeasible if cost-disease prone public services meet basic needs of the citizens such as healthcare or citizens attach a high value to these services.[8] In contrast, the government may be able to cut cost-disease affected public services temporarily (see Ryan, 1992, 277). The option to reduce the share of government services caught by the cost disease may be even technically unfeasible if these services amount to a large proportion of total government expenditure. Second, the government might try to bring about leaps in productivity of the public services contracted by the cost disease, which would reduce $\pi$. Since the cost disease is rooted in the personal-intensive production technology, however, this task is fraught with difficulties. A final option to reduce $\pi$ might be to curb the wage growth of civil servants. However, this strategy may cause labour-shortages in the public services in the long run. In addition, the government might not be able to recruit sufficiently qualified personnel, which can be detrimental to the quality of personal-intensive public services.

So far we have assumed that the government has recognised that Baumol's cost disease affects the public sector. If the government does not notice Baumol's cost disease, as Chen and Moul (2014, 223) assume for the US states, but wants to adhere to the debt-brake rule, the personal-intensive public services may crowd out other government services such as public infrastructure services, e.g. $\hat{G}_b^r > \hat{G}_o^r$. In this case, $\pi$ approaches $(\hat{p}_b - \hat{p})$ in the long run and the reduction of the ratio of the real primary public expenditure to real GDP is accelerated (see equation (8)). Nonetheless, the government may follow this strategy deliberately, for example, if citizens vote for increases in public expenditure on services caught by the cost disease.

In addition, if some government expenditure items are productive, adhering to a debt-brake rule would mean foregoing growth opportunities for the following reason. A well-known hypothesis of endogenous growth theory is that the ratio of productive public expenditure to GDP in real terms promotes the steady-state growth rate of an economy (see e.g. Colombier, 2009, 901). Empirical evidence confirms this hypothesis and shows that public expenditure items such as those in infrastructure and education are growth-enhancing (see Colombier, 2009, 909). Thus, the application of a debt-brake rule can lead to a slowdown in economic growth.

---

[8] Nevertheless, Chen and Moul (2014) provide evidence that the cost disease has led to shrinking teacher-pupil ratios in the public education sector of the US states from 1997 to 2010. Chen and Moul (2014), however, do not refer to the interplay between the cost disease and fiscal rules.

These results have crucial implications for the working of a balanced budget rule. A cost-disease affected government sector would mean a continuously downsizing of the government sector in real terms under a balanced-budget rule in the long run. As a consequence, governments are caught in a serious dilemma. Either they breach the balanced budget rule and risk a loss of credibility, or they risk a budget crowding-out of one kind or another and/ or foregoing growth opportunities. In the long run, even the proper working of governmental institutions might be at stake.

## 2.4. Method and Data

The empirical analysis is based on a sample of 23 OECD countries and the time spans from 1990 to 2010 (see 2.12 Appendix). To analyse the impact of Baumol's cost disease on the government sector we apply a new method introduced by Hartwig (2008) and Colombier (2017), the Baumol variable. The Baumol variable offers the advantage to avoid the usage of output measures or price indexes of the service sector, which are notoriously difficult to measure (see section 2.1). We apply the adjusted Baumol variable developed by Colombier (2017) as the Baumol variable introduced by Hartwig (2008) is only a special case of the adjusted Baumol variable, which prerequisites that the whole labour force is engaged in the Baumol sector. Given actual data, Hartwig's case (2008) is highly improbable. Since the service sector is commonly viewed as susceptible to Baumol's cost disease (Schettkat and Yocarini, 2006), we refer to the employment share of all service industries. The average employment share of the service industry of the 23 OECD countries of our sample is almost 70% ranging between 43% and 84%. Thus, the average employment share is considerably lower than the 100% as is assumed by Hartwig (2008).

Since we apply the adjusted Baumol variable as a rhs variable, we choose the first differences of real per-capita public expenditure in natural logarithms as the dependent variable (Colombier, 2017). The latter can be viewed as a proxy for unit costs of government services. To test the relevance of Baumol's cost disease, apart from total general government expenditure, government expenditure decomposed by function according to the COFOG classification are used as dependent variables. These are, namely, public expenditure on general administration, education, health, social security, public order and safety, economic affairs (including transport infrastructure), housing and community amenities, defence and recreation, culture and religion.[9]

The adjusted Baumol variable corresponds to the difference between the economy-wide average growth rate of wages and the labour productivity growth rate in real terms divided by the employment share of the sector possibly contracted by the Baumol's cost disease (Colombier, 2017). To err on the side of caution, we define the sector possibly caught by the cost disease very broadly and make the standard assumption that the whole service industry is affected by the cost disease (Schettkat and Yocarini, 2006). Therefore, we use the employment share of the service industry to calculate the adjusted Baumol variable. It is well-known that apart from Baumol's cost disease, Wagner's law is a prime explanation for the expansion of the public sector (e.g. Neck and Getzner, 2007). In contrast to Baumol's cost disease Wagner's law is a demand-side explanation of an expanding government sector. Empirically, Wagner's law is confirmed if the income elasticity of demand for government services is above one, e.g. publicly provided goods are luxury goods.[10] As a proxy for the working of Wagner's law, we include real GDP per capita (y) in our estimations.

Another source of explanations for government growth stems from the public-choice literature (see Neck and Getzner, 2007, 54). In democracies, voters may suffer from fiscal illusion, as they are not aware that, due to the inter-temporal budget restriction of the government, increases in the ratio of public outlays to GDP have to be financed in the future. According to public-choice theory, governments try to conceal the resulting financial burden of government growth from the voters by extending the credit financing of public expenditure or by increasing the complexity of the tax system. In order to take account of fiscal illusion, we follow Neck and Getzen (2007, 63) and use the extent of credit financed government expenditure as a proxy in our regressions. The extent of credit financed government expenditure is measured by the ratio of the primary public surplus to total government expenditure. Thus, if the fiscal-illusion hypothesis has some merits, the

---

[9] For a detailed description of public expenditure categories, see Classifications of the Functions of Government (COFOG), United Nations Statistics Division.

[10] Wagner's law can be viewed as a special case of the demand-side explanation for the expansion of the whole service sector in the economy. Note that with a rising share of the services industries in GDP the importance of Wagner's law diminishes. For an overview of explanations for an expansion of the service industries see Schettkat and Yocarini (2006).

coefficient of the primary public surplus assumes a negatively statistically significant coefficient.[11]

Our basic stochastic equation of the per-capita public expenditure item j and country i, $g_{j,i}$, can be written as follows:[12]

$$\Delta g_{j,i}(t) = \alpha_j \underbrace{\frac{1}{l(t)_{B,i}}(\hat{w}_i(t) - \hat{\mu}_i(t))}_{\text{adjusted Baumol variable}} + \beta_j \Delta y_i(t) - \delta_j d_i(t) + \omega_{j,i} + \lambda_j(t) + u_{j,i}(t) \qquad (9)$$

whereby j represents government expenditure item j, i represents country i, i:= 1,..., 22; t represents year t, t:= 1990,...,2010, $u_{j,i}(t)$ represent the residuals of the regression, $\alpha_j$, $\beta_j$ and $\delta_j$ stand for the regression coefficients of the adjusted Baumol variable, the per-capita GDP variable ($\Delta y$) and the ratio of the primary public surplus to total government expenditure (-d). Except for the adjusted Baumol variable, all variables are expressed in natural logarithms. As usually, $\Delta$ indicates first differences of the respective variable. Note that if $\alpha_j$ is equal to one government service j is fully contracted by Baumol's cost disease. If $\alpha_j$ is zero, government service j does not suffer from the cost disease.

Since the decomposition of the population can affect a range of public expenditure items, in particular, those on old-age pensions, healthcare, long-term care or education (e.g. European Commission, 2015), we also include proxies for the demographic development in further regressions. We use the youth-dependency ratio, e.g. the ratio of the up to 15-years old to the whole population, and the old-age-dependency ratio, e.g. the number of the above 64-years old to the whole population.

---

[11] Note that the proposal by Neck and Getzen (2007) suffers from some limitations. First, we cannot separate public-expenditure increases motivated by self-interests of politicians or bureaucrats from other sources such as business-cycle effects or welfare-enhancing spending increases. Second, the explanatory variable primary public surplus may suffer from reversed causation. Nonetheless, we think that the primary public surplus is useful to give a first indication for the fiscal illusion of voters.

[12] We are aware of the fact that using the same model for all functions of governments can only be viewed as a first approximation to test for Baumol's disease. However, an in-depth account of the possible determinants for each of the government functions goes beyond the scope of this analysis because our concern is to examine whether there is any evidence for Baumol's cost disease across the whole spectrum of government activities.

To estimate equation (9), we apply a two-way fixed effects approach with the unobserved country- ($\omega_i$) and time-fixed ($\lambda(t)$) effects. Panel data sets usually include several outliers due to heterogeneity and diversity across countries and times (see Aquaro and Cizek, 2013, 536). The standard fixed-effects estimator that is based on LSE is very sensitive to outlying observations. A crucial indicator for the sensitivity of an estimator to outliers is the breakdown point. This indicator provides the maximal fraction of outliers an estimator can withstand. Only a single observation can severely bias the within group fixed effects LSE, which implies that the breakdown point of the fixed effects LSE converges to zero (see Aquaro and Cizek, 2013, 537). In addition, using LSE runs the risk of masking outliers (*masking effect*) and that outliers can lead to a substantial loss of efficiency approximately between 10% and 100% (Hampel, 2000). In order to reduce the sensitivity to outlying observations substantially and achieve high efficiency, we apply the robust MM estimator proposed by Yohai et al. (1991). This estimator is a so-called high-breakdown estimator, which reconciles outlier-robustness and a high efficiency. Since the robust MM estimator identifies the most coherent part of the underlying sample, the drawback of parameter heterogeneity of panel-data regressions can also be mitigated. To deal with heteroscedasticity of the residuals, an outlier-robust heteroscedasticity-consistent (HC) covariance estimator proposed by Criberi-Neto and Da Silva (2011) is applied. Furthermore, we use the Chi-square test proposed by Marivana (2012) to test for bias and inefficiency of LSE. In addition, we use Hartung's (1999) combining p-test to apply the Ljung-Box test on auto-correlation and the Shapiro-Wilk test on normality to a panel data set. Since the adjusted Baumol variable may suffer from an endogeneity bias, also instrumented regressions are run. As instrumental variables (IV) for the adjusted Baumol variable, the productivity level and growth in the manufacturing industry are applied. This choice is based on Colombier (2017) who uses the productivity growth in the manufacturing industry as an IV for the adjusted Baumol variable to estimate the impact on healthcare expenditure. We use an outlier-robust IV estimator recently proposed by Desbordes and Veradi (2012).

## 2.5. Results

Before we report on the regression results, a few descriptive statistics are presented. In Figure 2.1, the development of the ratio of total government expenditure to GDP is shown for all countries in the sample from 1990 to 2010.

**Figure 2.1. General government expanditure (as % of GDP)**

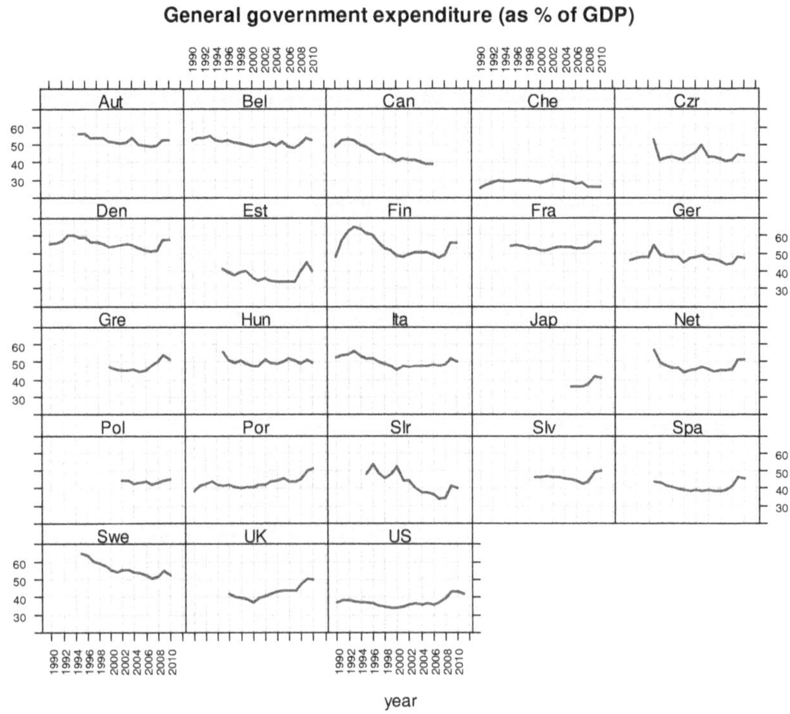


**Source**: OECD.

What is striking is that in almost all of the countries the public-expenditure ratio has been either stable or even has been diminished. The exceptions are the United Kingdom and Portugal. In addition, we can observe that the public-expenditure ratio surpasses pre-crisis levels only after the financial crisis and the Great Recession in some countries. Overall, Figure 2.1 suggests that an implementation of the balanced-budget rule would not appear to be necessary to stabilise the public-expenditure-to-GDP ratio.[13] One cannot infer from Figure 2.1 that forces such as Baumol's cost disease, Wagner's law or public-choice-related factors have driven up government expenditure in terms of GDP. Nonetheless, the development of the public-expenditure ratios shown in Figure 2.1 does not exclude the possibility that Baumol's cost

[13] Note to assess whether an implementation of a balanced-budget rule is pertinent, the development of the public-debt-to-GDP ratio has to be considered as well.

disease causes a reduction in the quantity of government services under fiscal restraints.

**Figure 2.2. Decomposition of public expenditure across 23 OECD countries, 1990-2010.**

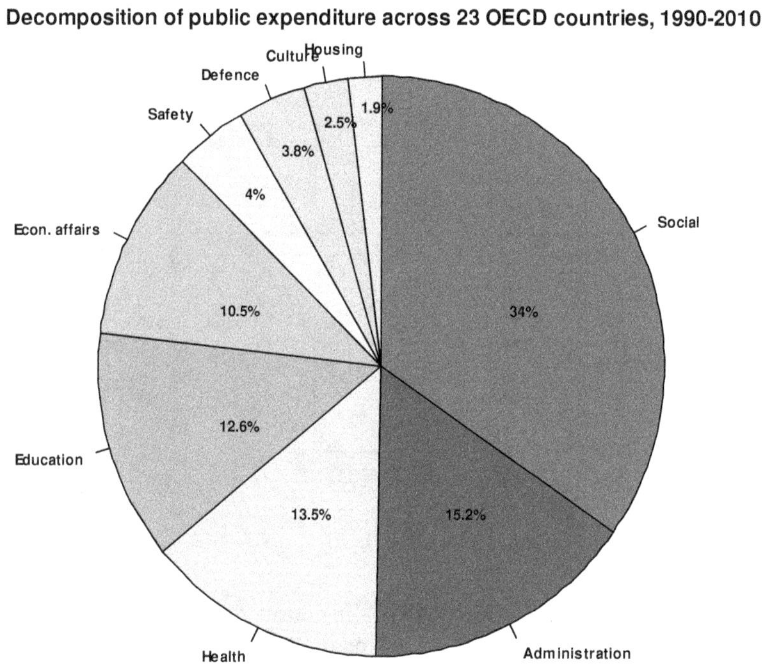


**Source: OECD and Swiss Government Finance Statistics**

In dependence of the fiscal relevance of government services, the impact of the cost disease can be more or less strong. The outlays on social security consume by far the highest share of government expenditure followed by general administration, health, education and economic affairs (including transport infrastructure) (see Figure 2.2). Consequently, the leeway of government shrinks if these fiscally important government expenditure items are affected by the cost disease.

In addition, our results strongly suggest using outlier-robust estimation methods. The Shapiro-Wilk tests indicate a non-Gaussian distribution of the residuals for over 50% of the regressions shown in Tables 2.1 and 2.2. The Chi-square tests show that the application of LSE would cause either inefficient or biased and inefficient estimates. In addition, the Chi-square tests of the IV estimations provide evidence that the Two-stage LSE would be biased.

## 2.6. Basic Estimations

Our regressions show that government expenditures are contracted by Baumol's cost disease (see Table 2.1). Apart from total government expenditure, a positive statistically significant coefficient of the adjusted Baumol variable can be ascertained for healthcare, education and general administration. However, the coefficient of the adjusted Baumol variable is far below one, which indicates that Baumol's cost disease has not exerted its full potential impact on public expenditure. Governments can temporarily mitigate the impact of the cost disease if they manage to reduce wage increases in the public sector to a level that is below the productivity growth in the progressive sector of the economy. Our regressions may, therefore, understate the impact of the cost disease. Nonetheless, our estimations indicate that a one percentage point increase in the adjusted Baumol variable causes an approximate 0.1 percentage point rise in the annual growth rate of per capita total government expenditure. What is striking is that we can observe a systematically negative correlation between the adjusted Baumol variable and public expenditure on housing and community amenities. This finding is at odds with Baumol's theory and rather counter-intuitive as the provision of housing amenities is a rather capital-intensive government activity. However, as housing amenities such as water supply may serve as a growth-promoting input for the private sector, this finding seems to be caused by reversed causation as we show in section 2.8.

**Table 2.1 The impact of Baumol's cost disease on government expenditure – basic estimations**

| Regressors | Dependent variable: public expenditure item | | | | | |
|---|---|---|---|---|---|---|
| | Total | Health | Education | General administration | Economic affairs | Transport infrastructure |
| Adjusted Baumolvariable | 0.09*** (0.03) | 0.15*** (0.04) | 0.09** (0.04) | 0.12* (0.06) | 0.10 (0.12) | 0.20 (0.14) |
| Real per capita GDP | 0.57*** (0.08) | 0.85*** (0.12) | 0.80*** (0.10) | 0.49*** (0.17) | 1.03*** (0.32) | 1.42*** (0.36) |
| Extent of credit financing[a] | -0.23*** (0.03) | -0.05 (0.04) | -0.08** (0.04) | -0.22*** (0.06) | -0.18 (0.12) | -0.39** (0.18) |

| Adjusted R squared | 26 | 9.8 | 9.3 | 2.4 | -3.4 | 2.2 |
|---|---|---|---|---|---|---|
| Panel Ljung-Box test | 1.51 | 0.68 | -0.12 | -0.10 | -0.63 | 0.54 |
| Panel Shapiro-Wilk test | -2.61*** | 2.45** | 2.09** | 1.27 | -4.45*** | -2.34** |
| Chi-square bias & inefficiency test LSE | 308*** | 293** | 34*** | 161*** | 708*** | 606*** |
| No. of observations | 296 | 296 | 296 | 296 | 294 | 189 |

**Notes:** 2-way fixed effects (FE) estimation with the outlier-robust MM estimator using an outlier-robust heteroscedasticity-consistent (HC) covariance estimator proposed by Cribari-Neto, Da Silva (2011). Dependent variable and per capita GDP are in first differences of logs. t tests: figures in parentheses are outlier-robust HC standard errors (SE); a robust Wald test is used as a redundant fixed-effects test; H0: FE are redundant; Panel Ljung-Box test based on Hartung's combining p-test (Hartung, 1999), $H_0$: no autocorrelation, t-test statistic; Breusch-Pagan tests with 2-way FE, HO: no heteroskedasticity, BP test statistic; Shapiro-Wilk test based on Hartung's combining p-test: $H_0$: Gaussian distribution, W-test statistic, Bias & inefficiency test (Maravina, 2012; T1 test), H0: Gaussian distribution; rejection of H0 means LSE is inefficient or inefficient and biased, chi-squared test statistic.If we detect serial correlation by the panel Ljung-Box test we apply the Cochrane-Orcutt method to deal with serial correlation. The results are shown in Table 2.A1; H0: LSE is not biased.

*** = 1% significance level

** = 5% significance level

* = 10% significance level

[a] Measured by the ratio of the primary surplus to total government expenditure.

**Table 2.1 continued**

| Regressors | Dependent variable: public expenditure item | | | | |
|---|---|---|---|---|---|
| | Housing & community amenities | Social security | Public order & safety | Recreation, culture & religion | Defence |
| Adjusted Baumolvariable | -0.49*** (0.16) | 0.05 (0.03) | 0.02 (0.05) | 0.02 (0.07) | -0.04 (0.09) |

| Real per capita GDP | 0.33 (0.43) | 0.43*** (0.08) | 0.34*** (0.12) | 0.37*** (0.17) | 0.24 (0.22) |
|---|---|---|---|---|---|
| Extent of credit financing[a] | -0.43*** (0.16) | -0.18*** (0.03) | 0.03 (0.04) | 0.03 (0.07) | -0.25*** (0.09) |
| Adjusted R squared | -6.4 | 19 | 2.6 | 6.0 | -0.3 |
| Panel Ljung-Box test | -0.85 | -1.26 | -0.34 | 1.86 | -1.46* |
| Panel Shapiro-Wilk test | -4.33*** | 1.83 | 0.04 | -3.27*** | 0.23 |
| Chi-square bias & inefficiency test OLS | 6092*** | 755*** | 712*** | 452*** | 24.7*** |
| No. of observations | 296 | 296 | 296 | 296 | 296 |

The estimations show that total government expenditure, as well as government expenditure on health, education and general administration, have a positive statistically significant correlation with real GDP per capita (see Table 2.1). However, Wagner's law would appear to be only relevant for public outlays on economic affairs, in particular, transport infrastructure, as these coefficients are statistically significant and above one. The confidence intervals at a 95% significance level and a 90% significance level respectively of the Baumol coefficient for health and education respectively include values above one, meaning that the validity of Wagner's law cannot be excluded for health and education. The variation of total government expenditure is positively correlated with the extent of credit financing. Accordingly, the coefficient of the primary public surplus is negative statistically significant. In addition, a negative statistically significant correlation between the primary public surplus and public spending on education, general administration, transport infrastructure, housing and community amenities, social security and defence can be ascertained. This is a first indication that governments might be able to increase government expenditure due to the fiscal illusion of voters.

## 2.7. Sensitivity Analysis

To test the sensitivity of our finding with respect to a different model specification, we take the demographic change as a further possible determinant of public expenditure into account (see section 2.4). Correspondingly, we include the youth- and old-age-dependency ratio in our estimations.

**Table 2.2 The impact of Baumol's cost disease on government expenditure – sensitivity analysis**

| Regressors | Dependent variable: public expenditure item | | | | | |
|---|---|---|---|---|---|---|
| | Total | Health | Education | General administration | Economic affairs | Transport infrastructure |
| Adjusted Baumolvariable | 0.09*** (0.03) | 0.17*** (0.04) | -0.03 (0.04) | 0.14** (0.07) | 0.09 (0.12) | 0.19 (0.14) |
| Real per capita GDP | 0.56*** (0.08) | 0.92*** (0.12) | 0.32*** (0.11) | 0.19 (0.17) | 0.88*** (0.33) | 1.27*** (0.38) |
| Extent of credit financing[a] | -0.23*** (0.03) | -0.05 (0.04) | -0.05 (0.04) | -0.25*** (0.06) | -0.17 (0.12) | -0.35** (0.18) |
| Young-age dependency ratio[b] | -0.06 (0.20) | 0.80*** (0.30) | 0.17 (0.26) | -0.97** (0.44) | -0.66 (0.82) | -0.35 (1.03) |
| Old-age dependency ration[c] | -0.04 (0.13) | 0.35* (0.20) | 0.05 (0.17) | 0.17 (0.29) | 0.46 (0.56) | 1.45** (0.63) |
| Adjusted R squared | 25 | 11 | 8.5 | 3.2 | -3.8 | 2.7 |
| Panel Ljung-Box test | 1.58 | 0.53 | 0.09 | 0.05 | -0.62 | 0.35 |
| Panel Shapiro-Wilk test | -2.52*** | -2.46** | -1.12 | 0.56 | -4.39*** | -0.84 |
| Chi-square bias & inefficiency test OLS | 360*** | 421*** | 571*** | 39.5*** | 777*** | 616*** |
| No. of observations | 295 | 295 | 295 | 295 | 293 | 189 |

Notes: see Notes Table 2.1.

*** = 1% significance level.

** = 5% significance level.

*:= 10% significance level.

[a] = Measured by the ratio of the primary surplus to total government expenditure.

[b] = This is the ratio of the 15 years old and below to the population of the respective country.

[c] = This is the ratio of the 65 years old and above to the population of the respective country.

**Table 2.2** ***continued***

| Regressors | Dependent variable: public expenditure item | | | | |
|---|---|---|---|---|---|
| | Housing & community amenities | Social security | Public order & safety | Recreation, culture & religion | Defence |
| Adjusted Baumolvariable | -0.47*** (0.15) | 0.06** (0.03) | 0.04 (0.05) | 0.15** (0.07) | -0.06 (0.09) |
| Real per capita GDP | -0.006 (0.41) | 0.49*** (0.08) | 0.40*** (0.12) | 0.79*** (0.18) | 0.23 (0.23) |
| Extent of credit financing[a] | -0.44*** (0.15) | -0.20*** (0.03) | 0.03 (0.05) | -0.001 (0.07) | -0.25*** (0.09) |
| Young-age dependency ratio[b] | -2.95*** (1.02) | -0.40* (0.21) | 0.30 (0.31) | 0.01 (0.46) | -0.46 (0.58) |
| Old-age dependency ration[c] | -0.94 (0.68) | -0.10 (0.14) | 0.14 (0.21) | 0.32 (0.30) | -0.41 (0.39) |
| Adjusted R squared | -16 | 19 | 7.1 | 4.6 | -0.8 |
| Panel Ljung-Box test | 1.11 | -1.46* | -0.30 | 1.82 | -1.15 |
| Panel Shapiro-Wilk test | -6.10*** | -0.11 | 1.04 | -3.34*** | 0.27 |
| Chi-square bias & inefficiency test OLS | 7308*** | 1253*** | 703*** | 224*** | 24.1*** |
| No. of observations | 295 | 295 | 295 | 295 | 295 |

By and large, the estimations shown in Table 2.2 confirm the findings of our first estimations with regard to the effect of Baumol's cost disease (see Table 2.1). However, the coefficient of the adjusted Baumol variable for spending on education turns insignificant. In contrast to the findings in Table 2.1, the estimations of Table 2.2 show that public expenditure on social security and recreation, culture and religion seem to be affected by the cost disease to some degree. However, if we correct for serial correlation, which is indicated by the Ljung-Box test, in the case of social security, the coefficient of the adjusted Baumol variable turns insignificant as in Table 2.1 (see Appendix, Table 2.1). Apart from two exceptions, the findings with respect to real GDP per capita and the extent of credit financing remain unchanged. In the case of education, the coefficient for the GDP per capita shrinks by more than 50%, and the coefficient of the primary public surplus even turns insignificant. Furthermore, the results change with respect to the correlation between real GDP per capita and public spending on general administration.

Our findings show that the age decomposition of the population affects positively public health spending, which is rather intuitive. In addition, expenditure on transport infrastructure has a positive statistically significant correlation with the old-age dependency ratio. Maybe the elderly prefer having well-maintained streets and highways. In response to the needs of an ageing population, communities may also have increased the construction of barrier-free side-walks and pedestrian zones. Moreover, our findings suggest that the younger generation would appear to use social transfers and services of the general administration to a lesser extent than the residual population. The latter might be due to a more computer-prone attitude of the younger generation so that governments can economise by increasing electronic government services. According to our results, the younger generation seems to put less emphasis on housing and community amenities such as street lighting and housing development.

### 2.8. Instrumental-variable Regressions

Baumol's model of unbalanced growth predicts that due to the cost disease the employment share of the Baumol sector increases and productivity growth shrinks. Consequently, the regressions shown in Tables 2.1 and 2.2 may suffer from an endogeneity bias. Therefore, we run estimations with IV. For the following reasons, one should read the findings of the IV estimations cautiously. First, due to a few short time series in our panel-data sample, we are not able to run reliable regressions with fixed effects. Therefore, we have to resort to pooled IV regressions. Second, to come up with valid IV for all government expenditure items is fraught with difficulties. The over-identification test in Table 2.3 suggests that either the level or the growth rate of manufacturing productivity may be endogenous with respect to public expenditure on general administration, transport infrastructure, social security, defence and recreation, culture and religion. We carry out additional regressions for these public-expenditure items with different IV for the adjusted Baumol variable (see Table 2.4).

**Table 2.3 The impact of Baumol's cost disease on government expenditure – instrumented regressions**

| Regressors | Dependent variable: public expenditure item | | | | | |
|---|---|---|---|---|---|---|
| | Total | Health | Education | General administration | Economic affairs | Transport infrastructure |
| Adjusted Baumolvariable | 0.42** (0.18) | 0.66** (0.25) | 0.28* (0.16) | 0.34 (0.37) | -1.19* (0.67) | -1.98 (3.12) |
| Real per capita GDP | 0.52*** (0.19) | 0.70** (0.32) | 0.08 (0.16) | 1.06*** (0.35) | -0.59 (0.69) | -1.43 (2.93) |
| Extent of credit financing[a] | -0.12*** (0.003) | -0.12** (0.07) | 0.05 (0.03) | -0.17** (0.07) | 0.29** (0.13) | 0.23 (0.29) |
| Adjusted R squared | 7.9 | -7.5 | -1.7 | 6.9 | -19 | -118 |
| Weak identification test | 18** (15%) | 17** (15%) | 20** (10%) | 9.1** (20%) | 13** (15%) | 0.64 |
| Under-identification test | 17.5*** | 16.6*** | 17.5*** | 14.7*** | 12.0*** | 1.47 |
| Over-identification test | 0.01 | 0.57 | 1.59 | 3.05* | 2.12 | 3.12* |
| Chi-square bias test 2SLS | 111*** | 19571*** | 349*** | 33.8*** | 10506*** | 2062*** |
| No. of observations | 103 | 87 | 88 | 88 | 89 | 56 |

**Notes:** We use an outlier-robust IV estimator based on the proposal by Desbordes and Verardi (2012) and implemented in the Stata-command 'robivreg'. The IV estimator is a weighted LSE so that the 2-stage LSE is run without outliers. The IV covariance estimator is a minimum covariance determinant and outlier-robust HC. We use a two-stage approach: first, the reduced form equations of the instrumented variable, the adjusted Baumol variable is estimated; second, the structural equation is estimated. The Baumol variable is instrumented by the productivity growth and the productivity level of the manufacturing industry. Dependent variable and per capita GDP are in first differences of logs. T-Tests: figures in parentheses are outlier-robust HC SE. Weak identification test: Wald F test statistic, H0: The instruments are weak, given that a maximum critical value of the IV-related size distortion of the Wald F test is not exceeded. In other words: H0 is rejected under the condition that a certain maximum size distortion, the critical value, is allowed for. Note that the IV size distortion is negatively correlated with the correlation between the instruments and the endogenous regressor. The percentage of the size distortion is given in parentheses if H0 is rejected. Under-identification test: Kleibergen-Papp LM test statistic, H0: The estimated reduced-form equation is under-identified, e.g. the instruments are weak (irrelevant). Note that a rejection of H0 does not necessarily imply that instruments are not weak. Therefore, we perform also the weak identification test; Over-identification test: Hansen's J statistic, H0: Instruments are valid (exogenous), e.g. the equation with all exogenous variables is over-identified. Chi-square bias test of 2-stage LSE; H0: LSE is not biased.

*** = 1% significance level.

** = 5% significance level.

* = 10% significance level.

a = Measured by the ratio of the primary surplus to total government expenditure.

**Table 2.3 *continued***

| Regressors | Dependent variable: public expenditure item | | | | |
|---|---|---|---|---|---|
| | Housing & community amenities | Social Security | Public order & safety | Defence | Recreation, culture & religion |
| Adjusted Baumolvariable | 3.39*** (1.17) | 0.50*** (0.17) | 0.68** (0.29) | 1.30*** (0.54) | 1.45*** (0.48) |
| Real per capita GDP | 2.90** (1.17) | 0.38** (0.16) | 0.73** (0.32) | 0.33 (0.45) | 1.96*** (0.48) |
| Extent of credit financing[a] | -0.88*** (0.23) | -0.11*** (0.04) | -0.03 (0.06) | -0.13 (0.11) | -0.07 (0.10) |
| Adjusted R squared | -36 | 4.9 | -10.6 | -20.1 | -15.6 |
| Weak identification test | 7.9** (25%) | 7.8** (25%) | 19** (15%) | 10** (20%) | 12** (15%) |
| Under-identification test | 10.7*** | 11.1*** | 17.4*** | 14.3*** | 14.1*** |
| Over-identification test | 0.01 | 8.96*** | 0.44 | 5.46** | 6.95*** |

| Chi-square bias test 2SLS | 1597*** | 6373*** | 968*** | 7418*** | 1657*** |
|---|---|---|---|---|---|
| No. of observations | 82 | 92 | 90 | 83 | 83 |

*** = 1% significance level.

** = 5% significance level.

* = 10% significance level.

[a] = Measured by the ratio of the primary surplus to total government expenditure.

**Table 2.4 The impact of Baumol's cost disease on government expenditure – further instrumented regressions**

| Regressors | Dependent variable: public expenditure item | | | | | |
|---|---|---|---|---|---|---|
| | General administration | Transport infrastructure | Housing & community amenities | Social Security | Defence | Recreation, culture & religion |
| Adjusted Baumolvariable | -1.00* (0.56) | 0.69 (0.55) | 0.34 (0.26) | 0.60*** (0.19) | -0.57 (0.44) | 0.34 (0.26) |
| Real per capita GDP | -0.01 (0.45) | 1.02 (0.66) | 0.39 (0.27) | 0.79*** (0.19) | -0.23 (0.53) | 0.39 (0.27) |
| Extent of credit financing[a] | -0.06 (0.08) | 0.08 (0.08) | 0.07 (0.06) | -0.26** (0.04) | 0.21 (0.14) | 0.07 (0.06) |
| Adjusted R squared | -13 | 8.1 | 1.5 | 1.2 | -8.2 | 1.5 |
| Weak identification test | 4.61 | 5.80 | 30** (10%) | 12** (15%) | 18** (15%) | 30** (10%) |
| Under-identification test | 7.84** | 8.62** | 28.0*** | 16.3*** | 17.9*** | 28.0*** |
| Over-identification test | 2.09 | 1.19 | 0.01 | 1.89 | 0.45 | 0.01 |

| | | | | | | |
|---|---|---|---|---|---|---|
| Chi-square bias test 2SLS | 318984*** | 7.22 | 30.3*** | 104*** | 122*** | 30*** |
| No. of observations | 92 | 81 | 102 | 106 | 76 | 102 |

**Notes:** see Table 2.3. The instrumental variables of the adjusted Baumol variable are chosen dependent on the regression model. In the equation of public expenditure on general administration the GDP deflator and the productivity of the manufacturing industry, both lagged by one year, are used as instruments. In the equation of transport infrastructure, the adjusted Baumol variable is instrumented by the GDP deflator lagged by one and two years. The productivity of the manufacturing industry and the adjusted Baumol variable itself, both lagged by one year, serve as instruments for spending on housing and community amenities and defence. In the case of social security, we use the productivity growth of the manufacturing industry of the contemporaneous year and lagged by one year as instruments. Finally, we apply the adjusted Baumol variable, lagged by one and two years, as instruments in the equation for public spending on recreation, culture, and religion.

*** = 1% significance level.

** = 5% significance level.

* = 10% significance level.

a = Measured by the ratio of the primary surplus to total government expenditure.

The IV regressions corroborate the findings of the original regressions that the total government sector, public health, and public education are affected by the cost disease. The coefficient of the adjusted Baumol variable is substantially higher than in the original regressions. This points to a possible endogeneity bias. For example, in the case of total government expenditure, the impact of the cost disease would be four times higher than according to the original regression (see Tables 2.1 and 2.3). In contrast, the IV regressions do not support the result of the original regressions concerning general government expenditure (see Table 2.4). However, given the shortcomings of our IV analysis, one cannot exclude the possibility that general government expenditure is affected by the cost disease. The IV regressions reject the findings for public expenditure on recreation, culture, and religion in Table 2.2 (see Table 2.4). In contrast to the results of the original regressions, the IV regressions indicate that services on public order and safety and social security suffer from the cost disease. Thus, the corresponding original regressions might suffer from an endogeneity bias. At first sight, one may not expect that social security services are caught by the cost disease. Rather than directly, the cost disease can affect social transfers through allowances for healthcare and education. The evidence of the IV regressions for housing and community amenities deviates from the results of the original regressions (see Tables 2.1, 2.2 and 2.4). The coefficient of the adjusted Baumol variable is statistically insignificant. Given that our analysis does not provide any evidence for the cost disease in this case along with the fact that housing and community amenities have a rather capital-intensive production technology leads us to the conclusion that this government function is not affected by the cost disease. We reach the same conclusion for economic affairs, which comprises subsidies and infrastructure, and the capital-intensive government function transport infrastructure (see Tables 2.3 and 2.4).

Overall, our analysis provides strong evidence that total government expenditure, public health, and public education are affected by the cost disease. For expenditure on general government, the evidence is less strong, but not weak. Inconclusive evidence is given for social security, public order and safety, and recreation, culture and religion. Furthermore, considerable uncertainty concerning the extent of Baumol's cost disease remains. First, the coefficient of the adjusted Baumol variable varies largely between the non-instrumented and instrumented regressions. Second, the standard errors of the instrumented regressions are comparatively large.

### 2.9. Cost Disease and Balanced-budget Rule: the Swiss Case

So far, we have shown that the cost disease infects a part of the government sector. In this section, we examine whether the debt-brake rule exerts an impact on the supply of government services caught, or possibly caught, by the cost disease. Since many OECD countries have only recently introduced a debt brake, Germany as a forerunner among EU countries implemented a balanced rule at the federal level only in 2011, we make use of the Swiss experience with debt-brake rules at the federal and cantonal level and apply a Swiss dataset that spans from 1990 to 2010. The cantons of Fribourg, St. Gallen, Grisons and Solothurn, had already a debt brake in place in 1990. The time sequence of the introduction of balanced-budget rules in Switzerland allows us to carry out a small natural experiment. We are able to apply a dummy variable for the debt-brake rule, $\overline{\pi}_{debtbrake}$, that distinguishes between two periods, from 1990 to 2002 and from 2003 to 2010. As a reference for this dummy variable, we use the share of public expenditure of the federation, the cantons and the communities that are controlled by balanced-budget rules. While in the first period, a comparatively low public-expenditure share of around 20% obeys balanced- budget rules, this share rises to over 50% in the second period (see Figure 2.3).

**Figure 2.3. Share of public expanditure under a balanced budget rule - the Swiss case 1990-2010.**

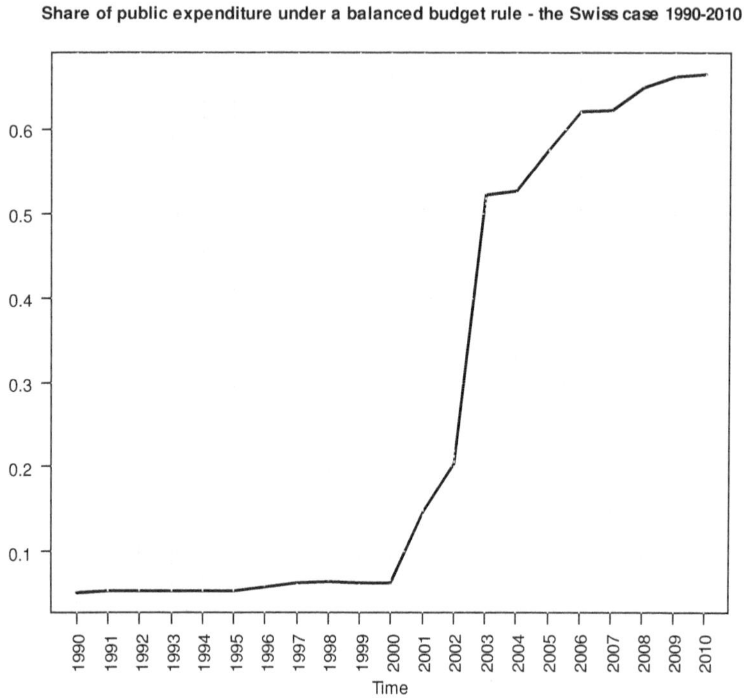


**Source: Luechinger and Schaltegger (2013), Swiss Government Finance Statistics, own calculations.**

Figure 2.3 shows that the public-expenditure share under a balanced-budget rule increased considerably between 2000 and 2003. From 2001 to 2003, the two most populous cantons, Zurich and Bern, and the federation implemented a debt brake consecutively. In particular, the implementation of the federal debt brake led to a huge jump in this share from about 20% in 2002 to over 50% in 2003. In contrast, the public-expenditure share controlled by debt-brake rules went up marginally from 5% in 1990 to 6% in 2000. In 2010 sixteen of twenty-six cantons and the federation had introduced a debt brake, and the share of public expenditure controlled by balanced-budget rules amounted to 65%. For the estimations, we use the following ARDL model:[14]

[14] ARDL:= Autoregressive distributed lag model.

$$g_j(t) = \alpha_0 + \alpha_{1j,h}\sum_{h=1}^{2} g_j(t-h) + \alpha_{2,h}\sum_{h=1}^{2} y(t-h) + \overline{\pi}_{\text{debt brake}} + \overline{\pi}_{\text{reformstatistics}} + e(t) \qquad (10)$$

whereby h, h = 1,..,2, represents the number of lags. We do not use the contemporaneous real GDP per capita to avoid drawbacks due to reversed causation. Apart from the dummy variable for the debt brake $\overline{\pi}_{\text{debtbrake}}$, we include a dummy variable, $\overline{\pi}_{\text{reformstatistics}}$, that takes the reform of the Swiss government finance statistics in 2008 into account. Since the dependent variables and the real per capita GDP are integrated of order one, we cannot exclude the possibility of spurious correlation (see Table 2.5). However, the Johansen cointegration test provides clear evidence for cointegration between real per capita GDP and real per capita public expenditure on total government, health, education and public administration respectively. The evidence regarding spurious correlation between real per capita GDP and real per capita public expenditure on public order and safety and recreation, culture and religion respectively is inconclusive. While the Johansen's cointegration test does not rule out spurious correlation, the Box-Ljung test indicates stationary residuals and, therefore, no spurious correlation. We test whether balanced-budget rules exert a more restrictive impact on government expenditure items possibly caught by the cost disease than on total government expenditure. The estimations confirm the expectation that debt-brake rules affect public expenditure in a restrictive manner. Although the coefficient of the debt-brake dummy variable is not statistically significant across all regression, it assumes a negative sign in each case (see Table 2.5). However, as the sample at our disposal is quite small, standard errors might be inflated.

**Table 2.5 The impact of the debt brake on public expenditure in Switzerland 1990 to 2010**

| Regressors | Dependent variable: public expenditure item | | | | | |
|---|---|---|---|---|---|---|
| | Total | Health | Education | General administration | Public order & safety | Recreation, culture & religion |
| Lag 1 of dependent variable | 0.54*** (0.13) | 0.74*** (0.03) | 1.53*** (0.06) | 0.22 (0.16) | 0.80*** (0.14) | 0.40* (0.21) |
| Lag 2 of | - | 0.07*** | - | - | - | - |

| dependent variable | | (0.03) | | | | |
|---|---|---|---|---|---|---|
| Real per capita GDP, lag 1 | - | - | 0.22*** (0.06) | 1.05*** (0.26) | - | 0.74*** (0.27) |
| Real per capita GDP, lag 2 | 0.64*** (0.19) | 0.86*** (0.10) | - | - | 0.39** (0.17) | - |
| *Dummy debt brake* | *-0.01 (0.02)* | *-0.02* (0.01)* | *-0.12*** (0.009)* | *-0.001 (0.02)* | *-0.01 (0.02)* | *-0.02** |
| Dummy reform finance statistic | -0.09*** (0.02) | -0.20*** (0.02) | -0.01* (0.007) | 0.03 (0.03) | -0.006 (0.02) | -0.02 (0.03) |
| Adjusted R squared | 84 | 50 | 79 | 78 | 96 | 74 |
| Box-Ljung test | 8.34 | 0.40 | 9.92 | 5.83 | 12.8 | 7.64 |
| Shapiro-Wilk test | 0.96 | 0.31*** | 0.71*** | 0.88** | 0.98 | 0.93 |
| Johansen's cointegration test | 23.7*** | 55.2*** | 21.9*** | 16.1** | 7.81 | 11.8 |
| No. of obs. | 19 | 19 | 20 | 20 | 19 | 20 |

Outlier-robust unit root test proposed by Abadir and Lucas (2000) (no drift, no trend)

| | GDP per capita | Total | Health | Education | General administration | Public order & safety | Recreation, culture & religion |
|---|---|---|---|---|---|---|---|
| Levels | 2.01 | 0.96 | 3.59 | 0.68 | 0.08 | 2.38 | 1.24 |
| First Diffs. | -1.84* | -3.15*** | -9.84*** | -3.68*** | -6.84*** | -1.53* | -2.56*** |

**Notes:** Regressions with the statistically robust MM estimator using the outlier-robust HC covariance estimator proposed by Cribari-Neto, Da Silva (2011). Model selection is made with the help of AIC.

Box-Ljung Chi-square test, H0: no autorcorrelation; Shapiro-Wilk W test, H0: Gaussian distribution; Johansen's eigenvalue cointegration test: H0: no cointegration; Outlier-robust unit root test (with 1 lag), t-statistic, H0: unit root.

*** = 1% significance level.

** = 5% significance level

* = 10% significance level.

Overall, we can infer from our regressions that debt-brake rules affect government expenditure on healthcare, education, and recreation, culture and religion more restrictively than total government expenditure. Thus, the empirical analysis provides evidence that possibly cost-disease prone government expenditure can be adversely affected by a balanced-budget rule and may be crowded out by other government expenditure items.

Nevertheless, one should read our results with some caution due to the following limitations. First, the sample size is very small so that a single further observation might change the results substantially. Yet, the outlier-robust estimation method applied takes care of this shortcoming to some extent. Second, we do not take into account that the balanced-budget rules of the cantons and the federation considerably differ in their degree of strictness (e.g. Luechinger and Schaltegger, 2013).

## 2.10. Conclusion

This charter shows that a balanced-budget rule is not consistent with Baumol's cost disease. Our empirical findings clearly support the view that the public sector suffers from Baumol's cost disease. Not only are government services as a whole affected by the cost disease but also government expenditure on health, education and general administration. As we have shown in this chapter, these findings mean that governments who adopt a balanced-budget rule face a serious dilemma. On the one hand, governments can adhere to the fiscal rule and risk a budget-crowding out and/ or foregoing growth opportunities. Empirical evidence shows that some public expenditure items such as healthcare, transport infrastructure or education can be productive (e.g. Colombier, 2011; Suhrke et al., 2006). Consequently, a budget-crowding out of these government expenditures may cause adverse consequences for economic growth. In the long run, the combination of Baumol's cost disease and a balanced-budget rule might even endanger the smooth functioning of governmental institutions. On the other hand, the breaching of the rule can imply a loss of the government's credibility and might put the fiscal sustainability at risk. Based on our findings we recommend the EU fine-tuning the Fiscal Compact in order to take Baumol's cost disease into account. Otherwise, EU member states risk impairing economic growth due to an over-proportional containment of productive public expenditure and a deterioration of the quality of government services in the long run. Future research should be devoted to studying if and how governments can simultaneously ensure fiscal sustainability, a good quality of government services and a growth-promoting fiscal policy in the presence of Baumol's cost disease. Additional insights could be gained from completing this present study by an in-depth analysis of each government expenditure function (possibly) affected by the cost disease.

## 2.11. References

AQUARO, M., ČÍŽEK, P. (2013). *One-step robust estimation of fixed-effects panel data models, Computational Statistics & Data Analysis,* 57(1), 536-548.

BATES, L. J., SANTERRE, R. E. (2013). *Does the U.S. health care sector suffer from Baumol's cost disease? Evidence from the 50 states,* Journal of health economics 32 (2), 386–391.

BATES, L. J., SANTERRE, R. E. (2015). *Does Baumol's Cost Disease Account for Nonfederal Public-Sector Cost Growth in the United States? A New Test of an Old Idea,* Social Science Quarterly 96 (1), 251–260.

BAUMOL, W.J. (1967). *Macroeconomics of unbalanced growth: The anatomy of urban crisis,* American Economic Review, 57(3), 415-426.

BAUMOL, W.J. (1985). *Productivity Policy and the Service Sector, in R.P. Inman (ed.),* Managing the Service Economy: Prospects and Problems, Cambridge University Press, Cambridge.

BAUMOL, W. J. (1993). *Health Care, Education and the Cost Disease: A Looming Crisis for Public Choice,* Public Choice, 77(1), 17-28.

BAUMOL, W.J., OATES, W.E. (1979). *Economics, Environmental Policy, and the Quality of Life,* 2nd ed.

CHEN, X., MOUL, CH. C. (2014). *Disease or utopia? Testing Baumol in education.* In: Economics Letters 122 (2), 220–223.

COLOMBIER, C. (2017). *Drivers of healthcare expenditure: What Role Does Baumol's Cost Disease Play?,* forthcoming in Social Science Quarterly.

COLOMBIER, C. (2011). *Does the composition of public expenditure affect economic growth? Evidence from the Swiss case,* Applied Economics Letters, 18 (16), 1583-1589.

COLOMBIER, C. (2009). *Growth Effects of Fiscal Policies: An Application of Robust Modified M-Estimator,* Applied Economics - Special Issue: The Applied Economics of Fiscal Policy, 41(7), 899 - 912.

COLOMBIER, C. (2006). *Does the Swiss Debt Brake Outperform the New Stability and Growth Pact in Terms of Stabilising Debt and Smoothing the Business Cycle?,* Schmollers Jahrbuch Journal of Contextual Economics, 126(4), 521-533. (published in German)

CRIBARI-NETO, F.; DA SILVA, W. B. (2011). *A new heteroskedasticity-consistent covariance matrix estimator for the linear regression model,* ASTA Adv Stat Anal 95 (2), 129–146.

DAHAN, M., STRAWCZYNSKI, M. (2013). *Fiscal Rules and the Composition of Government Expenditures in OECD Countries.* In: J. Pol. Anal. Manage. 32 (3), 484–504.

DESBORDES, R.; VERARDI, V. (2012). A robust instrumental-variables estimator, Stata Journal 12 (2), 169–181.

DEUTSCHE BUNDESBANK (2011). *The debt brake in Germany – key aspects and implementation,* Monthly Report, October 2011, 15-39.

EUROPEAN COMMISSION (2015). *The 2015 Ageing Report,* European Economy, 03/2015, Brussels.

EU-MEMO/11/647, *EU Economic Governance "Six Pack" – State of Play,* 28.09.2011, http://europa.eu/rapid/pressReleasesAction.do?reference=MEMO/11/647.

GRILICHES, Z. (ED.) (1992). *Output Measurement in the Service Sectors,* University of Chicago Press: Chicago and London.

HAMPEL, F. (2000). *Robust inference, Research Report No. 93,* Seminar for Statistics, Swiss Federal Institute of Technology Zurich (ETHZ).

HARTUNG, J. (1999). *A note on combining dependent tests of significance,* Biometrical Journal, 41(7), 849-855.

HARTWIG, J. (2008). *What drives health care expenditure? – Baumol's model of unbalanced growth revisited,* Journal of Health Economics, 27(3), 603-623.

LUECHINGER, S., SCHALTEGGER, CH (2013). *Fiscal rule, budget deficits and budget projections,* International Tax and Public Finance, 20 (5), 785-807.

MARAVINA, T. A. (2012). *Tests for Differences between Least Squares and Robust Regression Parameter Estimates and Related Topics,* Dissertation, University of Washington, Seattle.

NECK, R., GETZNER, M. (2007). *Austrian government expenditures: "Wagner's Law" or "Baumol's cost disease"?,* International Business and Economic Research Journal, 6(11), 49-65.

NOSE, M. (2015). *Estimation of Drivers of Public Education Expenditure: Baumol's Effect Revisited,* IMF Working Paper, WP/15/78, International Monetary Fund.

ROSSEN, B., FAROQUE, A. (2016). *Diagnosing the Causes of Rising Health-Care Expenditure in Canada. Does Baumol's Cost Disease Loom Large?,* American Journal of Health Economics 2 (2), 184–212.

RYAN, P. (1992). *Unbalanced growth and fiscal restriction: public spending on higher education in advances economies since 1970,* Structural Change and Economic Dynamics, 3(2), 261-288.

SCHETTKAT, R., YOCARINI, L. (2006). *The shift to services employment: A review of the literature,* Structural Change and Economic Dynamics, 17, 127-147.

STURM, J.-E., DE HAAN, J. (2001). *How Robust is the Relationship between Economic Freedom and Economic Growth,* Applied Economics, 33(7), 839-44.

TEMPLE, J. (2000). *Growth regressions and what the textbooks don't tell you,* Bulletin of Economic Research, 53(2), 181-205.

SUHRCKE, M., MCKEE, M., STUCKLER, D., SAUTO ARCE, R., TSOLOVA, S., MORTENSEN, J. (2006). The contribution of health to the economy in the European Union, Public health 120 (11), 994–1001.

TSCG, *Treaty on Stability, Coordination and Governance in the Economic and Monetary Union (2012).* signed by the EU head of governments on 12th March 2012.

VERARDI, V., WAGNER, J. (2011). *Robust Estimation of Linear Fixed Effects Panel Data Models with an Application to the Exporter Productivity Premium,* Journal of Economics and Statistics (Jahrbuecher fuer Nationaloekonomie und Statistik), 231(4), 546-557.

YOHAI, V. J., STAHEL, W. A., ZAMAR, R. H. (1991). *A procedure for robust estimation and inference in linear regression, in Directions in Robust Statistics – Part II,* Vol. 34 (Eds) W. A. Stahel and S. Weisberg, IMA Volumes in Mathematics and its Application, Springer-Verlag, New York, 365-374.

ZAMAN, A., ROOUSEEUW, P.J., ORHAN, M. (2001). *Econometric applications of high-breakdown robust regression techniques,* Economic Letters, 71(1), 1-8.

## 2.12. Appendix

### Data

The sample consists of 23 OECD countries, which include Austria, Belgium, Canada, Czech Republic, Denmark, Estonia, Finland, France, Germany, Greece, Hungary, Italy, Japan, Netherlands, Poland, Portugal, Slovak Republic, Slovenia, Spain, Sweden, Switzerland, United Kingdom and United States, and range from 1990 to 2010. The data originate from the OECD statistics and the AMECO database of the European Commission. Moreover, we use data from the Swiss government finance statistics. Except for the IV regressions that are run with the statistical software Stata, we carry out the statistical analysis with the open-source statistical software R.

**Table 2.A1. The impact of Baumol's cost disease on government expenditure – Cochrane-Orcutt estimations**

| Regressors | Dependent variable: public expenditure item | |
|---|---|---|
| | Defence | Social security |
| Adjusted Baumol variable | -0.13 (0.15) | 0.03 (0.04) |
| Real per capita GDP | 0.86** (0.39) | 0.33*** (0.08) |
| Extent of credit financing[a] | -0.17* (0.10) | -0.18*** (0.03) |
| Young-age dependency ratio[b] | | -0.49** (0.22) |
| Old-age dependency ration[c] | | -0.09 (0.14) |
| Adjusted R squared | 24 | 26 |
| Panel Ljung-Box test | -0.55 | -0.79 |
| Panel Shapiro-Wilk test | n.a.[d] | n.a.[d] |
| Chi-square bias & inefficiency test OLS | 65.7*** | 903*** |
| No. of observations | 140 | 249 |

**Notes:** see Notes Table 2.1. We use the Cochrane-Orcutt method to deal with auto-correlated residuals. We apply the Cochrane-Orcutt method to those estimations in Tables 2.1 and 2.2 for which the Panel Ljung-Box test indicates serial correlation.

*** = 1% significance level

** = 5% significance level

* = 10% significance level.

[a] = Measured by the ratio of the primary surplus to total government expenditure.

[b] = This is the ratio of the 15 years old and below to the population of the respective country.

[c] = This is the ratio of the 65 years old and above to the population of the respective country.

[d] = The number of data points at the country level does not suffice to carry out the Shapiro-Wilk test for every country.

Chapter 3

# Fiscal Union under Unsustainability of Public Debt

Gábor Kutasi

## 3.1. Introduction

In 2009, several EU members faced to years of the crisis with excessive initial public debt, but several others with broad room for fiscal stimulus. However, the prolonged duration of European economic depression expanded the public budgets and exhausted the stimulus policies and sovereign solvency. Meanwhile, one of the ways out of depression is supposed to centralize the EU by fiscal union.

As Benczes (2014:66) lamented about the fiscal union, this is not a new plan, as the idea or the necessity of a fiscal union incorporated with monetary integration has already appeared in the MacDougall Report (1977) and in the Delores Report (1989), too. Fuest and Peichel (2012) identified several elements of the fiscal union.[1] The current study is related to the risk pool originated in joint guarantees for each other's public debt or even each other's external debt through fiscal transfers and equalization. Are at least the eurozone countries or the whole EU ready for a risk pool in public finances? The study seeks the answer to this question.

There is a well developed and rich literature about budget constraint, default risk, fiscal vulnerability and debt sustainability indices. (Mankiw 1997, Barro 2008, Fatás et al. 2003, Buiter & Grafe 2004, Zee 1988, Tobin & Buiter 1976, Barnhill & Kopits 2003, Trehan & Walsh 1988, Blanchard 1990, etc.) The analysis is based on this state of the art. The methodological background is composed of the Blanchard indices of fiscal sustainability and the sovereign risk rating of the EURO19 and EU28 countries. The applied fiscal sustainability indicators are the primary gap indicator and the tax gap indicator by Blanchard (1990) After the calculation and collection of these

---

[1] Rules, crisis mechanism, joint guarantee for public debt, fiscal transfers, federal budget and taxes.

values, standard deviation and average risk indicators will be composed to verify the discouraging state of fiscal pool in the EU. The analysis results in a theoretical summary of fiscal sustainability, development of fiscal sustainability of EU member states, indicators of convergence or divergence of fiscal sustainability in the Community and conclusions from the indicators to the likelihood of a Fiscal Union.

The hypothesis of the chapter is that the sustainability of public finances deteriorated during the global and euro crisis in the majority of the eurozone and the EU, and this phenomenon is discouraging for the core countries to participate in a Fiscal Union.

### 3.2. Theory of Fiscal Sustainability and Empirical Literature Review

The fiscal spending in years of crisis and depression generally means a counter-cyclical policy. In a neoclassical model, the sustainability of such spending would not be a challenge as it assumes counter-cyclical behavior in years of economic growth, too. But since the 1970s, the European fiscal practice has been rather pro-cyclical with temporary adjustments. Many of the European national public budgets were already found in high indebtedness on the eve of the crisis in 2008. The concept of fiscal sustainability is that if sovereigns' solvency is ensured if the current debt equals with the net present value of the sum of future primary surpluses. (Benczes & Kutasi, 2010: 67) Otherwise, the continuous annual deficits will enforce adjustment in the structure of the public budget.

Namely, the basic form of fiscal sustainability is a net present value of revenues, expenditures and the existing debt. However, these budget items are affected by economic factors (particularly or completely) out of control of the fiscal policy.

This way we get the budget constraint, dependent on the interest rate, growth rate, and the past deficits.

$$(g_t - {}_t) + [(1+r_t) \;/\; (1+n_t)]\, b_{t-1} = b_t \qquad (1)$$

where $g$ is the governmental expenditure in ratio to GDP, $\tau$ is the tax revenue in ratio to GDP, $r$ is the real interest rate, $n$ is the growth ratio of GDP, $b$ is the debt ratio to the GDP.

Namely, according to Fatás et al. (2003), the change of debt is

$$\mathrm{b} = \mathrm{g} - \quad + (\mathrm{r}\text{-}\mathrm{n})\mathrm{b} \qquad (2)$$

De Grauwe (2000:167) extended this budget constraint by distinguishing seignorage revenues *(m)* as it follows:

$$b = g - \quad + (r\text{-}n)b - m \tag{3}$$

From equitation (1), (2) and (3), it can be established, that the public debt ratio can increase if *r* exceeds *n*, and/or if the fiscal balance is in deficit ( $g - \tau$ >0), and/or if seignorage income is decreasing. Equitation (2) makes it obvious that there are factors which cannot really be modified by the fiscal policy in the short term: real interest rate, growth of GDP, inherited public debt from the past. Quick adjustment can be implemented only through the tax revenues and the expenditures.

Of course, there are cyclical phenomena in the budget which must be taken into account in the understanding of fiscal solvency. That is why, according to Chalk and Hemming (2000), and Buiter and Grafe (2004), the determination of fiscal sustainability can be refined with the criterion as follows: the present value of the initial net public debt and the present value of the deficits in the future altogether should not exceed the present value of the sum of fiscal surplus in the future. McCallum (1984) considered it a vulnerable fiscal stance, too, if the accumulation of absolute debt value is faster than the rate of increase in the interest rate but slower than the speed of economic growth. Seemingly, it means decreasing debt in GDP-ratio, but the sustainability criterion is violated.

The budget constraint was refined by the concept of fiscal crowding-out effect (Tobin and Buiter, 1976) and overlapping generations (Zee, 1988). The approach extended with the crowding-out impact includes the effect of public debt on the stock of capital assets. It calculates with the effect of taxation on the income remains disposable for the private sector and the effect of public debt on capital markets, market rates and saving propensity. The microeconomic approach of overlapping generations involves the dynamics originated in the finite horizon of individuals standing behind the public bond acquisitions. Moreover, an individual has variable saving preferences and opportunities during his/her own life, which correlate strongly with the variable incomes in different ages. This way, the budget constraint can be derived from the individuals' income optimization, namely from the saving propensity, the interest rate elasticity of private investments and savings, and the capital elasticity of the production output. This way, besides the factors mentioned in the equitation (1)-(3), the higher capital-to-GDP ratio and the bigger interest rate elasticity results in extended budget constraint and improves the fiscal sustainability.

Nevertheless, the calculation of fiscal sustainability is just a simple technical, mathematical exercise, but keeping the budget constraint is a political game both in inter-temporal and in international sense. Former one depends on the preference of current society (or politicians) whether to finance the current expenditures or pass it on to the future generations by indebting. The latter is possible because of the globally interconnected community of states which has disciplined countries and governments having net savings.

There are several studies about European countries' fiscal sustainability which were written before the global financial and European debt crisis and numerous, too, which include the data of crisis years. For example, Afonso (2000) or Afonso and Rault (2010) made stationarity tests for the stock of public debt and co-integration tests between public expenditures and public revenues in case of Euro countries, and most of the (fifteen) eurozone countries had unsustainable debt according to the data before 2007. However, they state the overall European fiscal stance was sustainable, even though there were many challenges in a national level, what is, also, consistent with Claeys (2007) results from his test based on the cointegration relation between government revenues, expenditures and interest payments about data before 2002. But the repeated analysis by Afonso and Rault (2015) including crisis year data, too, does not confirm anymore the overall sustainability of EU fiscal policies, but discover the appearance of unsustainability.

There are future-oriented studies, e.g. Cournede and Gonand (2008) recommended and assessed scenarios how to restore sustainability. Or Checherita-Westphal et al. (2012) calculated the optimum debt target for long-term solvency. Balassone et al. (2008) focused on the long-term challenge of an aging population on public revenue and expenditure in the EU, thus, forecasted the very long-term future trends in fiscal sustainability. This approach of analysis was repeated in the European Commission (2012) analysis including already information about the crisis years.

Borgy at al. (2011) analyzed the risk premium in relevance to fiscal sustainability. They established that before the crisis year of 2009, there was a strong comovement among the risk premia of the eurozone countries. However, they also refer to Laubach (2011) who found that comovement among yield spreads has weakened since 2009. Namely, the impact of euro debt crisis caused not only deterioration but divergence in fiscal sustainability among members, which phenomenon is not supportive of a fiscal union. They concluded that because of the debt crisis, an explosion in EMU governments' bond yield spreads became a threat to national solvency and financial stability in Europe. They found evidence for that sharp increase in government debt, explains the bulk of the increase in spreads, what limits the fiscal stabilization opportunities. But what is more important, that "*the increase in spreads was to a large extent driven by increases in risk premia, implying that the deterioration of the economic and fiscal outlook during the crisis led to an endogenous increase in the market price of risk, thereby magnifying the effects on yield spreads much beyond pure compensation for perceived higher default risk.*" (Borgy et al., 2011:26)

Beritella and Zhang (2015) analyzed the public debt sustainability in the EU with a dynamic computable general equilibrium model to identify the short-term risk on the economy from the fiscal unsustainability, and to prove the convergence toward public debt threshold. They calculated short term fiscal risk in the well known PIIGS group of countries, but their long-term forecast showed no long-term risk but consolidation in public debt because of trends in GDP and taxation.

## 3.3 Methodology and Data

Sustainability simply means whether a *given* process, activity, or policy could be maintained either in a definite or indefinite future. When something is rated as unsustainable, it represents an expectation that certain phenomena might halt or altogether extinguish mechanisms that have been working fine. Translated into budget policy, it means that if the (primary) budget balance records constant deficit, it will increase the portfolio of public debt. And due to an increasing debt ratio, government bonds representing the debt will become riskier in terms of redemption and interest payment. Therefore, the sustainability of budget policy is primarily subject to real interest rates and economic growth. The fiscal sustainability can be measured with the indicators of Blanchard (1990), namely, the primary gap and the tax gap.[2] These indicators were used in the research to measure the fiscal sustainability of new member countries (2004 enlargement) before the global crisis.

The Blanchard indicators are composed as it follows. The primary gap indicator is rooted in the sustainability indicator by Buiter (1985) which was deducted as a difference of permanent (structural) deficit ($d$) and the current primary deficit ($d_t$) and scaled to the net size of public finances to the GDP. The primary gap indicator replaced the size of public finances to the public debt.

The permanent deficit term by Blanchard (1990) is

---

[2] Blanchard has a third indicator, too, the so called long-term tax gap (or tax rate stabilizing the debt).

$$d^{\frown} = ( n_t - r_t)^* b_t \tag{4}$$

and the difference is the primary gap, namely

$$d^{\frown} - d_t = ( n_t - r_t)^* b_t - d_t \tag{5}$$

where $d^{\frown}$ is the permanent deficit, $d_t$ is the current deficit. If the current deficit exceeds permanent deficit ($d^{\frown} < d_t$), the public budget is not sustainable, and the level of current deficit destabilizes the fiscal policy.

The tax gap indicator similarly assesses the difference between the current tax ($\tau_t$) rate and the permanent tax rate ($\tau^{\frown}$ ). The permanent tax rate

$$^{\frown} \quad g_t - ( n_t - r_t)^* b_t \tag{6}$$

and the difference is the tax gap, namely

$$_t - {}^{\frown} \quad {}_t + ( n_t - r_t)^* b_t - g_t \tag{7}$$

If ($\tau_t - \tau^{\frown}$ ) difference is less than zero, the current tax revenues are not sufficient to secure the long-term solvency. In case of tax gap, to simplify the calculation, the overall government revenues are taken into account, as in case of sustainability the origin of revenue is a secondary question.

As fiscal union is also a risk pool – which characteristic can be considered to be common pool resource of long-term solvency, – it is an important factor of overall solvency and willingness to participate. That is why we analyze the risk premium of the countries to see whether each of them would be a stabilizer or a free rider of the fiscal union.

The source of data is Eurostat, AMECO and indirectly Datastream: the GDP-ratio forms of general government's debt, revenues, and expenditures. In the case of real interest rate, there was a need for calculation as a difference of nominal interest rate and inflation. In the mentioned databases, the three months market rate was available historically for every currently eurozone countries, that is why this is the interest rate base of calculation. The inflation is the annual average change in consumer prices. The current primary balance is calculated as a difference of net lending/borrowing and the interest payable.

In the case of real interest rate calculation, it is the difference between nominal interest rate and the inflation ($r = i - HICP$). In the case of the empirical data, there were some dilemmas and constraints of statistics. First of all, as the gap indicators are about the sustainability of *public* finances, long-term government bond yields were taken into account as the nominal interest rate on borrowing. This is published as Maastricht criterion interest rates.[3] Where the Eurostat database was not complete, the following supplements were done in the database: There are no Estonian sovereign debt securities that comply with the definition of long-term interest rates for convergence purposes. No suitable proxy indicator has been identified. That is why the 3-months market rate was taken into account as Eurostat published historical data only of this rate in case of eurozone countries. For Cyprus, primary market yields are reported. The same applies to Bulgaria and Romania up to December 2005, Slovenia up to October 2003 and Lithuania up to October 2007. A harmonized long-term interest rate is presented starting mid-May 2010. Before, the Luxembourg Government did not have outstanding long-term debt securities with a residual maturity of close to ten years. Therefore, the yield on long-term bond(s) issued by a private credit institution with a residual maturity close to 10 years is presented for the period up to mid-May 2010 and is thus not fully harmonized for that period. In the following cases, the missing data was substituted with 3 and 12-month yields: Bulgaria 1999-2002, Malta, Poland, Slovakia, Latvia and Lithuania 1999-2000, Romania 1999-2005, Slovenia 1999-2001. There were no data for Croatia 1999-2000.

### 3.4. Analysis of EU Fiscal Indicators

The 28 member states of the EU are analyzed from the perspective of fiscal sustainability. As fiscal union would be built on a monetary integration, sustainability indicators are analyzed since the implementation of the single currency (1999), which was a strong commitment for EU-15 to seek fiscal convergence. According to the primary balance data (Table 3.1), calculated from net lending/borrowing reduced with the interest payable, it can be established that the initial commitment to fiscal balance in the eve of the euro disappeared particularly due to the pro-cyclical policy making of some undisciplined governments before the global recession (2009), and also because of broadly-used, massive, anti-cyclical stimuli during the economic crisis, even in many countries indebted deeply, alongside with sharply

---

[3] http://ec.europa.eu/eurostat/cache/metadata/en/irt_lt_mcby_esms.htm

increasing risk premium. A serious accumulation of fiscal reserves is only observable in the case of Italy among the indebted eurozone countries. Spain, Greece, Portugal, and France, or Ireland did not excel in primary surplus. In any case, only those countries created a primary surplus in the EU that earlier reformed their own public finances for sustainability: Germany, Sweden, Denmark, Belgium, Austria, Luxemburg, and the Baltic countries.

However, if we take into account every aspect of long-term solvency, the primary gap data (Table 3.2) strengthen the conclusion drawn from the primary balance data, with the addition of the UK and the Czech Republic to the list. The tax gap data (Table 3.3), however, do not confirm the restoration of fiscal sustainability after the stimulus period in 2011-2014, except in the case of Germany, Luxembourg and the UK. Namely, there is a serious challenge on the revenue side.

As it was mentioned, fiscal union is a risk community. In the case of the EU, the cyclical movement of the economy in time increases the difference of sovereign fiscal risks among the member countries (see standard deviation in Table 3.4 and Table 3.5). That is to say, it is very difficult to create fiscal solidarity between disciplined and free rider players of the European monetary community.

## 3.5. Conclusion

This study analyzed the fiscal sustainability of the EU member states, as well as the risk community of a potential European fiscal union. The theory of fiscal sustainability was summarized and explained to a better understanding, and, moreover, sustainability indicators were derived from the terms of budget constraint. It was established that government solvency is determined by economic growth and market rate levels, in addition to internal fiscal factors like inherited debt and the balance of revenues and expenditures. The empirical literature review presented the results of existing sustainability analysis regarding the EU. The review strengthened the assumption about the negative impact of the crisis and its anticipation of the vulnerability and room for maneuver of public finances, as well as about fiscal divergence in risk and sustainability indicators among the EU members.

The empirical analysis used the primary gap and the tax gap indicators of fiscal sustainability and the sovereign risk rating of the eurozone and other EU-28 countries. The following conclusions were established: 1) the enthusiasm in the majority of eurozone countries for debt sustainability lasted mostly until their accession to the single currency zone. 2) During the economic growth period of the 2000s, many of the EU countries had a pro-cyclical fiscal policy according to their primary deficit, which deteriorated their sustainability indicators too. 3) During 2012-2014, only a few EU countries managed to restore debt sustainability according to the primary gap indicator. 4) Although the single currency zone seemed to be an integrating community with declining and converging risk premium in the government bond market, the global financial crisis of 2008-2009 highlighted that the convergence of risk premia happened particularly because of the interim excess liquidity of global financial markets and because rating agencies misrated the risk of sovereign debtors.

Regarding the fiscal union, in the 2010s, the fiscal sustainability structure of the countries shows different engagement or capability to create a risk pool of fiscal federalism either in the eurozone or the whole EU. The divergence of debt sustainability in the eurozone countries and the EU means a potential moral hazard in case of a possible fiscal union in a macroeconomic sense. This conclusion does not exclude the feasibility of fiscal federalism in the EU, but, if it happens, it will be driven by political will and intent, which overwrites economic rationale.

### 3.6. References

AFONSO, A., RAULT, C. (2010). *What do we really know about fiscal sustainability in the EU?* A panel data diagnostic. Review of World Economics, 145(4), 731-755.

AFONSO, A., RAULT, C. (2015). *Multi-step analysis of public finances sustainability.* Economic Modelling, 48(8), 199-209.

AFONSO, A. (2000). *Fiscal Policy Sustainability: Some Unpleasant European Evidence (August 2000).* ISEG Working Paper, No. 12/2000/DE/CISEP.

BALASSONE, F., CUNHA, J., LANGENUS, G., MANZKE, B., PAVOT, J., PRAMMER, D., TOMMASINO P. (2008). *Fiscal sustainability and policy implications for the Euro Area.* Banque de France NER, 225.

BARNHILL, T. M., KOPITS, G. (2003). *Assessing fiscal sustainability under uncertainty.* IMF Working Papers, 79.

BARRO, R. J. (2008). *Macroeconomics: A modern approach.* Thomson South-Western.

BENCZES, I., KUTASI G. (2010). *Költségvetési pénzügyek. Hiány, államadósság és fenntarthatóság.* Budapest: Akadémiai kiadó (Public finances: Deficit, public debt and sustainability).

BENCZES, I. (2014) *Intergovernmentalism versus Supranationalism. Challenges and Controversies in European Economic Governance. In I. Benczes (Ed.), Crisis in the West and the East. Economic Governance in Times of Challenge (pp. 59-73).* Wien: Wiener Verlag.

BERITELLA, M., ZHANG, J. (2015). *Fiscal sustainability in the EU: From the short-term risk to the long-term challenge.* Journal of Policy Modeling, 37(2), 261-280.

BLANCHARD, O. J. (1990). *Suggestions for a New Set of Fiscal Indicators.* OECD Working Papers, 79.

BORGY, V., LAUBACH, T., MÉSONNIER, J-S., RENNE, J-P. (2011). *Fiscal Sustainability, Default Risk and Euro Area Sovereign Bond Spreads.* Banque de France Document de Travail, 315.

BUITER, W. H., GRAFE, C. (2004). *Patching up the Pact: Some Suggestions for Enhancing Fiscal Sustainability on Enlarged European Union.* CEPR Discussion Paper, 3496.

BUITER, W. H. (1985). *Guide to public sector debt and deficits.* Economic Policy, 1(3), 13-79.

CHALK, N., HEMMING, R. (2000). *Assessing Fiscal Sustainability in Theory and Practice.* IMF Working Papers, WP/00/81.

CHECHERITA-WESTPHAL, C., HUGHES HALLETT, A., ROTHER, P. (2012). *Fiscal sustainability using growth-maximising debt targets.* Applied Economics, 46(6), 638-647.

CLAEYS, P. (2007). *Sustainability of EU Fiscal Policies: a Panel Test.* Journal of Economic Integration, 22(1), 112-127.

COURNÈDE, B., GONAND, F. (2008). *Restoring Fiscal Sustainability in the Euro Area: Raise Taxes or Curb Spending? OECD Economics Department Working Papers, 520.*

DE GRAUWE, P. (2000). *Economics of Monetary.* Union Oxford University Press.

DELORS REPORT. (1989). *Report on Economic and Monetary Union in the European community.* Committee for the Study of Economic and Monetary Union.

EUROPEAN COMMISSION. (2012). *Fiscal Sustainability Report 2012.* European Commission.

FATÁS, A., VON HAGEN, J., HUGHES-HALLETT, A., STRAUCH, R. R., SIBERT, A. (2003). *Stability and Growth in Europe: Towards a Better Pact.* CEPR, ZEI.

FUEST, C., PEICHEL, A. (2012). *European fiscal union. What is it? Does it work? And are there really no alternatives?* IZA Policy Paper, 39.

HEINZ, F. F., SUN, Y. (2014). *Sovereign CDS Spreads in Europe—The Role of Global Risk Aversion, Economic Fundamentals, Liquidity, and Spillovers.* IMF Working Papers, WP/14/17.

LAUBACH, T. (2011). *Fiscal policy and interest rates: The role of sovereign default risk. In R. Clarida, F. Giavazzi (Eds.), NBER International Seminar on Macroeconomics 2010 (pp. 7-29).* Chicago: The University of Chicago Press.

MACDOUGALL REPORT. (1977). *Report of the study group on the role of public finances in the European integration. Vol. 1.* Brussels: Commission of the European Communities.

MANKIW, N. G. (1997). *Macroeconomics. 3rd edition.* New York.

MCCALLUM, B. T. (1984*). Are Bond-Financed Deficits Inflationary? A Ricardian Analysis.* Journal of Political Economy, 92(2), 123-135.

TOBIN, J., BUITER, W. (1976). *Long-run effects of fiscal and monetary policy on aggregate demand. In J. L. Stein (Ed.), Monetarism, studies in monetary economics (pp. 273-309).* Amsterdam: North-Holland.

TREHAN, B., WALSH, C. E. (1988). *Common Trends, The Government's Budget Constraint, and Revenue Smoothing.* Journal of Economic Dynamics and Control, 12(2-3), 425-444.

ZEE, H. H. (1988). *The sustainability and optimality of government debt.* IMF Staff Papers, 35(4), 658-685.

**Table 3.1 Primary balance**

| | 1999 | 2000 | 2001 | 2002 | 2003 | 2004 | 2005 | 2006 | 2007 | 2008 | 2009 | 2010 | 2011 | 2012 | 2013 | 2014 |
|---|---|---|---|---|---|---|---|---|---|---|---|---|---|---|---|---|
| **AT** | 0.8 | 1.6 | 3.0 | 2.2 | 1.4 | -1.8 | 0.7 | 0.6 | 1.8 | 1.6 | -2.1 | -1.5 | 0.2 | 0.5 | 1.3 | -0.2 |
| **BE** | 6.3 | 6.6 | 6.7 | 5.8 | 3.6 | 4.6 | 1.8 | 4.4 | 4.1 | 2.9 | -1.6 | -0.4 | -0.5 | -0.5 | 0.4 | 0.0 |
| **BG** | 3.7 | 3.6 | 5.3 | 1.0 | 1.8 | 3.6 | 2.6 | 3.1 | 2.2 | 2.4 | -3.4 | -2.5 | -1.3 | 0.2 | -0.1 | -4.9 |
| **HR*** | -6.4 | -3.8 | -0.3 | -1.8 | -2.8 | -3.1 | -1.8 | -1.4 | -0.6 | -0.8 | -3.5 | -3.4 | -4.8 | -1.9 | -1.9 | -2.1 |
| **CY** | -1.2 | 0.9 | 1.0 | -1.2 | -2.7 | -0.7 | 1.0 | 2.0 | 6.0 | 3.5 | -3.1 | -2.7 | -3.5 | -2.9 | -1.8 | -6.0 |
| **CZ** | -2.5 | -2.7 | -4.4 | -5.2 | -5.4 | -1.6 | -2.0 | -1.3 | 0.4 | -1.1 | -4.3 | -3.1 | -1.4 | -2.6 | 0.0 | -0.6 |
| **DK** | 5.0 | 5.6 | 4.5 | 3.1 | 2.7 | 4.6 | 7.1 | 6.8 | 6.6 | 4.6 | -0.9 | -0.8 | -0.1 | -1.8 | 0.4 | 3.0 |
| **EE** | -2.9 | 0.2 | 0.4 | 0.7 | 2.0 | 2.6 | 1.3 | 3.1 | 2.9 | -2.5 | -2.0 | 0.3 | 1.3 | -0.2 | 0.0 | 0.8 |
| **FI** | 4.6 | 9.6 | 7.6 | 6.1 | 4.2 | 3.9 | 4.2 | 5.4 | 6.5 | 5.6 | -1.2 | -1.3 | 0.4 | -0.7 | -1.2 | -2.1 |
| **FR** | 1.3 | 1.5 | 1.5 | -0.2 | -1.2 | -0.8 | -0.6 | 0.2 | 0.1 | -0.4 | -4.8 | -4.4 | -2.5 | -2.2 | -1.8 | -1.7 |
| **DE** | 1.3 | 4.0 | -0.1 | -1.0 | -1.3 | -0.9 | -0.7 | 1.0 | 2.9 | 2.5 | -0.6 | -1.7 | 1.5 | 2.2 | 1.9 | 2.1 |
| **EL**** | 4.2 | 3.5 | 1.9 | 0.7 | -0.7 | -2.5 | -0.9 | -1.5 | -2.2 | -5.4 | -10.2 | -5.3 | -2.9 | -3.7 | -8.4 | 0.3 |
| **HU** | 1.6 | 2.3 | 0.6 | -4.9 | -3.1 | -2.1 | -3.7 | -5.4 | -1.0 | 0.5 | -0.1 | -0.4 | -1.3 | 2.3 | 2.0 | 1.5 |
| **IR** | 4.8 | 6.8 | 2.4 | 1.0 | 1.9 | 2.5 | 2.3 | 3.8 | 1.3 | -5.7 | -11.8 | -29.3 | -9.1 | -3.9 | -1.4 | 0.1 |
| **IT** | 4.6 | 4.8 | 2.7 | 2.4 | 1.6 | 1.0 | 0.3 | 0.8 | 3.3 | 2.2 | -0.9 | 0.1 | 1.2 | 2.2 | 1.9 | 1.6 |
| **LV** | -3.1 | -1.8 | -1.1 | -1.5 | -0.9 | -0.3 | 0.1 | -0.2 | -0.3 | -3.5 | -7.6 | -6.8 | -1.6 | 0.8 | 0.6 | -0.1 |
| **LT** | -1.3 | -1.5 | -2.0 | -0.6 | -0.1 | -0.5 | 0.5 | 0.4 | -0.1 | -2.4 | -7.9 | -5.1 | -7.1 | -1.1 | -0.8 | 0.9 |
| **LU** | 4.0 | 6.1 | 6.3 | 2.6 | 0.8 | -0.9 | 0.4 | 1.6 | 4.5 | 3.6 | -0.1 | -0.1 | 1.0 | 0.7 | 1.1 | 1.8 |
| **MT** | -2.9 | -1.4 | -2.4 | -1.5 | -5.6 | -0.7 | 1.1 | 1.1 | 1.2 | -0.9 | 0.0 | -0.1 | 0.5 | -0.6 | 0.3 | 0.8 |
| **NL** | 4.2 | 5.2 | 2.6 | 0.5 | -0.6 | 0.6 | 1.9 | 2.2 | 2.2 | 2.2 | -3.4 | -3.2 | -2.5 | -2.3 | -0.9 | -1.0 |
| **PL** | 0.7 | 0.0 | -1.7 | -1.9 | -3.1 | -2.5 | -1.5 | -1.2 | 0.3 | -1.5 | -4.8 | -5.0 | -2.4 | -1.0 | -1.5 | -1.4 |
| **PT** | -0.1 | -0.2 | -1.8 | -0.5 | -1.7 | -3.6 | -3.6 | -1.5 | -0.1 | -0.7 | -6.8 | -8.3 | -3.1 | -0.8 | 0.1 | -2.3 |
| **RO** | 0.6 | -0.8 | -0.1 | 0.5 | 0.1 | 0.2 | 0.0 | -1.4 | -2.2 | -4.9 | -7.6 | -5.4 | -3.8 | -1.4 | -0.5 | 0.3 |
| **SK** | -4.0 | -8.0 | -2.5 | -4.6 | -0.2 | -0.2 | -1.2 | -2.2 | -0.5 | -1.1 | -6.5 | -6.2 | -2.6 | -2.4 | -0.7 | -0.9 |
| **SI** | -0.7 | -1.2 | -1.6 | -0.3 | -0.7 | -0.3 | 0.2 | 0.2 | 1.1 | -0.3 | -4.6 | -4.0 | -4.7 | -2.1 | -12.4 | -1.8 |
| **ES** | 2.1 | 2.2 | 2.5 | 2.2 | 1.9 | 2.0 | 2.9 | 3.8 | 3.6 | -2.9 | -9.3 | -7.5 | -7.0 | -7.4 | -3.5 | -2.5 |
| **SE** | 4.6 | 6.5 | 4.0 | 1.4 | 0.8 | 2.0 | 3.6 | 3.8 | 5.0 | 3.6 | 0.5 | 1.1 | 1.0 | 0.0 | -0.6 | -1.0 |
| **UK** | 3.5 | 3.8 | 2.6 | -0.2 | -1.5 | -1.7 | -1.5 | -0.9 | -0.8 | -2.9 | -8.9 | -6.8 | -4.5 | -5.4 | -2.8 | -3.0 |
| **EA19** | n/a | n/a | n/a | n/a | n/a | n/a | n/a | 1.3 | 2.3 | 0.7 | -3.5 | -3.5 | -1.2 | -0.7 | -0.2 | 0.1 |
| **EU28** | n/a | n/a | n/a | n/a | n/a | n/a | n/a | 1.0 | 1.7 | 0.2 | -4.1 | -3.7 | -1.6 | -1.4 | -0.6 | -0.5 |
| **mean** | 1.2 | 1.9 | 1.3 | 0.2 | -0.3 | 0.1 | 0.5 | 1.0 | 1.7 | -0.1 | -4.2 | -4.1 | -2.1 | -1.3 | -1.1 | -0.7 |
| **S.D.** | 3.59 | 3.47 | 2.90 | 2.55 | 2.37 | 2.31 | 2.49 | 2.60 | 2.93 | 3.87 | 4.63 | 4.49 | 2.51 | 2.62 | 2.56 | 2.04 |

**Source**: Eurostat, HR '99-'00 & EL '99-'05 IMF World Economic Outlook; mean = EU28 average, S.D.= EU28 standard deviation

**Table 3.2 Primary gap, if we demand d=0, gap=(nt-rt)*bt**

| | 1999 | 2000 | 2001 | 2002 | 2003 | 2004 | 2005 | 2006 | 2007 | 2008 | 2009 | 2010 | 2011 | 2012 | 2013 | 2014 |
|---|---|---|---|---|---|---|---|---|---|---|---|---|---|---|---|---|
| **AT** | -39 | -11 | -92 | -103 | -134 | 37 | 55 | 87 | 97 | 23 | -585 | 30 | 253 | 84 | 32 | 35 |
| **BE** | -6 | 77 | -208 | -167 | -190 | 130 | 111 | 90 | 76 | 72 | -615 | 153 | 99 | -21 | -126 | 10 |
| **BG** | -698 | 748 | 419 | 284 | 41 | 265 | 253 | 213 | 179 | 163 | -127 | -46 | -6 | -34 | -32 | -95 |
| **HR** | n/a | n/a | 53 | 183 | 172 | -44 | 40 | 141 | 110 | 72 | -625 | -393 | -296 | -341 | -264 | -361 |
| **CY** | -25 | 230 | -115 | 18 | 131 | 45 | 47 | 152 | 142 | 159 | -346 | -34 | -125 | -501 | -1226 | -946 |
| **CZ** | -55 | 48 | 29 | -49 | -17 | 76 | 125 | 145 | 117 | 125 | -308 | -15 | 16 | -8 | -54 | 35 |
| **DK** | 5 | 40 | -96 | -106 | -88 | -35 | 26 | 60 | -49 | -46 | -307 | 37 | 54 | 14 | -79 | 4 |
| **EE** | -33 | 45 | 32 | 33 | 33 | 35 | 50 | 51 | 35 | -7 | -143 | 24 | 68 | 86 | 46 | 34 |
| **FI** | 43 | 128 | 11 | -51 | -36 | -5 | 10 | 62 | 85 | 10 | -435 | 80 | 140 | -5 | -42 | -39 |
| **FR** | -37 | 18 | -66 | -112 | -73 | 66 | 6 | 32 | -19 | -57 | -510 | 47 | 92 | -13 | -46 | -83 |
| **DE** | -114 | -51 | -69 | -201 | -238 | -67 | -50 | 116 | 88 | -5 | -626 | 206 | 280 | 79 | 25 | 93 |
| **EL** | -97 | 99 | 220 | 263 | 464 | 364 | 50 | 560 | 203 | -107 | -1115 | -1551 | -3978 | -4703 | -2565 | -1402 |
| **HU** | -38 | 155 | 257 | 144 | 97 | 206 | 79 | 44 | 103 | -104 | -917 | -152 | -157 | -305 | -179 | -85 |
| **IR** | 401 | 363 | 160 | 172 | 110 | 74 | 135 | 125 | 98 | -155 | -781 | -607 | -645 | -495 | -233 | 343 |
| **IT** | -157 | 76 | -114 | -217 | -126 | -36 | -47 | 15 | -99 | -223 | -1014 | -85 | -223 | -614 | -607 | -408 |
| **LV** | -46 | 32 | 20 | 49 | 89 | 137 | 161 | 142 | 124 | 98 | -850 | -718 | 192 | 71 | -13 | 24 |
| **LT** | -161 | -46 | -1 | 14 | 57 | 62 | 118 | 122 | 196 | 118 | -713 | -100 | 184 | 86 | 34 | 17 |
| **LU** | 32 | 41 | -2 | 7 | 4 | 31 | 29 | 34 | 48 | -19 | -149 | 104 | 65 | 6 | 100 | 82 |
| **MT** | n/a | n/a | -202 | -14 | -44 | -114 | 122 | 5 | -1 | 200 | -355 | 89 | 8 | 106 | 17 | 115 |
| **NL** | 144 | 56 | 109 | -43 | -80 | -35 | 16 | 64 | 43 | -18 | -367 | -41 | 74 | -15 | 10 | -10 |
| **PL** | -114 | -149 | -156 | -145 | -69 | 82 | 22 | 107 | 191 | 95 | 24 | 33 | 161 | 16 | -108 | -6 |
| **PT** | 67 | 51 | 61 | -29 | -104 | 10 | -36 | 48 | 33 | -116 | -678 | -202 | -938 | -1478 | -907 | -397 |
| **RO** | -473 | -41 | -55 | 2 | 97 | 58 | 84 | 92 | 59 | 115 | -260 | -61 | -13 | -100 | 49 | -12 |
| **SK** | -258 | 240 | 119 | 45 | 366 | 315 | 192 | 258 | 245 | 138 | -335 | 79 | 106 | 34 | -16 | 18 |
| **SI** | 65 | 56 | 16 | 70 | 56 | 92 | 71 | 113 | 140 | 91 | -389 | -20 | -106 | -307 | -352 | 11 |
| **ES** | 120 | 190 | 91 | 79 | 104 | 100 | 157 | 156 | 81 | 33 | -410 | -135 | -231 | -511 | -438 | -149 |
| **SE** | 1 | 32 | -42 | -65 | 3 | 42 | 11 | 108 | 36 | -44 | -264 | 184 | 54 | -36 | -20 | 34 |
| **UK** | -26 | -29 | -37 | -40 | 4 | -45 | 27 | 27 | -7 | -73 | -353 | 110 | 297 | 194 | 242 | 202 |
| **EA19** | n/a | n/a | n/a | n/a | n/a | n/a | n/a | n/a | n/a | n/a | n/a | n/a | -3 | -192 | -181 | -68 |
| **EU28** | n/a | n/a | n/a | n/a | n/a | n/a | n/a | n/a | n/a | n/a | n/a | n/a | 43 | -130 | -108 | -18 |

**Source**: authors calculation based on Eurostat and IMF World Economic Outlook data, and Blanchard (1990) index

**Table 3.3 Tax gap, if we demand Tt = gt, gap = (nt-rt)*bt – gt**

| | 1999 | 2000 | 2001 | 2002 | 2003 | 2004 | 2005 | 2006 | 2007 | 2008 | 2009 | 2010 | 2011 | 2012 | 2013 | 2014 |
|---|---|---|---|---|---|---|---|---|---|---|---|---|---|---|---|---|
| **AT** | -90 | -61 | -143 | -154 | -185 | -16 | 4 | 37 | 48 | -27 | -639 | -22 | 202 | 33 | -19 | -18 |
| **BE** | -55 | 29 | -257 | -216 | -240 | 82 | 60 | 42 | 28 | 23 | -668 | 101 | 46 | -76 | -181 | -45 |
| **BG** | -737 | 708 | 379 | 245 | 3 | 227 | 216 | 179 | 140 | 125 | -167 | -84 | -40 | -69 | -71 | -134 |
| **HR** | n/a | n/a | 8 | 135 | 125 | -91 | -5 | 95 | 65 | 28 | -673 | -440 | -344 | -388 | -312 | -409 |
| **CY** | -59 | 195 | -150 | -19 | 90 | 6 | 7 | 113 | 104 | 120 | -389 | -76 | -168 | -543 | -1268 | -995 |
| **CZ** | -96 | 8 | -13 | -93 | -66 | 34 | 83 | 104 | 77 | 85 | -352 | -58 | -27 | -52 | -96 | -7 |
| **DK** | -49 | -13 | -149 | -159 | -142 | -88 | -25 | 10 | -98 | -97 | -363 | -20 | -3 | -45 | -136 | -53 |
| **EE** | -74 | 9 | -3 | -3 | -2 | 0 | 16 | 17 | 1 | -46 | -189 | -17 | 30 | 46 | 7 | -5 |
| **FI** | -8 | 80 | -37 | -100 | -85 | -54 | -39 | 14 | 39 | -38 | -490 | 25 | 86 | -61 | -100 | -97 |
| **FR** | -89 | -33 | -118 | -164 | -125 | 13 | -47 | -20 | -72 | -110 | -566 | -9 | 36 | -69 | -103 | -140 |
| **DE** | -161 | -95 | -116 | -248 | -286 | -114 | -96 | 71 | 45 | -49 | -673 | 159 | 235 | 35 | -19 | 49 |
| **EL** | -141 | 54 | 176 | 219 | 421 | 321 | 7 | 515 | 156 | -158 | -1169 | -1603 | -4032 | -4757 | -2625 | -1452 |
| **HU** | -87 | 108 | 210 | 93 | 48 | 157 | 29 | -8 | 53 | -152 | -967 | -202 | -207 | -354 | -229 | -135 |
| **IR** | 367 | 332 | 127 | 138 | 77 | 41 | 102 | 91 | 62 | -197 | -828 | -673 | -691 | -538 | -274 | 304 |
| **IT** | -204 | 30 | -162 | -264 | -173 | -83 | -94 | -32 | -146 | -271 | -1065 | -135 | -273 | -665 | -657 | -459 |
| **LV** | -87 | -6 | -15 | 14 | 56 | 102 | 126 | 106 | 91 | 61 | -894 | -762 | 153 | 34 | -49 | -13 |
| **LT** | -201 | -82 | -36 | -20 | 25 | 28 | 84 | 88 | 161 | 80 | -758 | -143 | 141 | 50 | -2 | -18 |
| **LU** | -8 | 5 | -39 | -34 | -39 | -12 | -14 | -6 | 10 | -58 | -194 | 60 | 22 | -37 | 56 | 38 |
| **MT** | n/a | n/a | -244 | -55 | -89 | -157 | 80 | -37 | -42 | 157 | -397 | 48 | -33 | 63 | -26 | 71 |
| **NL** | 101 | 15 | 66 | -87 | -125 | -79 | -26 | 20 | 0 | -62 | -415 | -89 | 27 | -63 | -37 | -57 |
| **PL** | -158 | -191 | -201 | -190 | -115 | 38 | -22 | 62 | 148 | 50 | -21 | -13 | 117 | -27 | -150 | -48 |
| **PT** | 25 | 8 | 17 | -72 | -150 | -36 | -83 | 3 | -12 | -161 | -728 | -254 | -988 | -1527 | -957 | -446 |
| **RO** | -512 | -79 | -91 | -33 | 64 | 25 | 51 | 57 | 21 | 76 | -300 | -101 | -52 | -136 | 14 | -46 |
| **SK** | -305 | 188 | 75 | 1 | 326 | 278 | 153 | 219 | 209 | 101 | -379 | 37 | 66 | -6 | -57 | -24 |
| **SI** | 20 | 10 | -31 | 25 | 10 | 46 | 26 | 69 | 98 | 47 | -438 | -69 | -155 | -355 | -412 | -39 |
| **ES** | 80 | 151 | 53 | 40 | 65 | 61 | 119 | 118 | 42 | -8 | -456 | -181 | -277 | -558 | -483 | -192 |
| **SE** | -55 | -22 | -95 | -119 | -51 | -11 | -42 | 56 | -14 | -94 | -317 | 132 | 3 | -89 | -73 | -19 |
| **UK** | -64 | -67 | -76 | -80 | -37 | -88 | -16 | -16 | -50 | -119 | -402 | 61 | 250 | 147 | 196 | 158 |
| **EA19** | n/a | n/a | n/a | n/a | n/a | n/a | n/a | n/a | n/a | n/a | n/a | n/a | -52 | -242 | -230 | -117 |
| **EU28** | n/a | n/a | n/a | n/a | n/a | n/a | n/a | n/a | n/a | n/a | n/a | n/a | -6 | -179 | -156 | -66 |

**Source**: authors calculation based on Eurostat and IMF World Economic Outlook data, and Blanchard (1990) index

**Table 3.4 Long-term government bond rates (Maastricht indicator)**

| | 1999 | 2000 | 2001 | 2002 | 2003 | 2004 | 2005 | 2006 | 2007 | 2008 | 2009 | 2010 | 2011 | 2012 | 2013 | 2014 |
|---|---|---|---|---|---|---|---|---|---|---|---|---|---|---|---|---|
| **EA** | 4.66 | 5.44 | 5.00 | 4.91 | 4.14 | 4.12 | 3.42 | 3.84 | 4.32 | 4.31 | 3.82 | 3.60 | 4.34 | 3.86 | 2.99 | 2.04 |
| **BE** | 4.75 | 5.59 | 5.13 | 4.99 | 4.18 | 4.15 | 3.43 | 3.81 | 4.33 | 4.42 | 3.90 | 3.46 | 4.23 | 3.00 | 2.41 | 1.71 |
| **BG** | : | : | : | : | 6.45 | 5.36 | 3.87 | 4.18 | 4.54 | 5.38 | 7.22 | 6.01 | 5.36 | 4.50 | 3.47 | 3.35 |
| **CZ** | : | : | 6.31 | 4.88 | 4.12 | 4.82 | 3.54 | 3.80 | 4.30 | 4.63 | 4.84 | 3.88 | 3.71 | 2.78 | 2.11 | 1.58 |
| **DK** | 4.91 | 5.64 | 5.08 | 5.06 | 4.31 | 4.30 | 3.40 | 3.81 | 4.29 | 4.28 | 3.59 | 2.93 | 2.73 | 1.40 | 1.75 | 1.32 |
| **DE** | 4.49 | 5.26 | 4.80 | 4.78 | 4.07 | 4.04 | 3.35 | 3.76 | 4.22 | 3.98 | 3.22 | 2.74 | 2.61 | 1.50 | 1.57 | 1.16 |
| **IR** | 4.71 | 5.51 | 5.01 | 5.01 | 4.13 | 4.08 | 3.33 | 3.76 | 4.31 | 4.53 | 5.23 | 5.74 | 9.60 | 6.17 | 3.79 | 2.37 |
| **EL** | 6.30 | 6.10 | 5.30 | 5.12 | 4.27 | 4.26 | 3.59 | 4.07 | 4.50 | 4.80 | 5.17 | 9.09 | 15.75 | 22.50 | 10.05 | 6.93 |
| **ES** | 4.73 | 5.53 | 5.12 | 4.96 | 4.12 | 4.10 | 3.39 | 3.78 | 4.31 | 4.37 | 3.98 | 4.25 | 5.44 | 5.85 | 4.56 | 2.72 |
| **FR** | 4.61 | 5.39 | 4.94 | 4.86 | 4.13 | 4.10 | 3.41 | 3.80 | 4.30 | 4.23 | 3.65 | 3.12 | 3.32 | 2.54 | 2.20 | 1.67 |
| **HR** | : | : | : | : | : | : | : | 4.43 | 4.93 | 6.04 | 7.83 | 6.29 | 6.54 | 6.13 | 4.68 | 4.05 |
| **IT** | 4.73 | 5.58 | 5.19 | 5.03 | 4.25 | 4.26 | 3.56 | 4.05 | 4.49 | 4.68 | 4.31 | 4.04 | 5.42 | 5.49 | 4.32 | 2.89 |
| **CZ** | : | : | 7.62 | 5.70 | 4.74 | 5.80 | 5.16 | 4.13 | 4.48 | 4.60 | 4.60 | 4.60 | 5.79 | 7.00 | 6.50 | 6.00 |
| **LV** | : | : | 7.57 | 5.41 | 4.90 | 4.86 | 3.88 | 4.13 | 5.28 | 6.43 | 12.36 | 10.34 | 5.91 | 4.57 | 3.34 | 2.51 |
| **LT** | : | : | 8.15 | 6.06 | 5.32 | 4.50 | 3.70 | 4.08 | 4.55 | 5.61 | 14.00 | 5.57 | 5.16 | 4.83 | 3.83 | 2.79 |
| **LU** | 4.66 | 5.52 | 4.86 | 4.70 | 3.32 | 2.84 | 2.41 | 3.30 | 4.46 | 4.61 | 4.23 | 3.17 | 2.92 | 1.82 | 1.85 | 1.34 |
| **HU** | : | : | 7.95 | 7.09 | 6.82 | 8.19 | 6.60 | 7.12 | 6.74 | 8.24 | 9.12 | 7.28 | 7.64 | 7.89 | 5.92 | 4.81 |
| **MT** | : | : | 6.19 | 5.82 | 5.04 | 4.69 | 4.56 | 4.32 | 4.72 | 4.81 | 4.54 | 4.19 | 4.49 | 4.13 | 3.36 | 2.61 |
| **NL** | 4.63 | 5.40 | 4.96 | 4.89 | 4.12 | 4.10 | 3.37 | 3.78 | 4.29 | 4.23 | 3.69 | 2.99 | 2.99 | 1.93 | 1.96 | 1.45 |
| **AT** | 4.68 | 5.56 | 5.08 | 4.96 | 4.14 | 4.13 | 3.39 | 3.80 | 4.30 | 4.36 | 3.94 | 3.23 | 3.32 | 2.37 | 2.01 | 1.49 |
| **PL** | : | : | 10.68 | 7.36 | 5.78 | 6.90 | 5.22 | 5.23 | 5.48 | 6.07 | 6.12 | 5.78 | 5.96 | 5.00 | 4.03 | 3.52 |
| **PT** | 4.78 | 5.59 | 5.16 | 5.01 | 4.18 | 4.14 | 3.44 | 3.91 | 4.42 | 4.52 | 4.21 | 5.40 | 10.24 | 10.55 | 6.29 | 3.75 |
| **RO** | : | : | : | : | : | : | : | 7.23 | 7.13 | 7.70 | 9.69 | 7.34 | 7.29 | 6.68 | 5.41 | 4.49 |
| **SI** | : | : | : | 8.72 | 6.40 | 4.68 | 3.81 | 3.85 | 4.53 | 4.61 | 4.38 | 3.83 | 4.97 | 5.81 | 5.81 | 3.27 |
| **SK** | : | : | 8.04 | 6.94 | 4.99 | 5.03 | 3.52 | 4.41 | 4.49 | 4.72 | 4.71 | 3.87 | 4.45 | 4.55 | 3.19 | 2.07 |
| **FI** | 4.72 | 5.48 | 5.04 | 4.98 | 4.13 | 4.11 | 3.35 | 3.78 | 4.29 | 4.29 | 3.74 | 3.01 | 3.01 | 1.89 | 1.86 | 1.45 |
| **SE** | 4.98 | 5.37 | 5.11 | 5.30 | 4.64 | 4.42 | 3.38 | 3.70 | 4.17 | 3.89 | 3.25 | 2.89 | 2.61 | 1.59 | 2.12 | 1.72 |
| **UK** | 5.01 | 5.33 | 5.01 | 4.91 | 4.58 | 4.93 | 4.46 | 4.37 | 5.06 | 4.50 | 3.36 | 3.36 | 2.87 | 1.74 | 2.03 | 2.14 |
| **mean** | 4.85 | 5.52 | 6.013 | 5.52 | 4.61 | 4.64 | 3.8 | 4.22 | 4.69 | 4.96 | 5.454 | 4.714 | 5.31 | 4.931 | 3.693 | 2.76 |
| **s.d.** | 0.43 | 0.19 | 1.558 | 1.02 | 0.8 | 1.06 | 0.86 | 0.9 | 0.71 | 1.06 | 2.762 | 1.954 | 2.86 | 4.117 | 1.955 | 1.45 |
| **EU28** | : | : | 5.32 | 5.06 | 4.35 | 4.44 | 3.70 | 4.08 | 4.56 | 4.55 | 4.11 | 3.82 | 4.27 | 3.65 | 2.96 | 2.21 |

**Source Eurostat, S.D.** = standard deviation, mean = unweighted average of EU28

**Table 3.5 CDS indicators**

| | AT | BE | BG | HR | CZ | EE | FR | DE | EL | HU | IR | IT | LV | LT | NL | PL | PT | RO | SK | SI | ES |
|---|---|---|---|---|---|---|---|---|---|---|---|---|---|---|---|---|---|---|---|---|---|
| **2009, March** | 207 | 123 | 589 | 495 | 257 | 649 | 77 | 72 | 219 | 547 | 295 | 171 | 1044 | 767 | 108 | 323 | 116 | 626 | 170 | 164 | 126 |
| **2010, May** | 71 | 97 | 242 | 234 | 92 | 113 | 71 | 46 | 683 | 238 | 219 | 170 | 357 | 261 | 46 | 139 | 309 | 256 | 84 | 76 | 203 |
| **2011, July** | 78 | 179 | 229 | 301 | 93 | 93 | 102 | 54 | 2314 | 294 | 985 | 265 | 213 | 211 | 48 | 163 | 1045 | 249 | 126 | 116 | 321 |
| **2012, June** | 181 | 262 | 346 | 530 | 135 | 117 | 200 | 103 | 10356 | 557 | 663 | 536 | 300 | 282 | 119 | 235 | 1022 | 437 | 255 | 394 | 586 |
| **change** | -26 | 139 | -243 | 35 | -122 | -532 | 123 | 31 | 10137 | 10 | 368 | 365 | -744 | -485 | 11 | -88 | 906 | -189 | 85 | 230 | 460 |

| | mean | S.D. |
|---|---|---|
| **2009, March** | 340.24 | 269.44 |
| **2010, May** | 190.81 | 145.54 |
| **2011, July** | 356.14 | 521.29 |
| **2012, June** | 838.86 | 2192.36 |

**Source**: Heinz & Sun (2014) refer to Datastream, S.D. = standard deviation, mean = average of the countries

missing data: CY, DK, SE, MT, LU, FI, UK

**country abbreviations**

EA = current eurozone, EA19 = 19 eurzone members, EU 28 = 28 EU members

AT = Austria, BE = Belgium, BG = Bulgaria, HR = Croatia, CY =Cyprus, CZ = Czech Republic, DK = Denmark, EE = Estonia, FI = Finland, FR = France, DE = Germany, EL = Greece, HU =Hungary, IR =Ireland, IT = Italy, LV = Latvia, LT = Lithuania, LU = Luxemburg, MT = Malta, NL = Netherlands, PL = Poland, PT = Portugal, RO = Romania, SK = Slovakia, SI = Slovenia, ES = Spain, SE =Sweden, UK = United Kingdom

Chapter 4

# The Principle of Proportionality

Stanisław Kasiewicz, Lech Kurklinski

## 4.1. Introduction

The development and implementation of effective and efficient legal regulations are addressed by many theoretical concepts, approaches, programs, and methods of regulatory improvement. In spite of constantly broadening knowledge, gathering more and more experience and skills in the development and enforcement of regulations, their quality, at a national or international level, raises many reservations. This situation results from a countless number of factors; one of them is a rapidly progressing process of creating more and more new regulations. Developing supranational regulations involves a problem; it relates to taking account of significant differences in the level of economic development of countries, differences resulting from different legal, political, social systems or established legal cultures. Undoubtedly, any significant differences between countries as well as internal differences affect attitudes and behaviors of the regulated entities. Their opinions, by different divisions (countries, industries, companies, key stakeholders), on a fair distribution of the assessment of regulatory benefits, costs and related risk differ significantly. If these differences are not included in the process of development and implementation of regulations, their effectiveness and efficiency decrease significantly. It manifests itself in the fact that some regulated entities may search for any actions aimed at delaying the process of implementing new regulations or at regulatory evasion, or try to implement regulations at a minimum level of burdens and costs, and even expose themselves to high costs of fines for non-compliance with these requirements. These behaviors will emerge when these entities consider that the distribution of benefits, costs or risk is a sign of absolute or relative injustice.

In this chapter, an attempt is made to assess regulatory impact concerning a popular principle of proportionality. However, this principle undergoes large modifications; its interpretation is broadened and it gets adapted to the factual assessment of legislative processes. The origin of the principle of proportionality cannot be indicated unambiguously. It has many dimensions; its functions, components, and scope of use are often hardly noticeable, and the scope of use depends largely on the legal system (Proportionality, 2006; 14) and the legislative context[1]. In the everyday interpretation, its essence comes down to the use of a relevant tool, so that the statement "Never use a cannon to kill a fly" does not become applicable. The origin of the principle of proportionality is attributed to a ruling of the European Court of Justice of 1956 that established it as a general principle of Community law (Białek et al., 2014; 5). The notion of the principle of proportionality has evolved (Engle, 2012); it has many alternative terms. For the purpose of this chapter, the following definition is adopted: "the principle of proportionality requires that acts of Community institutions not to exceed the limits of what is adequate and necessary to meet justified objectives set out by a specific regulation; it means that when there is a choice between several adequate means, the least restrictive means should be chosen, whereas arising inconveniences should not be excessive as compared to the intended objectives".[2] Thus, the principle of proportionality includes three significant elements: adequacy, necessity and proportionality *sensu stricto*. Consequently, the observance of the principle of proportionality in the law-making process comes down to three significant stages. The first one is an interpretation of the subjective scope of at least three abovementioned components. The second stage consists in the transformation of the adopted scope into clear and quite simple criteria. The third stage is attributing relevant measures to particular criteria.

The proposed approach to regulatory impact assessment has been termed as the model of the Observance of the Principle of Proportionality (OPP). In the chapter, the authors present the model assumptions, identify and particularize the criteria of main areas of the principle of proportionality, namely, the principle of adequacy, necessity and proportionality *sensu stricto*, and then determine its scoring methods. The final result of the chapter is a synthetic calculation: an ordered measure of the observance of the principle of proportionality for a specific regulation.

### 4.2. Idea and Justification for a Model for Observing the Principle of Proportionality (OPP)

We are convinced that a large number of actions should be taken in various areas to improve the quality of regulations, but the most important procedure in this respect is a consistent and reliable analysis of the legislative impact

---

[1] The principle of proportionality requires, for instance, a larger scope of restrictions for financial institutions and actions that generate a greater risk.

[2] Body of rulings of the National Farmers Union (Białek et al., 2015; 17).

assessment with the use of a structured methodology. It focuses, like in a lens, strengths, and weaknesses of a draft (planned) regulation. The starting point for building such a methodology is reliance on the approach we propose – the OPP model. It consists of two interacting parts, although works in each of them are autonomous. In the first part, a qualitative assessment is conducted; conditions, objectives, and threats related to a specific regulation are assessed. The analysis covers the observance of the principle of proportionality. This qualitative result is a substantive contribution to the development of another, quantitative part, namely quantification of the degree of observing the principle of proportionality. Apart from showing a summary result of the assessment of observing the principle of proportionality with the use of a standardized index, this model stresses weaknesses and strengths of its major components, namely of the principles of adequacy, necessity and proportionality *sensu stricto*.

An expanded hybrid approach is even more justified since these regulations are highly complex objects of research, due to the number of entities, large subjective scope, dynamic character of relations being analyzed and hardly examined relationships between key stakeholders. Moreover, a breakdown of this model into two parts results from the fact that each regulation is an innovation, to a smaller or greater degree; consequently, we do not have an adequate information base. Conducting a qualitative analysis of observing the principle of proportionality provides more reliable indications for the creation of databases of this type and, at the same time, development of quantitative methods that may be useful in the decision-making process.

This presentation of the model is also supported by the fact that the process of developing, implementing and applying regulations involves the participation of direct and indirect stakeholders with different preparation and perception of regulatory impact, and who represent different spheres of impact on economic, legal, social and ecological effects. Information and conclusions from the application of the OPP model must be thus clear and cannot come down only to one layer of assessment, namely to its qualitative or quantitative layer.

An important and even key condition of applying the OPP model is a growing share of international regulations in operations of companies and financial institutions. Consequently, it proved necessary to assess relatively quickly draft concepts of regulations in terms of their impact on operations of national entities and, at the same time, to develop adequate tactics and strategies of regulatory action, so as not to be doomed only to regulatory failures or accidental successes.

**Figure 4.1 Model for assessing the observance of the principle of proportionality (OPP)**

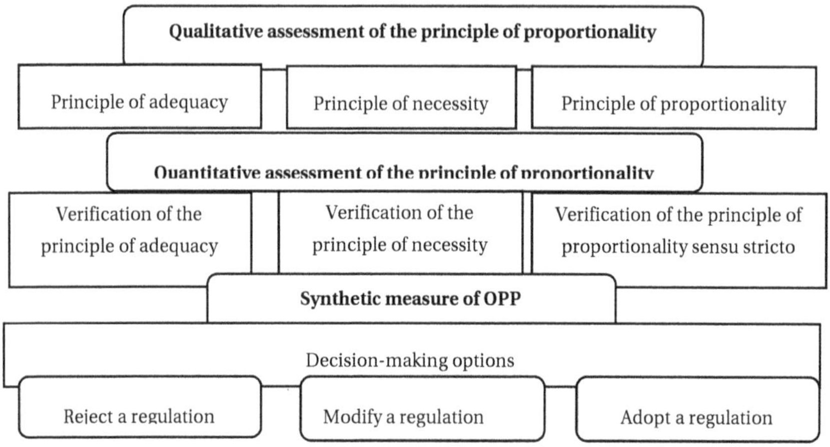


**Source**: prepared by the authors.

## 4.3. Qualitative Assessment of Observing the Principle of Proportionality

A theoretical and practical problem emerges: what are the criteria for assessing the use of the principle of proportionality in the law-making process? To some extent, to assess regulations, it is possible to use methods taken from the developing field of project management, taking account of various verification criteria. The team led by Professor M. Trocki recommends four groups of measures: adequacy, effectiveness, efficiency, and durability of effects (Trocki, Juchniewicz, 2013). In this chapter, we propose indexes similar to the ones for regulatory activity, which implies the use of the following criteria: management, legal, financial and socio-economic – see table 4.1 (Kasiewicz, et al., 2013). The management criterion defines the degree in which the whole process of drafting and implementing regulations is managed effectively. The legal criterion explains, in turn, the degree in which a specific regulation is consistent with the existing legal order. The financial criterion addresses financial burdens generated by the principle of proportionality and its impact on the autonomous effectiveness of regulations, expressed in monetary units. The socio-economic criterion tries to determine the degree in which a regulation takes account of general social and macroeconomic aspects.

**Table 4.1 Recommended criteria for testing the principle of proportionality**

| Elements of the principle of proportionality | Proposed criteria |
|---|---|
| **Adequacy** | **1. Management**<br>• Were the objectives specified adequately?<br>• Does the regulation result in meeting the objectives?<br>• Are there in place sufficient resources (tangible, human, intangible) and competences to implement the regulation?<br>• Was the unit responsible for implementing the regulation appointed?<br>• Were the draft regulation implementation schedule and budget prepared?<br>• Is cohesion of action maintained in the short, medium and long run?<br>• Does the organizational culture of units covered by the regulation foster its implementation?<br>• Is the determination to implement the regulation strong?<br>• Is regulatory success clearly formulated?<br>• Is the motivation system included in the process of drafting and implementing the regulation?<br>**2. Legal**<br>• Is the regulation contradictory or highly conflicting with the existing legal order?<br>• Were key legal risks identified?<br>• Were key stakeholders of the regulation identified?<br>• Does the regulation breach the effective competition principles?<br>• Does the regulation breach the market mechanism principles?<br>• Was the regulation monitoring method (scope, procedures, documents, dates) adopted?<br>**3. Financial**<br>• Will the regulation bring a significant deterioration in the financial position of the affected entities?<br>**4. Socio-economic**<br>• Will consultations associated with the draft regulation involve significant stakeholders?<br>• Will achievement of the regulation's objectives result in an increase in well-being of the society? |
| **Necessity** | **1. Management**<br>• Were justified alternative solutions chosen for the regulation?<br>• Were major burdens resulting from these solutions identified?<br>• Will the calculated burdens generate additional risk for the regulated units (excessively complex management, large scope of control, etc.)? |

| | |
|---|---|
| | • Were these burdens estimated?<br>• Were these solutions assessed in terms of efficiency and risk?<br><br>**2. Legal**<br><br>• What is the assessment of the regulated unit's ability to accept self-regulatory solutions?<br><br>**3. Financial**<br><br>• What will be the impact of estimated burdens resulting from the draft regulation on the regulated units' financial performance?<br>• What will be the impact of estimated burdens resulting from alternative solutions on the regulated units' financial performance?<br>• How large is the risk of errors in the valuation of regulatory burdens?<br><br>**4. Socio-economic**<br><br>• Will burdens result in a decline in trust in the State due to the unequal legal treatment of units, injustice, growing regulatory competition? |
| **Proportionality**<br><br>***sensu stricto*** | **1. Management**<br><br>• Are costs related to the specific regulation identified or valued?<br>• Are benefits related to the specific regulation identified or valued?<br>• Are measures to be achieved by the regulator defined?<br>• Is regulatory impact assessed in relation to the regulated entities, sectors and the economy?<br>• Are there in place resources and skills for the evaluation of social costs and benefits resulting from the specific regulation?<br><br>**2. Legal**<br><br>• Are institutions responsible for monitoring and assessing the achieved effects of the whole regulatory process identified?<br>• Is the regulator aware of the hierarchy of objectives of the regulation being implemented?<br>• Are the conditions for objective and reliable public consultations created?<br><br>**3. Financial**<br><br>• Is the regulatory impact assessment methodology (RIA, *Benefit-Cost Analysis*) applied?<br>• Are legal and regulatory risks measured?<br>• Is regulatory impact on risk reduction assessed?<br><br>**4. Socio-economic**<br><br>• Are preferences with regard to (national, EU) authorities' regulatory policy clearly addressed?<br>• Is progress in the regulatory impact assessment process shown? |

**Source**: prepared by the authors.

It is worth emphasizing that these are proposals of particularizing the principle of proportionality with regard to its main elements. The criteria can be changed completely, broadened or narrowed, depending on the special character of a draft regulation. Thanks to this description, the principle of proportionality is a highly flexible regulatory impact assessment method.

### 4.4. Quantification of the Principle of Adequacy

In December 2013, we presented a concept of assessing draft regulations in terms of the principle of proportionality (Kasiewicz, et al., 2013). The assessment was qualitative, and it consisted of an analysis of three pillars of the principle of proportionality, namely, adequacy, necessity and proportionality *sensu stricto*. We suggested that each of partial principles comprising the principle of proportionality should be subjected to numerous criteria in the analysis, which were relating to four problem areas: management, legal, financial and socio-economic area.

A shortcoming of this approach is, among other things, a difficulty in determining the general level of observing the principle of proportionality in respect of the specific regulation. To sum up, whether or not the regulation ignores the principle completely, observes it to a moderate or prevailing degree, maybe even in 100%. Apart from a general assessment of observing the principle of proportionality, which is useful for the legislative practice, it would be thus useful to search for quantifiable measures and aim at using a synthetic measure of the effectiveness of the analyzed regulation.

We can present that a measure of the principle of proportionality of a specific regulation fulfills the following condition:

$$\hat{}OPP = p_1 * PA + p_2 * PN + p_3 * PS \quad (1)$$

where: OPP = measure of observing the principle of proportionality (assumes discrete values from the range [0;6] points

PA = average measure of observing the principle of adequacy (assumes discrete values from the range [0;6] points

PN = average measure of observing the principle of necessity (assumes discrete values from the range [0;6] points

PS = average measure of observing the principle of proportionality *sensu stricto* (assumes discrete values from the range [0;6] points

$p_1$; $p_2$; $p_3$ = weights of importance of partial principles of proportionality (assume values from the range (0;1)
and the weights fulfill the condition:

$$p_1 + p_2 + p_3 = 1 \quad (2)$$

To obtain a standardized measure of observing the principle of proportionality, which assumes values from the range [ 0;1], it is sufficient to use the following formula:

$$OPP = \frac{\hat{}OPP}{6} \quad (3)$$

Following the pragmatics of the adopted OPP model, the entity that makes the decision on implementing the regulation may, on the basis of its value:

(a) reject the regulation because of non-observance of the principle of proportionality when the OPP index assumes values from the range < [0; 0.33].

(b) conclude that the regulation observes the principle of proportionality when the OPP index assumes values from the range [0.34; 0.66].

(c) conclude that the assessed regulation observes the principle of proportionality when the OPP index assumes values from the range < [0.67; 1].

### 4.4.1. Calculation Procedure of Observing the Principle of Adequacy

**Table 4.2 Assessing the observance of the principle of adequacy**

| Criterion | Criterion score from 0 to 6 points |
|---|---|
| 1. Relationship between the regulator's objectives and the regulation. | |
| 2. Scope of the regulatory impact on causes of a problem. | |
| 3. Available resources and motivation system of the regulator. | |

| | |
|---|---|
| 4. Stakeholders' interests versus the regulation. | |
| 5. Making use of behavior of key stakeholders. | |
| 6. Regulatory risk. | |
| 7. Enforcing the regulation. | |

**Source**: prepared by the authors.

### 4.4.2. Relationship Between the Regulator's Objectives and the Regulation

Prior to determining the causal relationship between the regulation's objectives and the adopted wording, it is worth analyzing general conditions that are decisive for the introduction of new draft regulations. Table 4.3, containing typical reasons for legislative action, is helpful in this respect.

**Table 4.3 Justifications for draft legislations**

| Type of legitimization | • Main area of regulation | Example |
|---|---|---|
| Natural and other monopolies | • Tendencies to price growth and decrease in production.<br>• Bundle of benefits resulting from scale effects.<br>• Identification of whether or not a monopoly is authentic. | Public utility companies. |
| Windfall gains | • Transfer of benefits, resulting from growth in windfall gains of a company to customers or a taxpayer. | A company discovers an extremely cheap source of supplies. |
| External effects | • Full costs of production or consumption that affect third parties or the society. | River contaminated by a factory. |
| Inadequate information | • Information for customers enabling them to make market decisions. | Pharmaceutical goods, foodstuffs, and beverages - labeling. |

| | | |
|---|---|---|
| Continuity and availability of services | • Ensured provision of desired services (or protection of a minimum level of basic service provision). | Transportation services have a hindered access to certain regions. |
| Anti-competitive and aggressive price behaviors | • Counteracting anti-competitive behaviors. | Offering services below costs. |
| Public goods and the so-called *moral hazard* | • Division of costs and benefits is determined, but there are certain players who want to take advantage of gaps so as not to incur costs or to get higher benefits, the so-called *free-riders*. | Defense services, safety services, health and medical services. |
| Unequal bargain force of competitors. | • Protection of sensitive interests that are not protected by the existing market mechanisms. | Health and medical and work safety services. |
| Scarcity of goods | • Determination of the principles of allocating scarcity goods. | Gasoline shortage. |
| Need for coordination | • Ensured effective production when transaction costs include positive network effects or scale effects.<br>• Standardization | Disproportions in agricultural production and fishery. |
| Planning | • Protection of future generations' interests.<br>• Coordination of altruistic behaviors. | Environmental protection |
| Human rights | • Protection of weaker citizens. | Discrimination Embryology. |
| Social protection | • Pursuing social solidarity. | Mass media. |

**Source**: Baldwin, et al., 2012.

Zero is granted when there is no causal relationship between the adopted objectives and rules of operations of the entities affected by the specific regulation. A huge problem emerges when the regulator's objectives are not formulated in regulatory provisions at all or are not particularized and are too general, insufficiently expressed (only in terms of quality) without exact terms and possibilities of verifying their achievement. As a matter of fact, when it is not possible to define the regulation's objectives unambiguously, 0 will be granted to this criterion.

A specific criterion obtains the maximum score when we have enough evidence confirming the conduct of national, foreign research, and an analysis of results of the previously adopted legislation, which indicate a causal relationship between the set regulator's objectives and the draft regulation. Moreover, it is understood that under these circumstances the regulation's objectives are logical and precisely defined.

### 4.4.3. Scope of the Regulatory Impact on Causes of a Problem

Regulations may determine causes or symptoms of a problem that was noticed, analyzed and resulted in the development of a draft regulation. Although the theoretical basis for regulatory assessment indicate that it should affect causes of a problem, in the present market conditions (not only in medicine but also in economy!) regulations are usually aimed at limiting alarming symptoms, for instance, most anti-crisis regulations after 2007. And thus, when they result in a reduction in factors which are the sources of alarming phenomena, e.g. increase in financial exclusion of bank customers, the maximum score can be granted. In turn, the worst score is granted to this criterion when problems are not analyzed reliably, and a regulation originates from stereotypical indications or relationships that are apparently logically justified but, in fact, meet other objectives and solve other problems.

### 4.4.4. Available Resources and the Motivation System of the Regulator

Resources and motivation fulfill an important role in the process of achieving regulatory efficiency and effectiveness. If the regulator is unable to determine the actual level of required expenditures on the development, implementation, and enforcement of a draft regulation, the risk of non-achievement of objectives grows and regulatory effectiveness decreases, which raises protests of the concerned parties and jeopardizes the reputation of state institutions. At this point, several alarming trends are worth mentioning. The regulatory administration aims at a situation where draft regulations can be executed nearly on a costless basis, as part of the standard and fixed employee tasks. This approach comes down to a situation with prevailing savings at every stage. As a result, conducting important analyses is limited, or cost assessment comes down only to the phase of developing a new draft since other items were not included in the regulators' annual budgets. Other items of regulatory costs remain beyond their sphere of interest. Owing to the complexity of draft regulations, the lack of analyses, experiments, and scenarios causes the emergence of unexpected threats, which, in turn, results in the low final quality of draft regulations. At the same time, employees of administration units who are necessary, to a different extent, in the legislative process feel formally taken for a ride since, not infrequently, these activities are not included in the scope of their duties. They are thus burdened with tasks to be executed without sufficient support. As a rule, the motivation system is not planned, either. In view of the above, employees try to reduce their involvement excessively, chose options that are careful from their point of view, delay various activities or evade them deliberately.

At this point, it is worth realizing that for example in Poland regulatory culture prevails, and this culture can be described as confrontational and repressive. It means that regulated entities are aware that authorities are characterized by a high degree of arrogance ("they know better", they reject most comments submitted during public consultations and sometimes they do not conduct public consultations). According to another prevailing belief, which is "a cultural heritage" of the period of real socialism, failure to adapt to regulatory obligations involves, first of all, numerous formal and informal penalties. As a result, draft regulations that would also contain positive incentives for their implementation (which is the case of many EU countries for instance in the UK) are missing.

The minimum score should thus be granted to regulations without approved regulatory budgets, which reduce excessively the scope of carried out analyses and stages of regulatory life cycle and do not try to make use of the elements of positive stimulation for the regulated entities to make them comply with the new legislations.

The maximum score is granted to regulations with adequate resources (tangible, human and information) and an organized motivation system (both penalties and awards).

### 4.4.5. Stakeholders' Interests versus the Regulation

When analyzing the character of the legislative processes, it can be concluded that effects of their works divide stakeholders into two classes: winners and losers. Regulation is effective if it is achieved as a result of a compromise of growth in social well-being. Thus, it is important to identify groups that obtain benefits from the regulation implementation and also groups that incur additional costs, which, however, do not result in administrative inhibition of their development, weakening innovation processes or willingness to invest. Therefore, in the case of developing initial regulatory assumptions, we cannot confine ourselves to an analysis of direct stakeholders; third parties also should be included.

Typical stakeholders are inhabitants; business entities (companies, financial institutions); customers; administrative units (local, regional, national and EU); third countries (beyond EU).

The principle of proportionality is breached directly if stakeholders are not identified correctly and if costs and benefits arising from regulation are not connected.

Consequently, the lowest score is granted to regulations that ignore an exact analysis of stakeholders, where the net impact of regulations is not calculated, public consultations are not conducted, and where regulators do not contact stakeholders in the process of developing assumptions and final versions of regulations. On the contrary, when regulations fulfill all the significant conditions, they can be granted the highest score.

### 4.4.6. Making Use of Behavior of Key Stakeholders

While assessing this criterion, it is worth paying attention, first of all, to all three groups of stakeholders, namely the regulator, the regulated entity and third parties. The lowest score is granted to the criterion when:

- the regulator shows a low level of involvement in the examination of regulatory impact on management and the necessity to issue additional rules, ordinances, in responding to presented interpretation doubts, or when it only takes account of the achievement of objectives of a narrow group of stakeholders
- the regulated entities have a strong negative attitude towards the scope of a regulation, severity of its rules, they challenge its reasonable character and, at the same time, their reservations are ignored (total lack of explanations of the reasons for rejection) or not considered, and a superficial justification is given for this state of affairs
- third parties show a high level of dissatisfaction and warn of taking actions aiming at limiting or holding back the introduction of a specific regulation.

This criterion is highly significant depending on circumstances that accompany the regulation development process, such as:

- regulatory rush or even "express delivery."
- the regulation is highly repressive
- the regulation contains parametric sizes, for instance, in relation to the applied means, with a high probability of frequent modifications (for instance in the case when values are assumed arbitrarily and are not supported by analyses)
- public consultations are accompanied by a disrespectful attitude to the regulated entities.

The maximum score is granted to this criterion when almost all key stakeholders give consent to the adopted objectives of a regulation and are convinced of the justified character of the applied regulatory means. Moreover, the regulator shows a high level of involvement and complies consistently with the agreed standards and requirements.

### 4.4.7. Regulatory Risk

Each regulation generates risk. Since the regulatory process involves two main parties: regulated entities and institution that initiates, develops and implements a regulation, termed as the regulator (for instance, the national government, the parliament, the European Commission, etc.), regulatory risk resembles a coin. On the one side, on the obverse, the regulator is placed; the regulator is responsible for the achievement of postulates or planned (anticipated) objectives of regulation. This type of risk is termed as regulatory risk (Kasiewicz, 2014a; 27-36 and Kasiewicz, 2012; 125-133). The regulator is almost always the strongest part, therefore, regulatory risk should be treated as a very important category in the legislative process. The regulator's task is to determine the possibility of achieving the formulated regulatory objectives. If the probability of their achieving is low, there is no point in making efforts, employing available resources, conducting further works towards the implementation of a draft regulation. Consequently, this criterion receives the lowest score. On the other hand, when a regulation generates a low risk of failure, there are reasons to carry on this process; it implies the maximum score in the OPP model. To assess this criterion, we can measure regulatory risk: the measurement is conducted based on experts' opinions, taking account of various aspects of the regulatory process (Kasiewicz, 2014b).

#### 4.4.8. Enforcing the Regulat

This criterion consists in the determination of the degree of the regulator's preparation to monitor and control compliance with a draft regulation. It should be assessed whether they have a plan, schemes, schedule and adequate funds and human resources to implement these actions.

The regulatory practice shows that some regulators are not aware of the fact that they are burdened with such an obligation or try to fulfill it to the smallest extent (using, for instance, simulated monitoring and control process). This situation takes place most often when a supervisory institution of a specific regulator assesses the regulator's work in this area of activity unsystematically.

### 4.5. Quantification of the Principle of Necessity

In quite a common legislative practice, considered alternatives to draft regulations are not described or those descriptions are too laconic as they lack solid arguments. Therefore it is difficult to assess explicitly whether this type of procedure, concerning legislative options, was executed. However, missing information in a report with justification for a specific regulation is alarming and indicates that authorities want to be effective only through their activity in the legislative sphere.

It seems that we should not have too high expectations in this respect. Most often the suggested analysis of an alternative action to a draft regulation is not conducted since this approach is costly, laborious and often generates new problems. A reasonable solution may be to adopt two or three options, which, in the opinion of experts, will define the limits of the regulator's decision-making area. In table 4.4 is proposed a typical (hypothetical) procedure for assessing the observance of the principle of necessity, covering the assessment of seven criteria.

#### 4.5.1. Calculation Procedure of Observing the Principle of Necessity

**Table 4.4 Assessing the principle of necessity**

| Criterion | Criterion score from 0 to 6 points |
|---|---|
| 1. Alternative solutions to the regulation. | |
| 2. Costs of alternative solutions. | |

| | |
|---|---|
| 3. Benefits of alternative solutions. | |
| 4. Regulated entities' ability to accept alternatives. | |
| 5. Regulatory risk of alternative solutions. | |
| 6. Type of criterion of the best alternative selection. | |
| 7. Ability to enforce implementation of the best alternative. | |

**Source**: prepared by the authors.

### 4.5.2. Alternative Solutions to the Regulation

According to a common belief prevailing, particularly among the public administration, the only effective solution in this respect is to adopt a legislation (mainly in the form of an act); then, the enforcement of the law will become far easier than the adoption of another form of regulation of operations of business entities. Even if we do not challenge this position, we see that the mere functioning in such a regulatory culture provides quite a big room for searching for alternative solutions. This approach may consist in examining an option that considers resignation from regulation (*status quo*) or introduction of more or less stringent activities, by broadening or narrowing the objective or subjective scope of the regulation, for instance shortening or prolonging of the waiting period. Moreover, regulations may use to different degree tools; for instance economic, management or psychological tools.

We should bear in mind that the regulator has a large room for selecting regulations. The applied non-statutory regulatory actions include the following actions and payments (Karpińska-Białek, 2014; 70): refraining from intervention, but conduct of monitoring; self-regulation (e.g. good practice); co-regulation; quasi-regulation; market impact tools (as taxes, expenses, loans and loan guarantees, fees for use, insurance, maintenance of the State property); information and education campaigns; direct product control (like price control, quantity control – production limits, determination of specific product features - technical standards, execution standards); input and output control; production process control (technical standards, execution standards); information control; marketable ownership rights.

When determining the score for this criterion, it is worth considering the following factors:

(a) whether or not regulatory alternatives were examined;

(b) whether or not the prevailing types of regulations with a similar scope of the draft problem were identified;

(c) whether or not the analysis covered options of a given act in terms of efficiency, effectiveness, and risk.

If none of these factors was the object of interest and deliberations of the regulator, then the score for this criterion is 0. If all the conditions are met, this criterion obtains the highest score.

### 4.5.3. Costs of Alternative Solutions

Having used the selected regulatory variants (options), an attempt should be made to estimate incurred expenditures, following the classification of direct, indirect costs, and regulatory enforcement (monitoring and control). As a result of quite laborious operations, it was possible to obtain a regulatory variant with the lowest cost. During these operations, one problem is to be solved, related to the fact that alternative regulations have a different structure of costs and, consequently, the issue of their comparability cannot be underestimated; for instance, regulatory activity in the form of a TV campaign because of the adoption of even a simple act.

The score is granted to the criterion depending on the scale of costs and precision of their measurement. If these costs are not measured, the minimum score should be granted. A low score is also granted when estimates are burdened with a very high uncertainty level. The maximum score is granted when the whole cost calculation process is characterized by the pursuit of complexity, observance of methodical rules, and a large divergence of opinions among experts.

### 4.5.4. Benefits of Alternative Solutions

This criterion is assessed similarly like in the previous case, related to the determination of regulatory costs. It should be mentioned that, when determining benefits, it is important to observe their distribution at a level of particular sectors of the whole economy and society (macroeconomic benefits).

The minimum score should be granted when high, non-quantified regulatory benefits are assumed a priori or when estimates are fragmentary.

On the other hand, when the whole of calculations is transparent; assumptions, justifications, and formulas of benefit calculations are determined, the discussed criterion can obtain a high score.

### 4.5.5. Regulated Entities' Ability to Accept Alternatives

The selection of alternative regulations should reflect such factor as the perception of these regulations by key stakeholders. At this point, the regulators' attitude collides with the regulated entities. A part of this first group can be excessively optimistic with regard to the possibility of fulfilling regulatory objectives. Another part can point at a significant sensitivity to risk of failure, and another part can approach the rational character of made regulatory decisions in a too simplified way. On the other hand, the regulated entities adopt, as a rule, various policies, strategies, and tactics for responding to regulations. These issues are poorly examined in the Polish conditions of managing companies and financial institutions, even in relation to statutory legislations. Based on the conducted observations, we can conclude that several regulated entities chose the procedure that is based on:

- avoiding, unconsciously or consciously, adaptation to the regulation; they conclude that they will be "lucky" and will not be subjected to regulatory compliance control or conclude that it is worth paying a low penalty, which is incommensurately low as compared to regulatory costs
- becoming a specialist in regulatory evasion, by searching for regulatory weaknesses, inaccurateness, lack of supplementary legislation, using skills and experience of own or external legal units (including, for instance, regulatory arbitrage)
- pursuing the minimization of regulatory costs
- using the regulation as a significant tool of competing and obtaining competitive advantage (it relates to relatively small groups of national companies).

It should be emphasized that entities with a positive attitude towards the best possible adjustment to the regulatory implementation change this attitude along with their growing number. It is important that a gap between the regulator's attitude towards a legislation not differ largely from the attitude of the regulated entities. If vast or prevailing part of the regulated entities accepts the chosen alternative, then this criterion can obtain the maximum score. Otherwise, the minimum score should be granted.

### 4.5.6. Regulatory Risk of Alternative Soluti

Regardless of the assessment of costs and benefits, it is necessary to evaluate regulations alternative from the point of view of risk (exposition level = the product of the probability of occurrence and effect scale). It can turn out that some of the specified alternatives have highly positive net effects, however, their implementation generates a high risk. Hence it is required to assess the degree in which quality of the regulatory development, results of public consultations, availability of resources and regulatory implementation techniques affect the level of regulatory alternatives. If these types of risk are not identified and when the measurement is not made, then 0 should be granted to this criterion. A substantive analysis of alternatives' risk enables the numerical value of this criterion of 6 points to be assumed.

### 4.5.7. Type of Criterion of the Best Alternative Selection

When selecting the examined regulatory variants, it is important to follow their assessment criteria. Depending on the degree of information and the scope of conducted evaluation of the analyzed variants, it is possible to use measures that relate to three categories: benefits, costs and regulatory risk (criteria are presented in Table 4.5).

**Table 4.5 Proposed measures for selecting variants in terms of the principle of necessity**

| Type of criterion | Measure of assessment |
|---|---|
| **1. Qualitative** | |
| • partial | maximum benefits; minimum costs; minimum regulatory risk |
| • bi-dimensional | maximum benefits net (benefits minus costs); minimum costs and risk; maximum benefits and risks |
| • synthetic | maximum benefits net including regulatory risk |
| **2. Quantitative** | |
| **2.1. Static** | |
| • partial | maximum benefits; minimum costs; minimum regulatory risk |

| | |
|---|---|
| • bi-dimensional | maximum benefits net (benefits minus costs); minimum costs and regulatory risk; maximum benefits and regulatory risks |
| • synthetic | maximum benefits net including regulatory risk |
| **2.2. Dynamic** | |
| • partial | maximum benefits; minimum costs; minimum regulatory risk |
| • bi-dimensional | maximum benefits net (benefits minus costs); minimum costs and risk; maximum benefits and risk |
| • synthetic | maximum benefits net including regulatory risk |

**Source**: prepared by the authors.

Qualitative measures result from an assessment conducted by experts, on the other hand, quantitative measures are built on the basis of gathered data, made estimates and obtained information. They can relate to one effective term of the regulation, excluding changes over time. At that time, they are static. Contrary to them, dynamic measures include the factor of time.

### 4.5.8. Ability to Enforce Implementation of the Best Alternative

A weakness of new regulations implemented in the economic practice is the lack of complex control and monitoring system. Unfortunately, this practice is common in Poland. It seems that this approach cannot be maintained in the long run since it involves too high costs for the economy and society. Therefore, the regulation being implemented into the practice of economic life should be accompanied by a document that indicates an effective system for monitoring and controlling regulatory impact assessment.

The minimum score is granted to this criterion in the cases when a regulation is accepted but without an element that indicates its enforceability. The better the planning of the implementation discipline, the higher the level of assessment of this regulation.

### 4.6. Quantification of the Principle of Proportionality *Sensu Stricto*

The quantification of the principle of proportionality may be conducted in two extreme versions: simplified and full. In the first version, entities that analyze the principle of proportionality try to justify the scoring of various dimensions of the principle of proportionality sensu stricto (table 4.6). On the other hand, full quantification of the principle of proportionality requires a quantitative analysis in monetary units of each significant dimension of the principle of proportionality sensu stricto.

#### 4.6.1. Calculation Procedure of Observing the Principle of Proportionality *Sensu Stricto*

**Table 4.6 Assessing the observance of the principle of proportionality *sensu stricto***

| Criterion | Criterion score from 0 to 6 points |
|---|---|
| 1. Macroeconomic proportionality | |
| 2. Functional proportionality | |
| 3. Sector proportionality | |
| 4. Proportionality by stakeholders | |

**Sources**: prepared by the authors.

#### 4.6.2. Macroeconomic Proportionality

This element of the regulatory impact assessment is the most important. It consists in determination of the degree in which the analyzed document affects social well-being, which can be defined on various bases (GDP, social consumption, broadly understood investments, safety, stability (Furtado, 1978; Zienkowski, 1979, Sztaba, 1994; Drewnowski, Scott,1966, Drewnowski, 1970; OECD, 1973; de Leon, 2012). If a legislation being assessed has no positive impact on social well-being, it obtains the minimum score, namely 0. If its impact is significant and positive, it obtains the maximum score.

#### 4.6.3. Functional Proportionalit

It is also purposeful to assess the observance of the principle of proportionality in functional terms, referring to key areas of impact of a specific regulation; namely economic, social and ecological area. If it relates only to fulfilling objectives from one area or its impact is prevailing, it should be concluded that we cannot refer to the observance of the principle of proportionality *sensu stricto.* A signal of such an assessment may be a result of social consultations, especially of key stakeholders. If representatives of social stakeholders, e.g. customers, local governments, trade unions, indicate a significant negative regulatory impact on their attitudes, positions and economic consequences than a specific regulation should obtain the minimum score. The greater the degree of a reasonable compromise between interests of groups of stakeholders, the greater the degree of the observance of the principle of proportionality *sensu stricto.*

### 4.6.4. Sector Proportionality

The sector dimension of the principle of proportionality *sensu stricto* refers to assessing the degree of regulatory impact on three problem areas related to responding, provided that:

- the regulation fosters achievement of the adopted economic policy objectives
- the regulation fosters the development of other sectors, including other entities
- the regulation creates development conditions, in particular for SMEs.

When regulations do not contribute to the implementation of the economic policy of the government, they largely inhibit the development of other economic sectors. Thus they can be classified as development barriers, in particular for SMEs. In this case, the minimum score should be granted to a specific regulation. In the case of highly positive potential regulatory impact on these problem areas, it is justified to grant the maximum score to this criterion.

### 4.6.5. Proportionality by Stakeholders

As it has been emphasized many times, each regulation has its beneficiaries and losers, who incur additional costs or face a higher level of risk with regard to running profitable business operations. Therefore it is not desired that only one, narrow group of stakeholders, for instance only customers, obtain disproportionately high benefits. In our opinion, it makes other stakeholders take in the short run actions aimed at compensating their "harm" or "regulatory injustice" with regard to equal rules of competition on the market. The list of possible methods of responding is very long and, more importantly, usually these actions are not anticipated by regulators and supervisors. In fact, it makes net benefits of regulations much lower than planned or forecasted. From this point of view, it is important to conduct marketing campaigns with clearly stressed indications in favor for introducing a regulation. Actions should refer to the fallibility of the market mechanism and an insufficient level of fulfilling objectives of the government's economic policy so that key stakeholders realize their presence. Moreover, it should be aimed at achieving a clear compromise between stakeholders, by showing regulatory benefits that can be ignored, unnoticed or interpreted inadequately.

Therefore, extreme disproportions in benefits, costs, and risk between stakeholders, resulting from a given regulation indicate that this criterion should obtain the minimum score. Higher consensus among key stakeholders involves higher score in the OPP model.

## 4.7. Version of a Full or Extended Quantification

We are convinced that the principle of proportionality will be evolving towards increasing quantification, where each criterion of proportionality sensu stricto will obtain more developed, more complex model depiction and will fulfill to a greater degree the pursuit of expressing the obtained results in monetary units. Thus decisions on the observance of the principle of proportionality can be made on the basis of unambiguous calculation results. At this point, statistical, econometric, simulation or experimental methods can be applied. It seems that the current state of progress in determining the degree of observance of the principle of proportionality does not enable a more complex and useful methodology to be applied. It requires testing a significant number of legislations, obtaining greater experience and building tools along with adequate databases.

## 4.8. Conclusion

To sum up these deliberations, we believe that, although the OPP model is at quite an embryo stage of development, it has several positive features, including but not limited to:

- it combines qualitative and quantitative assessment in the simplest possible way
- it is a flexible method, independent of the type of regulation; it enables various criteria to be applied, depending on the specific character of the area covered by regulation. Moreover, it includes management aspects, motivational aspects, attitudes and behaviors of stakeholders
- it permits unambiguous selection of regulations (regulations to be adopted or rejected, issues to be amended)

- it is more realistic than key regulatory impact assessment methods, namely cost-benefit analysis, regulatory impact assessment
- it indicates main advantages and disadvantages of the specific regulation
- it may be a useful or even necessary supplementation of key regulatory impact assessment methods
- it indicates possible directions of legislative process coordination
- it has a large methodological development potential.

## 4.9. References

BALDWIN, ROBERT, CAVE, MARTIN, LODGE, MARTIN (2012). *Understanding Regulation. Theory, Strategy, and Practice,* Oxford University Press, Oxford, New York.

BIAŁEK TADEUSZ, GRABOWSKA MONIKA, BREWIŃSKI PIOTR (2014). *Ekspertyza prawna dotycząca zasady proporcjonalności w europejskim prawie wspólnotowym i polskim porządku prawnym,* Center for Banking Law and Information of the Polish Bank Association, Warsaw.

DE LEON ERWIN (2012). *National Indicators and Social Wealth,* CPS Urban Institute. Washington DC.

DREWNOWSKI, JAN, SCOTT, WOLF (1966). *The Level of Living Index,* United Nations Research Institute for Social Development, Geneva.

DREWNOWSKI, JAN (1970). *Studies in the Measurement of Level of Living and Welfare,* United Nations Research Institute for Social Development, Geneva.

ENGLE, ERIC (2012). *The history of general principle of proportionality: an overview.* "The Dartmouth Law Journal" Vol. X.

FURTADO, CELSO (1978). *Mit wzrostu gospodarczego,* PWE, Warsaw.

KASIEWICZ, STANISŁAW (2012). *Wpływ złożoności i ryzyka regulacyjnego na konkurencyjność sektora bankowego w Polsce [in:] Partycki, Sławomir (ed.), Kryzys finansowy. Przebieg i skutki społeczno-gospodarcze w Europie Środkowej i Wschodniej, vol. 1,* Wydawnictwo KUL, Lublin.

KASIEWICZ, STANISŁAW, KURKLIŃSKI, LECH, SZPRINGER WŁODZIMIERZ (2013). *Raport Specjalny: Zasada proporcjonalności a polski system bankowy,* "Bank" 2013, No. 12.

KASIEWICZ, STANISŁAW (2014A). *Koncepcje regulacji sektora MŚP a pomiar ryzyka regulacyjnego [in:] Sobiecki, Roman (ed.), Gospodarka w sieciach relacji,* Wydawnictwo KUL, Lublin.

KASIEWICZ, STANISŁAW (2014B). *Problem ryzyka regulacyjnego na tle programu "Mieszkanie dla Młodych",* the 15th International Conference on Finance Management, Kołobrzeg.

KARPIŃSKA-BIAŁEK, KATARZYNA (2014). *Ekonomiczna ocena skutków regulacji w ochronie zdrowia,* Warsaw School of Economics, unpublished PhD dissertation, Warsaw.

OECD (1973). *List of Social Concerns, Common to Most OECD Countries,* The OECD Social Indication Development Programme nr 1, Paris.

TROCKI, MICHAŁ, JUCHNIEWICZ, MATEUSZ (2013). *Ocena projektów – koncepcje, modele, metody,* Oficyna Wydawnicza SGH, Warsaw.

PROPORTIONALITY AND BALANCING IN WTO LAW: A COMPARATIVE PERSPECTIVE, (2006*). EAIEL Policy Chapter No. 2.*

SZTABA, SŁAWOMIR (1994). *Ekonomia niekonwencjonalna,* Oficyna Wydawnicza READ ME, Warsaw.

ZIENKOWSKI, LESZEK (1979). *Poziom życia. Metody mierzenia i oceny,* PWE, Warsaw

Chapter 5

# Fiscal Policy of the EU Countries in the Time of Crisis

Jaroslaw Kundera

## 5.1. Introduction

Fiscal policies in the EU member's countries were considered as one of the most important methods of overcoming economic crisis and condition of their returning on the path of economic growth. The Maastricht Treaty is obliging the member states to comply with the rules as far as a balanced budget and public debts and not exceeding the level of the budget deficit over the 3% and public debt over 60% in reference with GDP (Protocol No 5, 1993). After 2008 the EU member countries burdened by excessive debt and budget deficits was forced to restore the balance to the Maastricht level with the implementation of austerity program that includes, among other things, an increase in several taxes or a reduction in budgetary expenditure. In the Euro Area where monetary policy is conducted by the ECB, hence is beyond the reach of member countries and their individual needs, the conduct of coordinated fiscal policy has gained in importance on both the expenditure and revenue during the crisis.

According to textbook definition, the fiscal policy means the use of taxation and expenditure to achieve economic ends, as tax structure and government expenditure create a pattern of incentives to determine how resources are allocated. Budgetary policy of the EU member countries have an important role in macroeconomic stabilization and need to perform at least a twofold aim: first, has a shock-absorption function at the national level, and second to allow the establishment of optimal budgetary spending for all the Euro Area.

After 2008 taxes and government spending are also essential tools to overcome the emerging economic downturn, particularly where budget deficits and excessive borrowing led to the fracture of the public finances. Need to change fiscal policy became apparent in the EU member states because changes to taxes and budget expenditure could not only stimulate the growth of investment and production in individual states but also have positive in the partner countries only when the actions act in harmony. The increasing awareness of the interlinkages of the EU economies in the time of crisis has led to an acknowledgement of the need to a detailed examination of the evolution of the tax systems. Therefore, the main objective of this chapter is to examine the evolution of the tax system in the EU member states during the economic crisis. Given the huge role played by fiscal policy in contemporary economic policy, the author tries to answer the question of what changes have been made in the fiscal policies of the EU countries to overcome the crisis of the Euro Area.

## 5.2. The Amount of Taxes in the EU Member Countries

The EU countries belong to areas with high levels of tax burdens, which put them in an inferior competitive position on international markets. The overall tax ratio (the sum of taxes and social security contributions) as % of the GDP in the EU-27 amounted to 35.7% in 2015, that is high not only compared to the USA (22.2%) and China (22%) and, but also compared to the other main trade partners as Japan - 28.3% or Switzerland -29.4%. Wide disparities in tax levels also exist across the European single market (see Table 5.1). The tax burden in the highest- taxing EU member country is over 75% higher than in the least taxing one. The highest taxes pay the inhabitants of Scandinavia countries. Record holders to Denmark, who gave the budget of 49% of GDP in the form of taxation and Sweden – 45.8%. Of the next places is Belgium where participation of taxes in GDP is 45.4%, in France is 44.6%, in Finland is 43%, in Italy is 42.6%. Overall tax levels are in general higher in the EU-15 than in new member countries. The smallest share of taxes in GDP shows such a new member countries as Lithuania (20.9%), Romania (28.1%), Croatia (26.6%), and Slovakia (29.5%). High taxation in many European countries is related to the applied model of the welfare State, but even in the Nordic countries the burden of taxes over the past decade has been the reduced on average in relation to GDP from 51.5% to 45.8% (in Finland the share of taxes fell by 5.1 percentage points, in Denmark about 1.8 percentage points). These tax reductions may be one of the secrets of the Scandinavian countries resistance to the last economic crisis.

**Table 5.1 Tax as % of GDP according to countries in 2015**

| Country | tax as % of GDP |
|---|---|
| Austria | 43.4 |
| Belgium | 45.4 |
| Bulgaria | 34.4 |
| Croatia | 26.6 |

| Cyprus | 39.2 |
|---|---|
| Czech Republic | 36.3 |
| Denmark | 49.0 |
| Estonia | 32.3 |
| Finland | 43.6 |
| France | 44.6 |
| Germany | 40.6 |
| Greece | 30.0 |
| Hungary | 39.1 |
| Ireland | 30.8 |
| Italy | 42.6 |
| Latvia | 30.4 |
| Lithuania | 20.9 |
| Luxembourg | 36.5 |
| Malta | 35.2 |
| Netherlands | 39.8 |
| Poland | 33.8 |
| Portugal | 37.0 |
| Romania | 28.1 |
| Slovakia | 29.5 |
| Slovenia | 39.3 |
| Spain | 37.3 |
| Sweden | 45.8 |
| United Kingdom | 39.0 |
| European Union | 35.7 |
| United States | 26.9 |
| China | 22.0 |
| Japan | 28.3 |
| Switzerland | 29.4 |

**Data based on Krajewska A. (2015), Heritage Foundation. "2015 Macroeconomic Data" and Index of Economic Freedom**

Fiscal policies differences between the EU member countries are applied to indirect taxation as well as to direct taxation and social contribution. While most EU 15 member states raise roughly equal shares of revenues from direct taxes, indirect taxes and social security contributions, new EU members (with the exception of Malta) display a lower share of direct taxes in the total. For many, especially the new EU member states indirect taxes are the primary source of revenue: Bulgaria-55.4%, Hungary-45.5%, Romania-45.2.%, Lithuania-44.7%, Cyprus-43.8%, Poland-43.5%, but for the EU-15 members the share of indirect taxes in general tax revenue is less than 40%, and Germany even less than 30%. Direct taxes are, in turn, the most important source of income in Denmark (62.7%), Finland (38.2%), just as important as indirect taxes the source of revenue in Italy (34.9% ), Spain, (30.9%), Germany (29.4%), or the Netherlands (31.5%), but they have the least importance of the three count revenue sources in Bulgaria (18.8%), Hungary (22.6%), Lithuania (10.8%), Poland (21.9%), Latvia (27.1%), Estonia (19.9%), Greece (25.2%), Slovenia (21.8%), Slovakia (19.1%), France (25.8%), the Czech Republic (20.8%) and Belgium (18.8%). The social contribution, which provides an important element of the competitiveness of any economy, differs also as source of public revenue from the small income the share of 18.1% in the general tax incomes in Sweden, 18.7% in the United Kingdom, 18.1% in Malta, to 43% of income revenue for Slovakia, 40.1% in Slovenia, 39.3% for France, 45.2% in the Czech Republic, 40.8% in Germany.

**Table 5.2 Structure of tax revenue in the EU by major type of taxes as % of the total burden in 2010.**

| | Share of indirect taxes | Share of direct taxes | Share of social contribution |
|---|---|---|---|
| Bulgaria | 55.4 | 18.8 | 25.6 |
| Hungary | 45.5 | 22.6 | 31.9 |
| Romania | 45.2 | 22.6 | 32.2 |
| Lithuania | 44.7 | 17.4 | 36.3 |
| Cyprus | 43.8 | 31.1 | 25.1 |
| Poland | 43.5 | 21.9 | 34,9 |
| Portugal | 43.1 | 28.4 | 28.5 |
| Latvia | 42.2 | 27.1 | 30.7 |

| | | | |
|---|---|---|---|
| Malta | 41.8 | 40.1 | 18.1 |
| Estonia | 41.7 | 19.9 | 38.5 |
| Ireland | 41.4 | 37.9 | 20.7 |
| Sweden | 38.5 | 42.2 | 18.1 |
| Greece | 39.7 | 25.2 | 35.1 |
| Slovenia | 38.5 | 21.8 | 40.1 |
| Slovakia | 37.2 | 19.1 | 43.7 |
| United Kingdom | 36.9 | 44.4 | 18.7 |
| France | 35.5 | 25.8 | 39.3 |
| Denmark | 35.4 | 62.7 | 2.1 |
| Austria | 35.0 | 30.3 | 34.9 |
| Czech Republic | 34.0 | 20.8 | 45.2 |
| Italy | 33.5 | 34.9 | 31.7 |
| Spain | 33.0 | 30.9 | 38.6 |
| Netherlands | 32.2 | 31.5 | 36.3 |
| Finland | 32.0 | 38.2 | 29.8 |
| Luxembourg | 32.0 | 38.8 | 29.2 |
| Belgium | 30.3 | 18.8 | 32.4 |
| Germany | 29.8 | 29.4 | 40.8 |

**Source**: Taxation trends in the European Union, Luxembourg 2012, and p.7

Indirect taxes are considered as the simplest form of a certain and quick public income. They have a strong link with economic turnover, especially large is their sensitivity to cyclical fluctuations. The data contained in Table 5.3 shows that the differences are very large in indirect taxes loads between the EU countries: from 9.8% in Spain, 11.5% in Ireland, 11.8% in Latvia, 11.9% in Lithuania to 18.6% in Sweden, 15.6% in France, 15.5% in Italy. Similar large disparities also exist between EU countries when it comes to consumption taxes: from 8.7% in Spain, 9.9% in Luxembourg to 15% in Denmark, 14.8% in Hungary. The high proportion of indirect taxes in GDP have both Hungary, the EU 15 members such as France, Italy, the countries of the South-Malta, Cyprus or the Scandinavian countries, which may be associated with their economic policy strategy and social preferences. Overall across the EU-27 share of indirect taxes in GDP amounted to 13.5%, slightly more than in the eurozone-13.1%, just slightly larger was also part consumption taxes in GDP EU-27-11. % than in the Euro Area-11.7%.

**Table 5.3 Indirect and consumption tax in the EU in 2012**

| | Share of indirect tax in total consumption | Indirect tax as % of GDP | Share of consumption tax in total taxation | Share of consumption tax as % of GDP |
|---|---|---|---|---|
| Belgium | 28.7 | 12.9 | 24.7 | 10.9 |
| Germany | 28.9 | 11.4 | 28.4 | 10.8 |
| Estonia | 42.4 | 13.9 | 39.8 | 13.6 |
| Ireland | 39.3 | 11.5 | 35.5 | 10.0 |
| Greece | 39.1 | 12.8 | 38.9 | 12.1 |
| Spain | 30.8 | 9.8 | 27.2 | 8.7 |
| France | 35.0 | 15.6 | 25.6 | 10.9 |
| Italy | 34.3 | 15.5 | 24.2 | 10.2 |
| Cyprus | 39.9 | 15.1 | 37.8 | 13.5 |
| Luxemburg | 31.6 | 12.0 | 26.8 | 9.9 |
| Malta | 43.4 | 15.3 | 39.5 | 13.2 |
| Netherlands | 29.6 | 11.5 | 31.0 | 12.0 |
| Austria | 33.9 | 14.5 | 28.1 | 11.8 |
| Portugal | 43.6 | 14.8 | 37.1 | 11.7 |
| Slovenia | 38.3 | 14.4 | 37.5 | 14.2 |
| Slovakia | 36.5 | 10.5 | 36.1 | 10.1 |
| Finland | 33.0 | 14.3 | 31.2 | 13.1 |
| Bulgaria | 53.3 | 14.6 | 53.0 | 14.5 |
| Czech Republic | 34.2 | 12.1 | 32.3 | 10.9 |
| Denmark | 36.1 | 17.0 | 31.5 | 15.0 |
| Latvia | 42.1 | 11.8 | 39.5 | 10.8 |
| Lithuania | 44.8 | 11.9 | 42.5 | 11.5 |
| Hungary | 45.6 | 17.4 | 39.2 | 14.8 |
| Poland | 41.4 | 14.0 | 38.6 | 12.3 |
| Romania | 45.6 | 12.7 | 42.4 | 11.5 |

| Sweden | 41.3 | 18.6 | 29.0 | 13.3 |
|---|---|---|---|---|
| UK | 35.4 | 13.4 | 31.5 | 11.2 |
| EU 27 | 33.9 | 13.5 | 29.1 | 11.0 |
| EA 17 | 32.5 | 13.1 | 27.7 | 10.7 |

**Source**: Tax reforms in EU member states 2012, European Economy 2012/6, p.63

## 5.3. Changes in Share of Indirect Taxation in Total Taxation the EU Countries

In the period of economic downturn, fiscal policy changes depend on the specific situation crisis-hit countries. Fight against crises may rely on both an increase in taxes and lowering taxes and evolution of individual taxes effects, of course, the structure of budgetary revenues. The arithmetic EU-27 countries average shows that the tax rate on consumption increase by 1.5 points in only four years of crisis at around 21%. In 2008-2012 most of the EU-27 members has risen the level of indirect taxation that among the major tax types are regarded as the least harmful for economic growth. Table 5.4 shows that growth was particularly high share of indirect taxes in the general income tax in Hungary (+11.2), Latvia (+5.9%), Romania (+5.5%), Lithuania (+5%), Estonia (+3.6), Sweden (+3.5%), the UK (+3.5%), Greece (3%), Finland (2.4 %). Only in Ireland (-1.8), France (-0.2), Cyprus (-2.2), Luxemburg (-1.1) Malta (-1.2), the Netherlands (-0.9), Portugal (-1.5) have reduced the share of indirect taxation in the global tax revenues during the crisis.

The increase in the tax, concessions and rates differences creates, of course, numerous opportunities for tax evasion in the single market. Tax avoidance is still a major problem in the exchange between the EU members: the total tax losses due to the fiscal fraud ranging from 170 to 250 billion euro, that correspond to 1.8-2.25 % of the member countries GDP and about 10% of all their VAT revenue (Economic and Social Committee of the European Communities, 1995). The tax system seal can be an important factor in improving the budgetary situation, especially in the EU new member countries. While for example in Germany the VAT gap was assessed at 1% of GDP and 12% of potential VAT revenue, in Austria as 1.2% of GDP and 13% of VAT revenue, tax evasion were much more intensive in new EU countries like in Hungary where the gap represented 3.7% of GDP (3.7 billion euro) that means 30% of the total VAT revenue, in Slovakia the gap was 4% of GDP and 37% of the total VAT revenue, in the Cheech Republic was measured at 2.7% of GDP and 28% of potential VAT revenue (Takacs et al, 2015).

**Table 5.4 Share of indirect taxation in total taxation the EU in the period 2011-2012 (change 2008/2011)**

| | Share of indirect tax in total taxation 2011 | Share of indirect tax in total taxation 2012 | Change 2008/2011 |
|---|---|---|---|
| Belgium | 30.5 | | 0.9 |
| Germany | 33.1 | | 0.5 |
| Estonia | 42.6 | | 3.6 |
| Ireland | 40.8 | | -1.8 |
| Greece | 42.4 | | 3.0 |
| Spain | 33.4 | | 2.5 |
| France | | 34.9 | -0.2 |
| Italy | | 34.5 | 1.7 |
| Cyprus | 44.0 | | -2.2 |
| Luxemburg | 32.5 | | -1.1 |
| Malta | 42.4 | | -1.2 |
| Netherlands | 31.5 | | -0.9 |
| Austria | 35.0 | | 1.2 |
| Portugal | 43.1 | | -0.5 |
| Slovenia | 38.5 | | -0.1 |
| Slovakia | 38.6 | | 1.7 |
| Finland | 32.9 | | 2.4 |
| Bulgaria | | 55.3 | 0.1 |
| Czech Republic | 33.8 | 35 | 3.1 |
| Denmark | 37.0 | | 0.9 |
| Latvia | 44.1 | | 5.9 |
| Lithuania | 44.5 | | 5.0 |
| Hungary | 47.2 | 50.8 | 11.2 |
| Poland | 42.8 | | 0.7 |

| | | | |
|---|---|---|---|
| Romania | | 47.2 | 5.5 |
| Sweden | 39.6 | 42.3 | 3.5 |
| UK | 37.5 | 38.5 | 5.7 |
| EU 27 | 34.9 | | 1.1 |
| EA 17 | 33.8 | | 0.5 |

**Source**: Tax reforms in EU member states 2011, European Economy, Luxembourg2012/6, p.94, Taxation trends in the European Union, Eurostat 2014, Luxembourg,p.20-21

After the Schengen agreement, it has become possible to set up fictitious movements of goods to dubious and insolvent firms in one the EU country while the goods themselves "disappear into the untaxed sector in partner country (missing trader). Therefore it is thought that the best solution for tax avoidance practices would be the application of uniform tax rates between partners with the least amount of exemptions. Table 5.5 compares the VAT revenue in the EU countries with the revenue that would accrue if all private consumption were taxed at the standard rate and all revenue were effectively collected. Standard rate includes most of the goods and preferential rates applied to goods and services considered to be particularly important socially (primary goods, drugs, public services). As we see from data of the last column of Table 5.5 in the EU countries, there are large savings from VAT and its collection after the standard rate. A low value of the ratio indicates that exemptions, reduced rates or tax evasion have a significant impact. If all countries give up with reduced rates and the increased efficiency of the VAT collection, their tax revenues increase, on average, by about 50%. The lowest level of a pointer to countries such as Greece, Italy, Spain, which means that the changing the system of VAT reduced rates and raising to the standard would increase their budget revenue importantly.

**Table 5.5 The VAT rates in the EU in 2014/2015 and revenues as a percentage of revenues at standard rates**

| | Standard rates 2014 | Standard rates 2015 | Preferential rates | Revenues as a percentage of revenues at standard rates |
|---|---|---|---|---|
| Belgium | 21 | 21 | 6/12 | 49.1 |
| Germany | 19 | 19 | 7 | 54.7 |

| Estonia | 20 | 20 | 9 | 72.2 |
|---|---|---|---|---|
| Ireland | 23 | 23 | 9/13,5 | 55.8 |
| Greece | 23 | 23 | 6.5/13 | 42.8 |
| Spain | 21 | 21 | 4/10 | 45.3 |
| France | 20 | 20 | 5.5/10 | 48.8 |
| Italy | 22 | 22 | 10 | 40.4 |
| Cyprus | 19 | | 5/9 | 93.1 |
| Luxemburg | 15 | 15 | 6/12 | 93.9 |
| Malta | 18 | | 5/7 | 57.2 |
| Netherlands | 21 | 21 | 6 | 58.8 |
| Austria | 20 | 20 | 10 | 61.0 |
| Portugal | 23 | 23 | 6/13 | 50.0 |
| Slovenia | 22 | 22 | 9.5 | 66.4 |
| Slovakia | 20 | 20 | 10 | 51.4 |
| Finland | 24 | 24 | 10/14 | 57.9 |
| Bulgaria | 20 | | 9 | 69.5 |
| Czech Republic | 21 | 21 | 15 | 57.5 |
| Denmark | 25 | 25 | no | 62.0 |
| Latvia | 21 | | 12 | 50.2 |
| Lithuania | 21 | | 12 | 55.2 |
| Hungary | 27 | 27 | 5/18 | 55.3 |
| Poland | 23 | 23 | 5/8 | 50.5 |
| Romania | 24 | | 5/9 | 53.5 |
| Sweden | 25 | 25 | 6/12 | 57.7 |
| UK | 20 | 20 | 5 | 46.6 |
| EU 27 | 18.7 | | | 50.3 |
| EA 17 | | | | 50.1 |

**Source**: Tax reforms in EU member states 2011, European Economy, Luxembourg2011/5, p.110, www.europa.eu, 1 July 2014, National delegates - position as at 1 January 2015

## 5.4. Changes in the Direct Taxation in the EU Countries During the Crisis

Overall the decrease in budget revenue in the EU in the crisis period was aligned with the more indirect than direct taxes. The rate of the PIT, tax paid by individuals during crisis period increased only slightly during the crisis. The EU the top personal income tax (PIT) amounts to 38.1% on average, but this rates varies substantially ranging from a minimum rates of 10% in Bulgaria, 15% in Czech Republic and Lithuania, 16% in Romania, 19% in Slovakia and 21% in Estonia to 59.7% in Sweden, 54.6% in Denmark, 52% in Spain and in Netherlands, 50% in Austria and 45% in UK (Table 5.6). In 2008-2012 eight EU members countries had increased top tax rate on personal income (Greece, Spain, France, Italy, Luxembourg, Portugal, Sweden, UK), but four countries had decreased top tax rates on personal income (Denmark, Hungary, Poland, Finland). The increase was noticeable in Greece from 40% to 49% and Spain from 43% to 52%, but fall was noticeably in Hungary from 40% to 20.3%, Denmark from 62.3% to 55.4%. The comparatively lower taxation of labor in new member countries symmetrically tends to improve their economic competitiveness and boost the share of consumption taxation.

**Table 5.6 Top statutory tax rates on personal income**

| | 2008 | 2009 | 2010 | 2011 | 2012 | 2015 |
|---|---|---|---|---|---|---|
| Belgium | 53.7 | 53.7 | 53.7 | 53.7 | 53.7 | 53.7 |
| Bulgaria | 10.0 | 10.0 | 10.0 | 10.0 | 10.0 | 10.0 |
| Czech Republic | 15.0 | 15.0 | 15.0 | 15.0 | 15.0 | 20.1 |
| Denmark | 62.3 | 62.3 | 55.4 | 55.4 | 55.4 | 55.6 |
| Germany | 47.5 | 47.5 | 47.5 | 47.5 | 47.5 | 47.5 |
| Estonia | 21.0 | 21.0 | 21.0 | 21.0 | 21.0 | 21.0 |
| Ireland | 41.0 | 41.0 | 41.0 | 41.0 | 41.0 | 40.0 |
| Greece | 40.0 | 40.0 | 49.0 | 49.0 | 49.0 | 42.0 |
| Spain | 43.0 | 43.0 | 43.0 | 45.0 | 52.0 | 49.0 |
| France | 45.8 | 45.8 | 45.8 | 46.8 | 46.8 | 45.0 |
| Italy | 44.9 | 44.9 | 45.2 | 47.3 | 47.3 | 47.8 |
| Cyprus | 30.0 | 30.0 | 30.0 | 30.0 | 38.5 | 35.0 |
| Latvia | 25.0 | 23.0 | 26.0 | 25.0 | 25.0 | 24.0 |
| Lithuania | 24.0 | 15.0 | 15.0 | 15.0 | 15.0 | 15.0 |

| | | | | | | |
|---|---|---|---|---|---|---|
| Luxembourg | 39.0 | 39.0 | 39.0 | 42.1 | 41.3 | 43.6 |
| Hungary | 40.0 | 40.0 | 40.6 | 20.3 | 20.3 | 16.0 |
| Malta | 35.0 | 35.0 | 35.0 | 35.0 | 35.0 | 35.0 |
| Netherland | 52.0 | 52.0 | 52.0 | 52.0 | 52.0 | 52.0 |
| Austria | 50.0 | 50.0 | 50.0 | 50.0 | 50.0 | 50.0 |
| Poland | 40.0 | 32.0 | 32.0 | 32.0 | 32.0 | 32.0 |
| Portugal | 42.0 | 42.0 | 45.9 | 50.0 | 49.0 | 48.0 |
| Romania | 16.0 | 16.0 | 16.0 | 16.0 | 16.0 | 16.0 |
| Slovenia | 41.0 | 41.0 | 41.0 | 41,.0 | 41.0 | 50.0 |
| Slovakia | 19.0 | 19.0 | 19.0 | 19.0 | 19.0 | 25.0 |
| Finland | 50.1 | 49.1 | 49.0 | 49.2 | 49.0 | 49.0 |
| Sweden | 56.4 | 56.5 | 56.6 | 56.6 | 56.6 | 59.7 |
| United Kingdom | 40.0 | 40.0 | 50.0 | 50.0 | 50.0 | 45.0 |
| Norway | 40.0 | 40.0 | 40.0 | 40.0 | 40.0 | 46.9 |
| Iceland | | | 46.1 | 46.1 | 46.0 | 46.0 |

**Source**: Taxation trends in the European Union, Eurostat, Luxembourg 2012, and p.28., Top statutory personal axe rates and top marginal tax rates for employees, OECD, stats.org./index.aspx.data

During the economic downturn, of course, increase pressure on taxes the people to tax with the highest incomes to share the cost of the crisis. In this way, tax policy was going to bring the distribution effects, reduce the resulting from excessive income differences. Many member states have increased personal income tax to speed up fiscal consolidation. Hikes in statutory rates have often been implemented on a temporary basis, and they have taken the form of general surcharges or solidarity contributions for high-income earns (Belgium, Greece, Italy, Cyprus, Luxembourg, Portugal and Spain). Solidarity contributions are levied on high income: Italy and Portugal levy surcharges on high-income at rates of 3% and 2.5% respectively, Belgium brought in a 4% solidarity charges on financial income above a threshold. Greece, Cyprus, and Spain have increased taxes progressively for all income brackets and Greece is also considering an additional charge to the wealthiest citizens. Notable examples of this type of action were France where President Francois Hollande proposed a 75 percent tax, which had to pay those who have income above 1 million euros and included about 1500 the richest French citizens. Income taxes were to bring the 300 to 500 million euros per year in revenue for the budget, but the French Constitutional Court objected to tax for the richest and acknowledged unconstitutional the new rules, which had come into force from the beginning of 2013.

The tax burden on labor consists of personal income taxes and social security contribution. Similarly like income taxes, the diversity was the share of social security contribution among the EU member states: more than 40% of the budget revenue in the Czech Republic, Slovakia, Germany, Slovenia, less than 20% of the income of Denmark, Sweden, Malta, UK. In most member states, social security contribution accounts for a much greater share of labor taxes than personal income tax. On average about two-thirds of the labor taxes consists of non-wage labor costs paid by employees. Only in three countries: Denmark, Ireland, and the UK are personal income tax a relatively large part of the total charges paid by the labor force. In Poland, Greece, and Slovakia less than 20% of charges paid on labor force consists of personal income tax (Tax reforms in EU member states 2011 by European Economy, 2012)

During the crisis in the EU countries, tax reliefs were granted to low and medium income earners. The special focus was concentrated on incentives for vulnerable groups. In 2011 Netherlands decreased the tax rate in the lowest tax bracket. Denmark introduced a temporary deduction for wage expenses for household services. Sweden raised basic income tax allowances for labor income of people older than 65 years. In France, a household comprising two adults and three children is considered to be a household of 4 persons for tax purpose. In Germany, child allowance with a view for tax deduction was given at the level of 7008 euro per child. Spain reintroduced the general 15% tax credit for buying a taxpayer primary residence. To attract foreign specialists, Ireland granted an exemption from income tax on 30% of their annual salary between 75 000 euro and 500 000 euro if they were employed for a minimum of one year to a maximum of five years.

The second next to the work an important production factor for overcoming the economic crisis is capital and obtained by him the profits that a significant impact is its level of taxation. The capital taxes include taxes on income earned from savings and investments by households and corporation and taxes on stocks of capital from savings and investments. At the begin of the crisis, the tax on capital had decreased considerably since 2007 to 2010 in the EU, but it stabilized in 2010 when the tax on capital and business income clusters was around 20% in the EU countries ([20]). This average hides however

[20] Ibidem, p. 28, 34.

significant differences in the taxable capital between the member state. The ratio between taxes on capital and aggregate capital and savings income ranging from 39% in Denmark to a mere 9.1% in Estonia. It should be taken into account that there is strong tax competition on corporate income in the EU, where some countries impose significantly lower taxes to profit companies in order to attract foreign capital.

Table 5.7 shows that the adjusted statutory tax rate on corporate income still varies between the EU member countries with a minimum of 10% in Bulgaria and Cyprus, 12.5% in Ireland, 15% in Lithuania and Latvia to 34.41% in France, 30.18% in Germany, 35% in Malta, 33% in Belgium. Although some countries fought the crisis through a reduction in taxes on corporate income, the other measures have typically increased the tax burden on capital. For example, in Belgium the withholding tax rate on interest and dividends was increased from 15% to 21%, in Cyprus the rate increased from 10% to 15% for interest and from 17% to 20% for dividends, in France the optional final levy on dividends and interest was increased from 18% to 19%, in Ireland taxes on capital and interest were aligned at 30%. in Portugal tax on income from dividends was risen from 15% to 21.5%, in Finland the tax rate on capital income increased from 28% to 30% and for income exceeding 50 000 euro to 32%, in Spain taxes saving and capital gains depending on income: 21% on the first 6000 euro, 25% up to 24 000, and 27% on income above.

**Table 5.7 Adjusted top statutory rates on corporate income in 2008- 2015**

| | 2008 | 2009 | 2010 | 2011 | 2012 | 2015 |
|---|---|---|---|---|---|---|
| Belgium | 34.0 | 34.0 | 34.0 | 34.0 | 34.0 | 33.0 |
| Bulgaria | 10.0 | 10.0 | 10.0 | 10.0 | 10.0 | 10.0 |
| Czech Republic | 21.0 | 20.0 | 19.0 | 19.0 | 19.0 | 19.0 |
| Denmark | 25.0 | 25.0 | 25.0 | 25.0 | 25.0 | 23.5 |
| Germany | 29.8 | 29.8 | 29.8 | 29.8 | 29.8 | 30.18 |
| Estonia | 21.0 | 21.0 | 21.0 | 21.0 | 21.0 | 20.0 |
| Ireland | 12.5 | 12.5 | 12.5 | 12.5 | 12.5 | 12.5 |
| Greece | 35.0 | 35.0 | 43.0 | 30.0 | 30.0 | 26.0 |
| Spain | 30.0 | 30.0 | 30.0 | 30.0 | 30.0 | 28.0 |
| France | 34.4 | 34.4 | 34.4 | 34.4 | 36.1 | 34.43 |
| Italy | 31.4 | 31.4 | 31.4 | 31.4 | 31.4 | 27.5 |

| Cyprus | 10.0 | 10.0 | 10.0 | 10.0 | 10.0 | |
|---|---|---|---|---|---|---|
| Latvia | 15.0 | 15.0 | 15.0 | 15.0 | 15.0 | 15.0 |
| Lithuania | 15.0 | 20.0 | 15.0 | 15.0 | 15.0 | 15.0 |
| Luxembourg | 29.6 | 28.6 | 28.6 | 28.8 | 28.8 | 29.22 |
| Hungary | 21.3 | 21.3 | 20.6 | 20.6 | 20.6 | 19.0 |
| Malta | 35.0 | 35.0 | 35.0 | 35.0 | 35.0 | |
| Netherland | 25.5 | 25.5 | 25.5 | 25.5 | 25.0 | 25.0 |
| Austria | 25.0 | 25.0 | 25.0 | 25.0 | 25.0 | 25.0 |
| Poland | 19.0 | 19.0 | 19.0 | 19.0 | 19.0 | 19.0 |
| Portugal | 26.5 | 26.5 | 29.0 | 29.0 | 31.5 | 29.5 |
| Romania | 16.0 | 16.0 | 16.0 | 16.0 | 16.0 | 16.0 |
| Slovenia | 22.0 | 21.0 | 20.0 | 20.0 | 20.0 | 17.0 |
| Slovakia | 19.0 | 19.0 | 19.0 | 19.0 | 19.0 | 22.0 |
| Finland | 26.0 | 26.0 | 26.0 | 26.0 | 24.5 | 20.0 |
| Sweden | 28.0 | 26.3 | 26.3 | 26.3 | 26.3 | 22.0 |
| United Kingdom | 30.0 | 28.0 | 28.0 | 28.0 | 24.0 | 20.0 |
| Norway | 28.0 | 28.0 | 28.0 | 28.0 | 28.0 | 27.0 |
| Iceland | 15.0 | 15.0 | 18.0 | 20.0 | 20.0 | 20.0 |

**Source**: Taxation trends in the European Union, Eurostat, Luxembourg 2012, and p.29

During the euro crisis only in two, the EU member states raised CIT taxes (Italy, Portugal), while eight countries lowered taxes on business profits (Czech Republic, Greece, Luxembourg, Malta, Netherlands, Finland, Sweden, United Kingdom). The average rate of CIT in the EU member countries was 24% in 2008 while 23% in 2013. Tax reduction of CIT coincided with a period of particularly out of the crisis after 2013, when the twelve EU countries have reduced the taxes on businesses by 2015, including some as far as the United Kingdom from 30% to 20%, Greece from 35% to 26%, Sweden from 28% to 20%, Finland 26% to 20%. Some the EU countries apply attractive tax advantages for foreign investors and SME, such as the Baltic States where in Lithuania the rate of 10% was applied to the interest and royalty income paid to non-resident companies. After 2008 several the EU members reduced their headline tax rates on corporate income. Some members introduced tax relief on investments in physical capital or R+ D, while restricting the deductibility of other items (operational losses).

Many investigations support the claim that a move from income taxation to consumption taxation would raise the rate of long-term economic growth. The European Commission research shows that a 1% GDP consolidation achieved by raising consumption taxes would lead to an initial decline in GDP of only 0.1- 0.2% and in the long run, the GDP would be higher by 0.-04.% in comparison with no consolidation scenario ([21]). D. Botman and S. Danninger stimulated the impact of the German tax reforms assuming an increase in VAT rates partly compensated by lower payroll taxes and corporate taxes. In their conclusions, the initial negative effects on GDP growth in Germany would turn slightly positive in the medium turn (Botman, Danninger, 2007). For Italy shift from taxing labour to taxing consumption should reduce disincentive in labour market and lead to an increase in the level of employment and output (Annicchiaro et al., 2011).

According to austerity programs, the EU member countries undertook sizeable consolidation efforts to increase their tax revenues during the crisis. If however governments are forced to increase taxes, it is better to achieve it through the increase in indirect taxes, which are less harmful to investment or work than direct taxes. Generally, EU countries had evolved in these ways their tax systems during the crisis, when they increased mostly taxes which inhibit less economic growth. This was particularly the countries most affected by the crisis as Greece, Spain, Portugal or Ireland. The potential for taxes increases was considered to be high if: tax to GDP ratio was relatively low and there was scope for increasing the least distortionary taxes. Table 5.8 shows estimates of the increase in tax charges as in the EU countries in the medium and long term with the aim to reach budgetary equilibrium and reduction the public debt in accordance with the Maastricht level. The indicator of fiscal sustainability gap in the medium term S1 is high if more than 3, which corresponds to the very top of the indicator distribution. The indicator of fiscal sustainability in the long term S2 is high if more than 6, which corresponds to the very top of the indicator distribution. Both indicators signify that initial budgetary position component of the sustainability gap (initial budgetary deficit) and the long-term budgetary projections are very unfavorable.

[21] Ibidem,p.54

**Table 5.8 Sustainability GAP and primary balance**

| | S1 medium term | S2 long term | Initial Budgetary position | Ageing component |
|---|---|---|---|---|
| Belgium | 6.2 | 7.5 | 0.5 | 7.0 |
| Germany | 0.6 | 1.8 | -0.5 | 2.3 |
| Estonia | -2.1 | 2.1 | 1.2 | 0.8 |
| Spain | 3.7 | 4.3 | 2.3 | 2.0 |
| France | 3.0 | 2.2 | 1.3 | 0.9 |
| Italy | -0.9 | 2.8 | -3.4 | 0.5 |
| Cyprus | 2.3 | 5.5 | -0.2 | 5.7 |
| Luxemburg | 0.3 | 9.8 | 1.2 | 8.7 |
| Malta | 2.9 | 6.1 | 1.3 | 4.8 |
| Netherlands | 4.1 | 7.9 | 2.4 | 5.4 |
| Austria | 2.3 | 3.7 | 0.2 | 3.5 |
| Slovenia | 2.2 | 7.5 | 0.6 | 6.8 |
| Slovakia | 4.4 | 8.6 | 3.5 | 5.1 |
| Finland | 1.2 | 4.9 | 0.3 | 5.1 |
| Bulgaria | 1.7 | 2.6 | 0.4 | 2.2 |
| Czech Republic | 0.4 | 4.9 | 1.1 | 3.8 |
| Denmark | 0.6 | 3.3 | 0.5 | 2.9 |
| Latvia | 1.9 | 0.7 | 0.9 | 1.6 |
| Lithuania | 0.1 | 4.3 | 0.8 | 3.5 |
| Hungary | 0.7 | 0.54 | 0.5 | 1.0 |
| Poland | 0.1 | 1.5 | 0.5 | 1.0 |
| Romania | 1.5 | 3.6 | 0.1 | 3.5 |
| Sweden | 2.9 | 1.8 | 1.1 | 2.9 |
| UK | 5.1 | 5.2 | 2.6 | 2.5 |
| EU 27 | 2.2 | 2.9 | 0.7 | 2.3 |
| EA 17 | 2.1 | 2.4 | 0.3 | 2.2 |

**Source**: Tax reforms in EU member states 2012, European Economy 2012/6, p.58

S1 corresponds to the required adjustment of the primary balance until 2020 to reach public debts of 60% and the debt threshold fixed in the Treaty by 2030. As one can see in Table 5.8 Belgium, Spain, UK, Slovenia, Netherlands need a strong fiscal adjustment to make their public finance sustainable in the medium term. As far as long-term perspective is concerned fiscal adjustment was particularly high in Belgium, Luxembourg, Spain, Netherlands, Slovenia, Slovakia, Czech Republic, UK, and Lithuania. Among Euro Area member states Belgium, Spain, Luxembourg, Malta, the Netherlands, Slovenia, Slovakia and the UK faced particular consolidation challenges due to serious sustainability issues both in the medium and long run. At the same time Spain, Malta Slovenia, and Slovakia showed some overall tax space (relatively low tax to GDP ratio) which might be used to contribute to consolidation on the revenue side.

## 5.5. Evolution of Government Expenditure in the EU Countries During Crisis

The Economic crisis has a significant impact not only on level and structure of taxes but also on budgetary expenditure. The Euro Area crisis has affected the public spending in member countries by at least four main factors: 1. automatic stabilisers reaction to the crisis; 2. introduction of discretionary measures and increase spending; 3. fall in budgetary revenue; 4. austerity programs.

During the crisis, the Euro Area countries tipped the austerity tendency and reduced the share of budgetary expenditure in the GDP of 51.2% to 49% in 2009-2013 and to 48.8% in 2015. In 2008- 2015 even deeper decreased the share of public expenditure in the GDP of EU member states from 51.1% to 48.2%. Among the Euro Area countries, particularly the share of Estonian government expenditure in GDP decreased from 45.2% to 39.1%, in Greece from 53.8% to 50.5%, Italy by 52.0% to 50.69%, Portugal from 49.7% to 47.89%, in Spain with 46.3% to 42.04%. Of concern was the decline in the share of budgetary expenditure in GDP in Germany with 48.1% to 43.87% given the huge role in stimulating demand across the European single market. Austerity programs have not only carried out the countries of the Euro Area, but also the other EU countries, such as Romania where the share of public expenditure in GDP decreased to 25.5% from 33.77%, UK downgraded the share of public expenditure in GDP from 46.3% to 40.29%, Sweden from 54.7% to 50.07%, or Poland from 47.7% to 41.81%.

**Table 5.9 Government expenditure of the EU member countries in 2009 – 2015 (as % of GDP)**

| | 2009 | 2010 | 2011 | 2012 | 2013 | 2015 |
|---|---|---|---|---|---|---|
| Denmark | 57.8 | 57.6 | 57.8 | 58.6 | 56.6 | 54.41 |
| Estonia | 45.2 | 40.6 | 38.2 | 41.2 | 39.3 | 39.14 |
| Ireland | 48.8 | 66.8 | 48.8 | 44.1 | 43.1 | 35.6 |
| Greece | 53.8 | 50.0 | 50.0 | 49.7 | 50.6 | 50.5 |
| Spain | 46.3 | 45.6 | 43.6 | 42.4 | 42.0 | 42.04 |
| France | 56.8 | 56.5 | 55.9 | 56.3 | 56.2 | 57.01 |
| Lithuania | 43.8 | 40.9 | 37.5 | 36.8 | 36.1 | 34.1 |
| Malta | 43.5 | 43.3 | 43.0 | 44.4 | 43.8 | 44.86 |
| Netherland | 51.6 | 51.3 | 50.2 | 50.8 | 50.8 | 44.47 |
| Poland | 44.5 | 45.4 | 43.6 | 43.1 | 42.4 | 41.81 |
| Romania | 41.1 | 40.2 | 37.7 | 36.2 | 35.4 | 33.77 |
| Slovakia | 41.5 | 40.0 | 37.4 | 37.7 | 37.3 | 41.76 |
| Hungary | 51.5 | 49.4 | 48.6 | 48.6 | 47.6 | 49.07 |
| Italy | 52.0 | 50.6 | 50.0 | 50.4 | 49.5 | 50.69 |
| Slovenia | 49.3 | 50.3 | 50.9 | 48.7 | 47.9 | 44.48 |
| United Kingdom | 46.3 | 47.3 | 48.3 | 49.3 | 50.3 | 40.29 |
| Belgium | 53.7 | 52.7 | 53.2 | 53.9 | 53.7 | 53.44 |
| Bulgaria | 40.7 | 37.4 | 35.2 | 35.2 | 35.3 | 37.77 |
| Czech Republic | 44.9 | 44.2 | 43.4 | 43.3 | 43.1 | 42.02 |
| Germany | 48.1 | 47.9 | 45.7 | 45.6 | 45.2 | 43.87 |
| Cyprus | 46.2 | 46.4 | 47.3 | 46.0 | 45.3 | |
| Latvia | 44.5 | 43.9 | 39.1 | 38.1 | 37.0 | 36.51 |
| Luxembourg | 43.0 | 42.4 | 42.0 | 43.6 | 44.0 | 41.79 |
| Austria | 52.9 | 52.6 | 50.5 | 51.4 | 50.6 | 51.98 |
| Portugal | 49.7 | 51.2 | 48.7 | 47.7 | 46.1 | 47.89 |
| Finland | 55.9 | 55.2 | 53.7 | 54.3 | 54.7 | 58.73 |
| Sweden | 54.7 | 52.2 | 51.1 | 52.1 | 51.8 | 50.07 |
| EA 17 | 51.2 | 51.0 | 49.4 | 49.4 | 49.0 | 48.8 |
| EU 27 | 51.1 | 50.6 | 49.1 | 48.9 | 48.4 | 48.2 |

**Source**: Report on Public Finances in EMU, European Economy 2012/4, Luxembourg 2012, p.2, www.statistica.com/statistics/263220/public-spending -ration-in EU countries, 2016-02.26

On the basis of the statistical data we can find, that the EU countries have not opted for the classic methods of fight against the crisis by increasing public expenditure. The overall support of the EU' member countries finances was substantial in the critical period 2009- 2013, as measured by the deterioration in the governments' balance amounted to 5%. After 2013 the EU members rather stabilized budgets in austerity program by public savings or increased taxes. In the EU only three member countries increased budget expenditure share in GDP in the period 2009-2015: Finland from 55.9% to 58.73%, France from 56.8% to 57.01%, Malta from 43.5% to 44. 86% (see Table 5.9). Belgium and Slovakia, have maintained the level of public expenditure in relation to GDP more or less at the same level. Other countries have significantly reduced the share of spending in GDP budgetary due to stabilization program. Some like Ireland, UK, and Portugal after a short-lived increase in public expenditure finally reduced their expenditure relative to GDP.

## 5.6. Expenditure Multipliers and Fiscal Space

In economic theory, it is considered that consolidation by increasing taxes may not be harmful to economic growth if the increase in taxes is used to increase the expenditure. The so-called balanced budget theorem says that a change in real GDP is equal to the change in government purchases when government purchases and taxes change by the same amount and in the same direction (Arnold, 1996). However, in the short term consolidation might have a negative impact on aggregate demand and growth before the positive impacts from reduced interest payments begin. The main factors driving the success of a budgetary consolidation in reducing the debt ratio are the value of the fiscal multiplier. The fiscal multiplier measures the reaction of the economic output to a budgetary expansion or consolidation. Tax and transfer multipliers used to have a smaller short term impact than government expenditure. A euro spend by any governments is euro spend, but euro tax cut is a euro partly saved and partly spent (Heller, 2005). The size of the first year multipliers used to be then larger if fiscal consolidation is based on government expenditure. There is growing conviction that fiscal multipliers are not linear and become larger in the crisis period. The negative output consolidation is larger if the measures taken are not credible, for example, if the monetary policy is enabling to reduce real interest rates.

**Table 5.10 Expenditure multipliers in Euro Area countries**

| Studies | Sample | Short term multiplier | Medium Term multiplier |
|---|---|---|---|
| Perotti (2004) | Germany(1960 1974) | 0.36 | 0.28 |
| Heppke – Falk (2006) | Germany ( 1974 2004) | 0.62 | 1.27 |
| Baum - Koester (2011) | Germany (1976 2009) | 0.7 | 0.69 |
| Benassy-Quere Cimadomo (2006) | Germany (1971 2004) | 0.23 | -0.23 |
| Biau- Girard (2005) | France (1978-2003) | 1.9 | 1.5 |
| Giordano (2007) | Italy (1982- 2004) | 1.2 | 1.7 |
| De Castro (2006) | Spain (1980-2001) | 1.14-1.54 | 0.58-1.04 |
| De Castro- H. de Cos (2008) | Spain (1980 -2004) | 1.3 | 1.0 |
| De Castro – Fernandez (2011) | Spain | 0.94 | 0.55 |
| IMF (2005) | Portugal (1995 2004) | 1.32 | 1.07 |
| Perotti (2004) | UK (1963-1979) | 0.48 | 0.27 |
| Benassy- Quere Cimadomo (2006) | UK (1971-2004) | 0.12 | -0.3 |
| Burriel (2010) | Euro Area (1981 2007) | 0.87 | 0.85 |

**Source**: Report on Public Finances in EMU, European Economy 2012/4, Brussels 2012, p. 123

Fiscal and spending multipliers were quite different between the EU member states as well between the USA as in Euro Area. Expenditure multiplier for the Euro Area as a whole was higher than in the USA and UK. Government consumption multipliers were lying between 0.5 and 0.8 in most of the EU member countries; larger multipliers correspond to cuts in their government wages and government investments, while smaller multipliers correspond to VAT and labor tax increases. Table 5.10 summarizes some of the available empirical evidence in the literature concerning fiscal multipliers to government expenditure shocks in the case of Germany, France, Italy, Spain, and Portugal. The effect of consolidation depends not only on individual actions implemented but also on budgetary policy undertaken in main partner's countries. The most of the available empirical shows smaller expenditure multiplier in the medium term than in the short run. Public expenditure multiplier differs clearly among the Euro Area member countries in the long period 1960- 2007. Short term -one-year multipliers usually rank between 0.4 and 1; for a longer period, the dispersion is even higher. A much higher multiplier was obtained for France, Italy, Spain, and Portugal than for Germany. The government spending shocks displayed little persistence and the influence on the economy in the case of Germany (multiplier is somewhat below 0.7), as well as spending multipliers, were usually found to be low in the United Kingdom (from 0.12 to 0.48). For France, Italy, Spain, and Portugal one year spending multiplier was above unity, whereas they turned out to be fairly persistent, so fiscal consolidation might have influenced the economic growth in these countries negatively.

Overall most of the empirical estimates for Euro Area have revealed that the tax shocks usually entail lower effects on GDP than public expenditure. The success of government's policy to increase taxes depends however also on the so-called fiscal space: to be effective fiscal consolidation must have a certain freedom of manoeuvre in budgetary policy. P. Heller defined fiscal space as "room in a government's budget that allows it to provide resources for the desired purpose without jeopardizing the sustainability of its financial position or the stability of the economy" ([22]). Table 5.11 shows the estimated critical multipliers for the EU 27 for 2011 taking into consideration the reaction of automatic stabilizers to the change in growth induced by budgetary consolidation. Given the size of the fiscal multiplier in the EU countries, each partner should have taken into account its critical size, which may not be exceeded. If the multiplier is very high, then too ambitious a program budgetary consolidation may have brought about the prolonged recession and an increase in debt.

---

[22] Ibidem, p.3-5

**Table 5.11 Critical first-year multipliers in the EU member states at constant interest rates in 2011**

| | Cyclical semi-elasticities | Debt in 2011 | Critical multiplier |
|---|---|---|---|
| Belgium | 0.51 | 98.0 | 0.7 |
| Bulgaria | 0.33 | 16.3 | 2.0 |
| Czech Republic | 0.36 | 41.2 | 1.3 |
| Denmark | 0.65 | 46.5 | 0.9 |
| Estonia | 0.30 | 6.0 | 2.8 |
| Ireland | 0.44 | 108.2 | 0.7 |
| Greece | 0.42 | 165.3 | 0.5 |
| Spain | 0.43 | 68.5 | 0.9 |
| France | 0.53 | 85.8 | 0.7 |
| Italy | 0.49 | 120.1 | 0.6 |
| Cyprus | 0.43 | 71.6 | 0.9 |
| Latvia | 0.30 | 42.6 | 1.4 |
| Lithuania | 0.29 | 38.5 | 1.5 |
| Luxembourg | 0.44 | 18.2 | 1.6 |
| Hungary | 0.44 | 80.6 | 0.8 |
| Malta | 0.38 | 72.0 | 0.9 |
| Netherland | 0.62 | 65.2 | 0.8 |
| Austria | 0.47 | 72.2 | 0.8 |
| Poland | 0.38 | 56.3 | 1.1 |
| Portugal | 0.45 | 107.8 | 0.7 |
| Romania | 0.32 | 33.3 | 1.5 |
| Slovenia | 0.45 | 47.6 | 1.1 |
| Slovakia | 0.33 | 43.3 | 1.3 |
| Finland | 0.58 | 48.6 | 0.9 |
| Sweden | 0.61 | 38.4 | 1.0 |
| United Kingdom | 0.46 | 85.7 | 0.8 |

**Source**: Report on Public Finances in EMU, European Economy 2012/4, Luxembourg 2012, p.138.

Table 5.11 shows that nearly all the cyclical elasticities of semi-figures fall below critical multiplier. In some countries, the space to increase taxes is even much (Estonia, Latvia, Lithuania, Luxembourg, Austria, Slovenia, Slovakia) but the other countries, such as France, Ireland or Italy could no longer afford to further boost up tax without exceeding the critical multipliers. Particularly large were the differences between the cyclical semi-elasticities and critical multiplier in Bulgaria, where the level of public debt was just 16.3%, in Estonia, where the level of public debt was only 6% in reference with GDP. Greece was a unique country in Euro Area where short run debt could increase even its composition between expenditure and revenue would be balanced. If consolidation is repeated, and the multiplier is large, the effect on the economy tends to cumulate with possible adverse effect on the economy and debt increases. The same spiral can happen with the budget deficit, so it is relevant that policy recommendations are formulated carefully and long term taking into consideration growth, employment, structural balance rather than actual headline debt and deficit ratios.

## 5.7. Conclusion

In a situation of crisis that started in 2008, the EU countries took the entire package of activities to restore macroeconomic equilibrium comprising various instruments from fiscal policy. During the crisis majority of the EU partners used taxation to consolidate their public finances, but the increase in the tax to GDP ratio appeared fairly modest, and the tax increases did not cover equally all taxes and in the same way all partner countries in their consolidation effort. Overall the euro crisis reshaped the tax structure of the EU members with the noticeable shift from direct taxes to indirect taxes as a less harmful for economic growth. Roughly half the EU member states have raised their VAT rates. Increasing the consumption taxes in the EU was accompanied by "fiscal devaluation" indirect taxation. The rate of income tax from companies progressively declined, and tax reduction coincided with a period of particularly out of the crisis after 2013. The rate of the PIT, tax paid by individuals during crisis period increased slightly on the solidarity basis, but among the EU countries prevailed policy to reduce the tax on labor aimed mainly to increase work incentive.

The economic crisis has influenced not only budgetary revenue in the EU countries but also budgetary expenditure. Only three EU members increased budget expenditure share in GDP, but other countries the stabilization programs have reduced the share of spending in GDP, some countries after a short-lived increase in public expenditure finally reduced their expenditure relative to GDP. Due to the low value of fiscal multiplier, the tax increases in the EU countries might have had a moderate impact on economic activity during the crisis. The level of GDP and a deep recession in Euro Area could have been the result of the method of restoring fiscal balance by reducing more spending than increase taxes. Confronting the crisis the EU would be much more effective when that was not carried out by the member states individually, but together at the EU level. There are valid arguments for jointly imposing discipline and budgetary stabilization coordination as well as optimal budgetary spending in all area in the time of crisis.

## 5.8. References

ANNICCHIARO B., DIO B.,FELICI F., NUCCI F. (2011). *Macroeconomic modelling and the effects of policy reforms: an assessment for Italy using ITEM and Quest,* Ministry of Economy and Finance Working paper,

ARNOLD R.A. (1996). *Economics,* New York

BOTMAN D., DANNINGER S. (2007). *Tax reform and debt sustainability in Germany: an assessment using the Global Fiscal Model,* IMF Working Paper 07/46/ 2007.

HELLER P, S. (2005). PDP/05/4 , *IMF Policy Discussion Paper,* Fiscal Affairs Department , March 2005,p.3-5

KRAJEWSKA A. (2015). *Podatki w Unii Europejskiej,* PWN Warszawa 2010., 2015 Macro-economic Data" and Index of Economic Freedom, Heritage Foundation.

*Protocol No 5 on the excessive deficit procedure.* European Union (1993). Selected instruments taken from the Treaties. Luxembourg

Economic and Social Committee of the European Communities (1995). *Opinion on direct and indirect taxation.* Brussels, 20-21 December 1995,

*Report on Public Finances in EMU,* European Economy 2012/4, Luxembourg 2012, p.2, www.statistica.com/statistics/263220/public-spending -ration-in eu countries, 2016-02.26

TAKACS V., MATE A., NAGY S.G (2015). *Changes in tax structures in European Union member states (in ) Society and Economy in Central and Eastern Europe,* Journal of the Corvinius University of Budapest, November 2015, vol. 37.

*Tax reforms in EU member states (2011).* European Economy, Luxembourg2012/6

Taxation trends in the European Union (2012), Eurostat, Luxembourg 2012, and p.28.

*Top statutory personal taxes rates and top marginal tax rates for employees,* OECD, stats.org./index.aspx.data

Chapter 6

# Inflation Expectations and Long-term Interest Rates

Rajmund Mirdala

## 6.1. Introduction

Euro Area member countries suffering an economic downturn are no longer able to improve their competitiveness by devaluating national currencies. While internal devaluation may improve price competitiveness and boost both internal and external demand, the risk of deflationary pressures substantially reduces vital growth incentives (Hetzel, 2015). Moreover, ECB by inflating its monetary base fueled by another wave of quantitative easing does not primarily follow the idea of economic recovery. Low-interest rate environment may be followed by euro depreciation improving the competitiveness of European producers on the foreign markets. However, as the most of the transactions on the EU single market are conducted in euro among its member countries, Euro Area seeks common reasonable automatic mechanisms that would help to improve its internal competitiveness (Peersman, 2011).

There are still many opened issues according to the suitability of the common monetary policy in the Euro Area provided a relative heterogeneity of the single market (Micossi, 2015). Time-varying exchange rate pass-through effects to domestic prices under fixed euro exchange rate perspective represent one of the most challenging implications of the common currency (Bussière, 2013). The problem is even more crucial when examining crisis related redistributive effects associated with relative price changes. The degree of the exchange rate pass-through to domestic prices reveals its role as the external price shocks absorber especially in the situation when the leading path of exchange rates is less vulnerable to the changes in the foreign nominal variables (Campa, Goldberg and González-Mínguez, 2005). Resulted adjustments in domestic prices followed by exchange rate shifts induced by sudden external price shocks are associated with changes in the relative competitiveness among member countries of the currency area. Moreover, distribution of the exogenous price shock across the internal pricing chain may be biased by country-specific conditions and cross-country distortionary effects induced by the recent economic crisis.

Risks of a deflationary spiral in the Euro Area together with low nominal interest rates policy conducted by European Central Bank (ECB) are drawing the attention of increasing number of empirical studies. Changes in the relative importance of inflation expectations and expected real interest rates in determining nominal interest rates are generally induced implications of the zero inflation environment (Labadie, 1994; Evans, 1998; Den Haan, 1995). Moreover, deflationary pressures and tightened financial conditions provided contradictory effects on the determination of long-term interest rates and even emphasized changed market fundamentals during the crisis period (Christensen, Lopez and Rudebusch, 2008).

Nominal interest rates in the Euro Area member countries followed generally criticized decreasing and mutually converging trend since the beginning of the Euro Area establishment (Acharya and Steffen, 2015). The introduction of the single currency on a very heterogeneous group of countries induced undesirable convergence especially in the long-term interest rates on the government bonds. Reduction of differences among interest rates of the Euro Area member countries resulted from decreased expected risk premium recognized by financial markets being supported by (un)conventional operations of ECB that many economists criticized and indicated as one of the key design failures of the Euro Area (De Grauwe, 2013).

In the chapter, we examine the influence of inflation expectations and expected real interest rates on the long-term nominal interest rates of government bonds with 10-year maturity in the Euro Area member countries by employing SVAR (structural vector autoregression) methodology. We also decompose nominal interest rates on government bonds into inflation expectations and expected real interest rates components. Our results indicate that both components significantly determined main trends in the development of interest rates on government bonds since 2000. At the same time, the role of both types of shocks in determining sovereign debt yields differs when comparing our results for periphery countries with those of core of the Euro Area.

## 6.2. Interest Rates Determination in Empirical Literature

Gerlach-Kristen and Rudolf (2010) compared three monetary operating procedures by examining optimal policy reaction functions, impulse responses and simulated volatilities of inflation, the output gap and the yield curve to examine volatility of interest rates and other main macroeconomic variables. Their results suggest that volatilities in key variables under different monetary-policy framework (commitment vs. discretion) are strongly dependent on general preconditions (normal times vs. financial distress). Eiffinger, Schaling, and Vehagen (2000) analyzed the relevance of the term structure of interest rates for the transmission process of the monetary policy. Authors identified and empirically tested the long-term interest rates as a crucial indicator for monetary policy discretionary changes. Emiris (2006) decomposed long-term interest rates into term premium and inflation premium to investigate the sources of an average premium on 10-year government bonds variability. The author also examined responses of the term premia to the different shocks. Fendel (2009) intended to support the empirical findings on the information content of the term structure of interest rates for monetary policy. Kulish (2007) analyzed two roles (first, as a key determinant of the reaction function of the monetary authority; second, as instruments of policies) that long-term nominal interest rates can play in the conduct of the monetary policy. McGough, Rudebusch, and Williams (2005) investigated the problem of short-term versus long-term interest rates suitability to operate as a monetary policy instrument. Authors highlight and discuss a crucial role of inflation expectations and real interest rate for selecting the most appropriate interest rate as a key pillar of a monetary policy framework. Michaud and Upper (2008) identified the origins of interbank interest rates volatility by examining the possible determinants of the risk premium contained in the money market interest rates. Rudebusch, Sack, and Swanson (2006) examined the origins and implications of changes in bond term premiums for economic activity to analyze the stability of long-term interest rates. Authors also analyzed empirical relationship between short-term and long-term interest rates.

St-Amant (1996) employed bivariate SVAR model to analyze the impact of expected inflation and ex-ante real interest rates on the nominal interest rates volatility of government bonds with maturity one year and ten years in the U.S.A. Following the author's results, we may conclude that the inflation expectations seem to the prevailing determinant of nominal interest rate volatility since the beginning of the 1970s till the middle of the 1980s, whereas shifts in expected real interest rates substantially contributed to the nominal interest rates volatility during the first half of the 1990s. Deacon a Derry (1994) provided a variety of methods for identification of market interest rate and inflation premium from the interest rates associated with government bonds. Engsted (1995) implemented cointegration analysis and VAR methodology to examine properties of interest rates and inflation time series. Neely and Rapach (2008) analyzed time series for real interest rates employing growth equilibrium model. Authors dedicated extra effort to investigate a presence of persistence patterns, especially in the medium and long period. Ragan (1995) analyzed time structure of nominal interest rates to estimate inflation expectations of agents. Results of his empirical investigation provided interpretation of the real interest rate volatility over time. Crowder a Hoffman (1996) analyzed mutual interconnections between inflation and interest rates. Implemented SVAR methodology helped authors to isolate permanent and temporary sources of volatility for nominal interest rates and inflation time series. Lai (2004) examined properties of time series for real interest rates. The author investigated conditions to maintain a time series stationary under changing the length of the base period. Garcia and Perron (1996) analyzed long-run features of time series for real interest rates in the U.S.A. Lanne (2001) verified a validity of Fisher effect following the results of long-run interconnections testing between inflation and nominal interest rates in the U.S.A.

### 6.3. Econometric Model

VAR models represent dynamic systems of equations in which the current level of each variable depends on past movements of that variable and all other variables involved in the system. Residuals of vector $\varepsilon_t$ represent unexplained movements in variables (effects of exogenous shocks hitting the model); however, as complex functions of structural shocks effects, they have no economic interpretation. Structural shocks can be still recovered using the transformation of the true form representation into the reduced-form by imposing a number of identifying restrictions. Applied restrictions should reflect some general assumptions about the underlying structure of the economy, and they are obviously derived from economic theory.

In the chapter, we employ methodology introduced by Blanchard a Quah (1988) who estimated a bivariate model with two types of exogenous shocks. To identify structural shocks, authors implemented identification scheme based on decomposing effects of the shocks into permanent and transitory components. Long-run identifying restrictions were applied on the variance-covariance matrix of reduced form VAR residuals.

Following our objective, we estimate a model consisting of the vector of endogenous variables $X_t$ and the same number of primitive (structural) shocks. An unrestricted true form of the model is represented by the following infinite moving average representation:

$$X_t = A_0\varepsilon_t + A_1\varepsilon_{t-1} + A_2\varepsilon_{t-2} + \dots = \sum_{i=0}^{\infty} A_i\varepsilon_{t-i} = \sum_{i=0}^{\infty} A_i L^i \varepsilon_t \qquad (1)$$

or

$$\begin{bmatrix} ir_{n,t} \\ p_t \end{bmatrix} = \begin{bmatrix} a_{11} & a_{12} \\ a_{21} & a_{22} \end{bmatrix} \begin{bmatrix} \varepsilon_{p^e,t} \\ \varepsilon_{ir_r^e,t} \end{bmatrix} \tag{2}$$

where $X_t = [ir_{n,t}, p_t]$ is $n$ x 1 vector of the endogenous macroeconomic variables ($ir_{n,t}$ - long-term nominal interest rate, $p_t$ - rate of inflation), $A(L)$ is a $n$ x $n$ polynomial consisting of the matrices of coefficients to be estimated in the lag operator $L$ representing the relationship among variables on the lagged values, $\varepsilon_t$ is $n$ x 1 $\left(\varepsilon_t = \left[\varepsilon_{p^e,t}, \varepsilon_{ir_r^e,t}\right]\right)$ vector of identically normally distributed, serially uncorrelated and mutually orthogonal errors (white noise disturbances that represent the unexplained movements in the variables, reflecting the influence of exogenous shocks):

$$E(\varepsilon_t) = 0, \quad E(\varepsilon_t \varepsilon_t') = \Sigma_\varepsilon = \mathrm{I}, \quad E(\varepsilon_t \varepsilon_s') = [0] \quad \forall t \neq s \tag{3}$$

we assume two exogenous shocks that contemporaneously affects endogenous variables - inflation expectations shock $\left(\varepsilon_{p^e,t}\right)$ and expected real interest rates shock $\left(\varepsilon_{ir_r,t}\right)$.

Structural exogenous shocks from equation (1) are not directly observable due to the complexity of information included in true form VAR residuals. At the same time, the shocks in the reduced form are likely to be correlated so they cannot be considered as true structural shocks. As a result, structural shocks cannot by correctly identified. It is then necessary to transform the true model into following reduced form:

$$X_t = u_t + C_1 u_{t-1} + C_2 u_{t-2} + \ldots = \sum_{i=0}^{\infty} C_i u_{t-i} = \sum_{i=0}^{\infty} C_i L^i u_t \tag{4}$$

or

$$\begin{bmatrix} ir_{n,t} \\ p_t \end{bmatrix} = \begin{bmatrix} c_{11} & c_{12} \\ c_{21} & c_{22} \end{bmatrix} \begin{bmatrix} u_{i^e,t} \\ u_{ir_r^e,t} \end{bmatrix} \tag{5}$$

where $C(L)$ is a $n \times n$ polynomial of matrices with coefficients representing the relationship among variables on the lagged values and $u_t$ is a $n \times 1$ vector of normally distributed errors (shocks in reduced form) that are serially uncorrelated but not necessarily orthogonal:

$$E(u_t)=0, \quad \Sigma_u = E(u_t u_t') = A_0 E(u_t u_t') A_0' = A_0 A_0', \quad E(u_t u_s') = [0] \quad \forall t \neq s \tag{6}$$

The relationship between reduced-form VAR residuals $(u_t)$ and structural shocks $(\varepsilon_t)$ can be summarized from equations (1) and (4) as follows: $u_t = A_0 \varepsilon_t$. Matrices $C_i$ we obtain from estimated equation (1). Considering $A_i = C_i A_0$, we can now identify matrix $A_0$. To estimate the coefficient of the matrix $A_0$, it is necessary to impose four restrictions. Two restrictions are simple normalizations, which define the variance of the shocks $\varepsilon_{p^e,t}$ and $\varepsilon_{ir_r,t}$ (it follows the assumption that each of the disturbances has a unit variance, $\text{var}(\varepsilon) = 1$). The third restriction comes from an assumption that identified shocks are orthogonal. Normalization together with an assumption of the orthogonality implies $A_0' A_0 = \Sigma$, where $\Sigma$ is the variance-covariance matrix of $\varepsilon_{p^e,t}$ and $\varepsilon_{ir_r,t}$. SVAR methodology decomposes the series into its permanent and temporary components. The final restriction, which allows the matrix C to be uniquely defined, represents the long-run identifying restriction providing that a cumulative effect of expected real interest rate shock to the nominal interest rates variability is zero. Long-run identifying restrictions enable us to isolate temporary and permanent sources of nominal interest rates volatility and thus to distinguish effects of both structural shocks on endogenous variables of the model.

The equation (2) we can now rewrite to the following form:

$$\begin{bmatrix} ir_{n,t} \\ p_t \end{bmatrix} = \begin{bmatrix} 1 & 0 \\ . & 1 \end{bmatrix} \begin{bmatrix} \varepsilon_{i^e,t} \\ \varepsilon_{ir_r^e,t} \end{bmatrix} \tag{7}$$

The correctly identified model can be finally estimated employing SVAR methodology as the system is now just-identified. Variance decomposition and impulse-response functions are computed to observe a relative contribution of inflation expectations and expected real interest rates shocks to the nominal interest rates conditional variance as well as the overall responsiveness of nominal long-term interest rates to one standard deviation inflation expectations and expected real interest rates shocks.

### 6.4. Data and Results

We've estimated bivariate SVAR model for each Euro Area member country to estimate variance decomposition and impulse-response functions for long-term nominal interest rates. In order to estimate the sources of conditional variability of long-term interest rates as well as their responsiveness to the identified structural shocks we have employed monthly data for the period of 2000M1-2007M12 (model A) consisting of 96 observations and for the period of 2000M1-2016M5 (model B) consisting of 197 observations were employed for the interest rates on government bonds with 10-year maturity and inflation based on consumer prices. Estimation of two models for each individual country should be helpful in examining crisis related effects on calculated results. Time series for inflation were seasonally adjusted. Time series for all endogenous variables were collected from IMF database (International Financial Statistics, August 2016).

#### 6.4.1. Testing Procedures

Estimation of both models and correct identification of structural shocks affecting both endogenous variables it is necessary to preserve stationarity of the VAR model. To test the stationarity of both models, it is necessary to check the time series for unit roots and cointegration. To test the stability of the VAR model we have also applied a number of diagnostic tests of the VAR residuals (normality, serial correlation, heteroskedasticity).

Augmented Dickey-Fuller (ADF) and Phillips-Perron (PP) tests were computed to test endogenous variables for the unit roots presence. Both ADF and PP tests indicate that all variables are non-stationary on values. As a result, the null hypothesis of a unit root presence cannot be rejected for any of time series. Testing variables on first differences indicate that time series are stationary. We may conclude that variables are integrated of order 1 I(1).

Because all endogenous variables have a unit root, it is necessary to test time series for cointegration using the Johansen and Juselius cointegration test. The test for the cointegration was calculated using three lags as recommended by the AIC (Akaike Information Criterion) and SIC (Schwarz Information Criterion).

The results of Johansen cointegration tests confirmed our results of unit root tests. Both the trace statistics and maximum eigenvalue statistics (both at 0.05 level) indicate that there is no cointegration among endogenous variables of the model.

To test the stability of VAR models, we also employed a number of diagnostic tests. We found no evidence of serial correlation, heteroskedasticity and autoregressive conditional heteroskedasticity effect in disturbances. The model also passes the Jarque-Bera normality test, so that errors seem to be normally distributed. VAR models seem to be stable also because inverted roots of the model for each country lie inside the unit circle. Detailed results of time series testing procedures are not reported here to save space. Like any other results, they are available upon request from the author.

### 6.4.2. Variance Decomposition

Instability of the correlation between long-term interest rates and inflation as well as changing patterns in the price level dynamics during the pre-crisis and crisis periods reveals questions associated with a stability of long-term inflations expectations (Chernov and Mueller, 2012). Moreover, the relative importance of inflation expectations in determining long-term interest rates requires rigorous investigation. Increasing importance of this objective is even highlighted considering that near zero inflation environment makes the relative importance of inflation expectations quite ambiguous. Moreover, expected real interest rates do not seem to be the only (though still significant) driver of the nominal interest rates movements during the deflationary periods (Arouba, 2014). However, increased uncertainty on the financial markets, excessive liquidity fueled by the conduction of the unconventional monetary policy and time deformation of the yield curves provide mixed suggestions on the relative importance of expected real interest rates in determining long-term nominal interest rates (Rudebusch and Swanson, 2012).

Table 6.1 summarizes relative contributions of the inflation expectations and expected real interest rates shocks to the conditional variance of long-term nominal interest rates on 10-year government bonds in the Euro Area member countries during pre-crisis (model A) and extended (model B) periods. Variance decomposition enables us to examine the relative importance of both structural shocks in explaining long-term nominal interest rates fluctuations over different time horizons. Because we have employed bivariate VAR model and employed a scheme to identify just two (mutually uncorrelated) structural shocks the sum of both shocks in each particular horizon in both models for all countries is equal to 100 per cent. Moreover, following our identification scheme considering that shock of expected real interest rates is neutral in determining nominal interest rates, in the long run, the contribution of this shock to the variance of nominal interest rates gradually approaches zero percent.

Our results indicate that expected real interest rate clearly dominates in explaining immediate and short-term fluctuations of the long-term nominal interest rate in models for both pre-crisis and extended period in all countries. However, over increasing time horizon its contribution, the variability in nominal interest rate clearly decreases and is equal to zero in the long run as we have assumed. It also implies that the role of inflation expectations in explaining short-term movements of nominal interest rate is quite low though their importance continuously raises with increasing time horizon and dominates in the long run.

**Table 6.1 Variance Decomposition of Long-term Nominal Interest Rates (in percentage)**

| **Austria** | | | | |
|---|---|---|---|---|
| Horizon (Months) | Expected Real Interest Rates | | Expected Inflation | |
| | A | B | A | B |
| 1 | 73.24 | 71.75 | 26.76 | 28.25 |
| 6 | 68.87 | 65.22 | 31.13 | 34.78 |
| 12 | 60.36 | 57.23 | 39.64 | 42.77 |
| 24 | 41.70 | 36.29 | 58.30 | 63.71 |
| 48 | 24.09 | 22.62 | 75.91 | 77.38 |
| long-term | 0.00 | 0.00 | 100.00 | 100.00 |

| **Belgium** | | | | |
|---|---|---|---|---|
| Horizon (Months) | Expected Real Interest Rates | | Expected Inflation | |
| | A | B | A | B |
| 1 | 72.56 | 70.12 | 27.44 | 29.88 |
| 6 | 69.23 | 66.19 | 30.77 | 33.81 |
| 12 | 61.49 | 59.35 | 38.51 | 40.65 |
| 24 | 42.70 | 40.22 | 57.30 | 59.78 |
| 48 | 22.10 | 21.76 | 77.90 | 78.24 |
| long-term | 0.00 | 0.00 | 100.00 | 100.00 |

| Cyprus | | | | |
|---|---|---|---|---|
| Horizon (Months) | Expected Real Interest Rates | | Expected Inflation | |
| | A | B | A | B |
| 1 | 74.56 | 70.18 | 25.44 | 29.82 |
| 6 | 70.17 | 64.12 | 29.83 | 35.88 |
| 12 | 53.76 | 51.09 | 46.24 | 48.91 |
| 24 | 35.56 | 34.75 | 64.44 | 65.25 |
| 48 | 18.90 | 21.59 | 81.10 | 78.41 |
| long-term | 0.00 | 0.00 | 100.00 | 100.00 |

| Germany | | | | |
|---|---|---|---|---|
| Horizon (Months) | Expected Real Interest Rates | | Expected Inflation | |
| | A | B | A | B |
| 1 | 76.29 | 73.53 | 23.71 | 26.47 |
| 6 | 73.15 | 69.36 | 26.85 | 30.64 |
| 12 | 65.88 | 62.28 | 34.12 | 37.72 |
| 24 | 45.05 | 42.45 | 54.95 | 57.55 |
| 48 | 24.17 | 22.16 | 75.83 | 77.84 |
| long-term | 0.00 | 0.00 | 100.00 | 100.00 |

| Estonia | | | | |
|---|---|---|---|---|
| Horizon (Months) | Expected Real Interest Rates | | Expected Inflation | |
| | A | B | A | B |
| 1 | 78.71 | 60.03 | 21.29 | 39.97 |
| 6 | 69.38 | 53.56 | 30.62 | 46.44 |
| 12 | 59.45 | 48.21 | 40.55 | 51.79 |
| 24 | 40.49 | 35.69 | 59.51 | 64.31 |
| 48 | 21.86 | 20.54 | 78.14 | 79.46 |
| long-term | 0.00 | 0.00 | 100.00 | 100.00 |

| Spain | | | | |
|---|---|---|---|---|
| Horizon (Months) | Expected Real Interest Rates | | Expected Inflation | |
| | A | B | A | B |
| 1 | 70.51 | 74.29 | 29.49 | 25.71 |
| 6 | 65.84 | 70.41 | 34.16 | 29.59 |
| 12 | 52.25 | 57.14 | 47.75 | 42.86 |
| 24 | 33.68 | 36.27 | 66.32 | 63.73 |
| 48 | 16.22 | 17.42 | 83.78 | 82.58 |
| long-term | 0.00 | 0.00 | 100.00 | 100.00 |

| **Finland** | | | | |
|---|---|---|---|---|
| Horizon (Months) | Expected Real Interest Rates | | Expected Inflation | |
| | A | B | A | B |
| 1 | 71.33 | 68.49 | 28.67 | 31.51 |
| 6 | 67.09 | 63.24 | 32.91 | 36.76 |
| 12 | 50.14 | 58.98 | 49.86 | 41.02 |
| 24 | 41.77 | 35.63 | 58.23 | 64.37 |
| 48 | 23.32 | 19.44 | 76.68 | 80.56 |
| long-term | 0.00 | 0.00 | 100.00 | 100.00 |

| **France** | | | | |
|---|---|---|---|---|
| Horizon (Months) | Expected Real Interest Rates | | Expected Inflation | |
| | A | B | A | B |
| 1 | 74.21 | 71.33 | 25.79 | 28.67 |
| 6 | 71.18 | 68.08 | 28.82 | 31.92 |
| 12 | 64.23 | 60.56 | 35.77 | 39.44 |
| 24 | 42.32 | 41.29 | 57.68 | 58.71 |
| 48 | 22.89 | 21.24 | 77.11 | 78.76 |
| long-term | 0.00 | 0.00 | 100.00 | 100.00 |

| **Greece** | | | | |
|---|---|---|---|---|
| Horizon (Months) | Expected Real Interest Rates | | Expected Inflation | |
| | A | B | A | B |
| 1 | 79.08 | 81.16 | 20.92 | 18.84 |
| 6 | 73.22 | 75.72 | 26.78 | 24.28 |
| 12 | 66.90 | 68.57 | 33.10 | 31.43 |
| 24 | 45.47 | 46.23 | 54.53 | 53.77 |
| 48 | 25.04 | 27.31 | 74.96 | 72.69 |
| long-term | 0.00 | 0.00 | 100.00 | 100.00 |

| **Ireland** | | | | |
|---|---|---|---|---|
| Horizon (Months) | Expected Real Interest Rates | | Expected Inflation | |
| | A | B | A | B |
| 1 | 73.29 | 76.26 | 26.71 | 23.74 |
| 6 | 69.23 | 71.49 | 30.77 | 28.51 |
| 12 | 61.43 | 64.11 | 38.57 | 35.89 |
| 24 | 42.56 | 45.81 | 57.44 | 54.19 |
| 48 | 22.79 | 23.09 | 77.21 | 76.91 |
| long-term | 0.00 | 0.00 | 100.00 | 100.00 |

| Italy | | | | |
|---|---|---|---|---|
| Horizon (Months) | Expected Real Interest Rates | | Expected Inflation | |
| | A | B | A | B |
| 1 | 73.54 | 75.02 | 26.46 | 24.98 |
| 6 | 68.42 | 71.79 | 31.58 | 28.21 |
| 12 | 54.29 | 60.92 | 45.71 | 39.08 |
| 24 | 36.16 | 41.11 | 63.84 | 58.89 |
| 48 | 20.44 | 22.63 | 79.56 | 77.37 |
| long-term | 0.00 | 0.00 | 100.00 | 100.00 |

| Luxembourg | | | | |
|---|---|---|---|---|
| Horizon (Months) | Expected Real Interest Rates | | Expected Inflation | |
| | A | B | A | B |
| 1 | 71.17 | 68.56 | 28.83 | 31.44 |
| 6 | 67.64 | 62.15 | 32.36 | 37.85 |
| 12 | 58.22 | 56.38 | 41.78 | 43.62 |
| 24 | 41.83 | 38.27 | 58.17 | 61.73 |
| 48 | 22.07 | 20.19 | 78.93 | 79.81 |
| long-term | 0.00 | 0.00 | 100.00 | 100.00 |

| Lithuania | | | | |
|---|---|---|---|---|
| Horizon (Months) | Expected Real Interest Rates | | Expected Inflation | |
| | A | B | A | B |
| 1 | 77.21 | 64.18 | 22.79 | 35.82 |
| 6 | 70.44 | 60.37 | 29.56 | 39.63 |
| 12 | 56.22 | 45.29 | 43.78 | 54.71 |
| 24 | 32.74 | 31.36 | 67.26 | 68.64 |
| 48 | 18.16 | 16.22 | 81.84 | 83.78 |
| long-term | 0.00 | 0.00 | 100.00 | 100.00 |

| Latvia | | | | |
|---|---|---|---|---|
| Horizon (Months) | Expected Real Interest Rates | | Expected Inflation | |
| | A | B | A | B |
| 1 | 74.29 | 67.29 | 25.71 | 32.71 |
| 6 | 68.98 | 59.21 | 31.02 | 40.79 |
| 12 | 51.14 | 48.61 | 48.86 | 51.39 |
| 24 | 31.05 | 29.40 | 68.95 | 58.60 |
| 48 | 22.45 | 23.26 | 77.55 | 76.74 |
| long-term | 0.00 | 0.00 | 100.00 | 100.00 |

| Malta | | | | |
|---|---|---|---|---|
| Horizon (Months) | Expected Real Interest Rates | | Expected Inflation | |
| | A | B | A | B |
| 1 | 75.29 | 70.88 | 24.71 | 29.12 |
| 6 | 69.07 | 66.49 | 30.93 | 33.51 |
| 12 | 51.80 | 54.21 | 48.20 | 45.79 |
| 24 | 32.31 | 37.04 | 67.69 | 62.96 |
| 48 | 16.66 | 20.45 | 83.34 | 79.55 |
| long-term | 0.00 | 0.00 | 100.00 | 100.00 |

| Netherlands | | | | |
|---|---|---|---|---|
| Horizon (Months) | Expected Real Interest Rates | | Expected Inflation | |
| | A | B | A | B |
| 1 | 74.29 | 70.22 | 25.71 | 29.78 |
| 6 | 71.15 | 66.29 | 28.85 | 33.71 |
| 12 | 64.27 | 61.71 | 35.73 | 38.29 |
| 24 | 40.15 | 38.14 | 59.85 | 61.86 |
| 48 | 18.78 | 18.06 | 81.22 | 81.94 |
| long-term | 0.00 | 0.00 | 100.00 | 100.00 |

| Portugal | | | | |
|---|---|---|---|---|
| Horizon (Months) | Expected Real Interest Rates | | Expected Inflation | |
| | A | B | A | B |
| 1 | 69.56 | 72.15 | 30.44 | 27.85 |
| 6 | 65.12 | 69.54 | 34.88 | 30.46 |
| 12 | 54.26 | 60.03 | 45.74 | 39.97 |
| 24 | 37.09 | 42.77 | 62.91 | 57.23 |
| 48 | 22.15 | 23.51 | 77.85 | 76.49 |
| long-term | 0.00 | 0.00 | 100.00 | 100.00 |

| Slovakia | | | | |
|---|---|---|---|---|
| Horizon (Months) | Expected Real Interest Rates | | Expected Inflation | |
| | A | B | A | B |
| 1 | 73.15 | 71.23 | 26.85 | 28.77 |
| 6 | 69.53 | 65.67 | 30.47 | 34.33 |
| 12 | 62.67 | 56.22 | 37.33 | 43.78 |
| 24 | 43.18 | 38.12 | 56.82 | 61.88 |
| 48 | 17.97 | 16.95 | 82.03 | 83.05 |
| long-term | 0.00 | 0.00 | 100.00 | 100.00 |

| Slovenia | | | | |
|---|---|---|---|---|
| Horizon (Months) | Expected Real Interest Rates | | Expected Inflation | |
| | A | B | A | B |
| 1 | 71.49 | 68.11 | 28.51 | 31.89 |
| 6 | 65.24 | 61.27 | 34.76 | 38.73 |
| 12 | 58.56 | 50.14 | 41.44 | 49.86 |
| 24 | 39.16 | 35.05 | 60.84 | 64.95 |
| 48 | 15.17 | 14.77 | 84.83 | 85.23 |
| long-term | 0.00 | 0.00 | 100.00 | 100.00 |

***Note:*** Relative contributions of structural shocks to the conditional variance of long-term nominal interest rates on 10-year government bonds in models A (2000M1-2007M12) and B (2000M1-2015M4).

***Source:*** Author's calculations.

While the response patterns of the long-term nominal interest rates followed a quite similar scenario in all Euro Area member countries, we have observed some differences in the relative contributions of both shocks to the nominal interest rates determination in individual countries. Results seem to be also sensitive to the underlying period as the contribution of both shocks to the nominal interest rates determination has slightly changed when comparing models for the pre-crisis and extended period. However, differences between both models are less considerable because the model for the extended period includes time series for the pre-crisis period.

The relative importance of expected real interest rates during the first year since the shock in explaining unexpected movements in nominal interest rates clearly dominated during the pre-crisis period in all countries. However, the role of inflation expectations continuously increased and generally dominated since the sixteenth month since the shock. It seems that inflation expectations are more persistent and sudden changes in inflation expectations require more time to induce changes in the long-term interest rates. While the relative contribution of both shocks to the unexplained fluctuations in the nominal interest rates followed a rather similar pattern in all countries from the group, crisis period brought some changes to the determination of nominal interest rates. Results for the extended period indicate a slight reduction in the relative importance of the expected real interest rates in all countries but periphery economies (Greece, Italy, Portugal, and Spain). We suggest that the crisis-induced reduction in the role of inflation expectations, and the increased role of expected real interest rates in the periphery countries reflects well-known problems with liquidity (and the associated increase in the risk premium) on the markets with their government bonds in the early stage of the crisis period. The second important implication of the effects associated with the crisis period is represented by the more significant increase in the relative importance of inflation expectations in determining long-term nominal interest rate in Baltic countries in comparison with the core countries of the Euro Area. Estonia, Latvia, and Lithuania experienced the most significant drop in the dynamics of the price level during the early stage of the crisis period that is why the more significant increase in the more significant increase in the role of inflation expectations seems to be reasonable.

**Figure 6.1 Responses of Long-term Interest Rates to Shocks of Inflation Expectations and Expected Real Interest Rates**

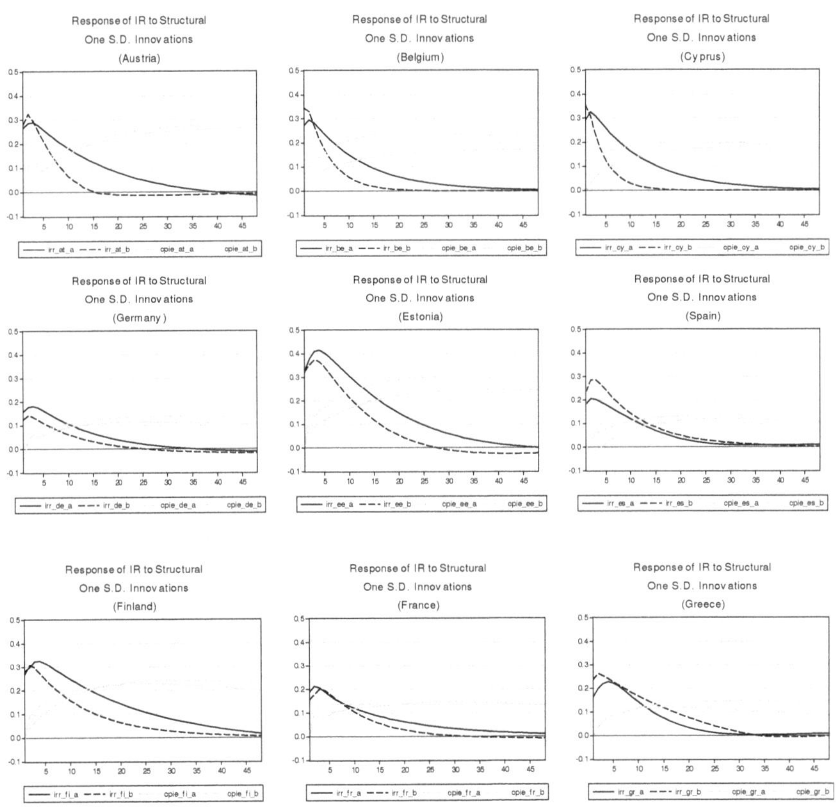

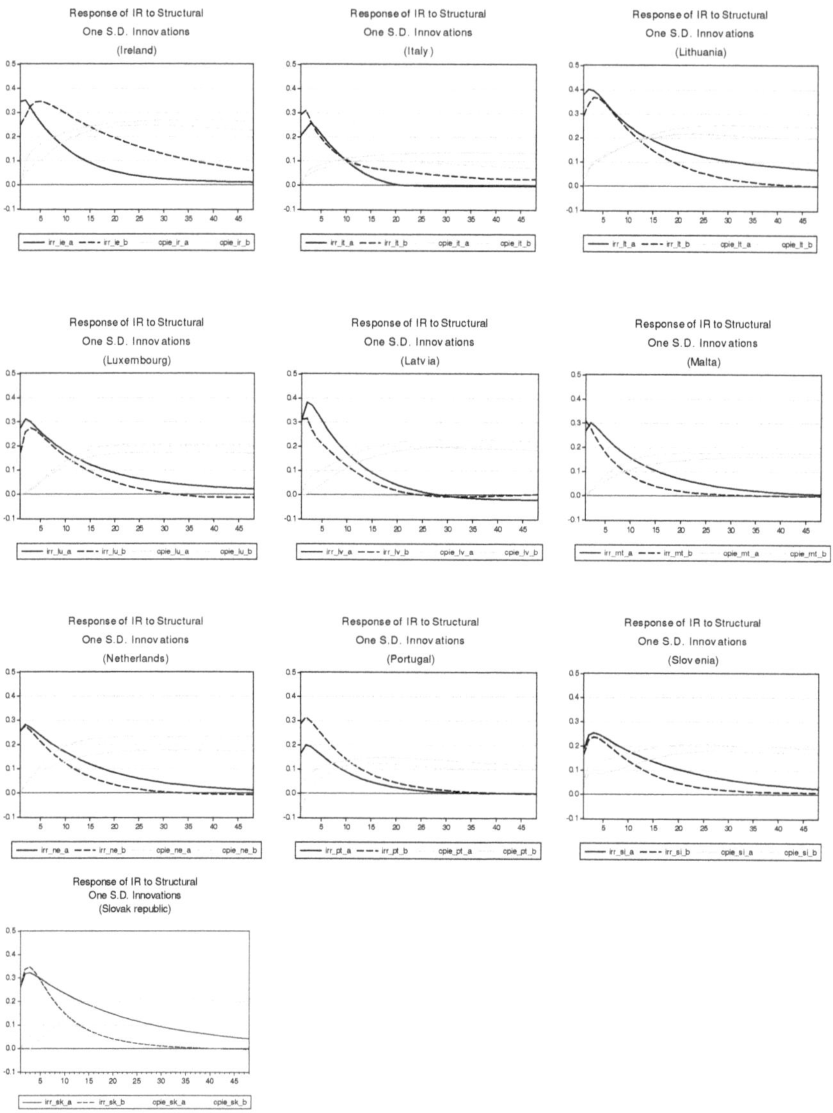


***Note:*** Curves represent responses of long-term nominal interest rates (IR) to the positive one standard deviation inflation expectations shock (CPIE) and expected real interest rates shock (IRR) in models A (2000M1-2007M12) and B (2000M1-2015M4).

***Source:*** Author's calculations.

Impulse-response functions of long-term nominal interest rates revealed mostly similar response patterns of interest rates on 10-year government bonds to the underlying shocks across all countries though we have observed some differences between periphery economies (PIGS) and Euro Area core countries. Moreover, differences in the response patterns of nominal interest rates between both groups of countries are reasonable in both models covering both pre-crisis and extended periods.

Expected real interest rates dominated in determining long-term interest rates during the almost whole first year since the shock in all Euro Area member countries. Nominal interest rates immediately increased after the positive expected real interest rate shock. However, the responsiveness of nominal interest rates to the shock of expected real interest rates was slightly higher in the periphery countries. Effect of the shock culminated within the first three months and then steadily died out during the subsequent two years of the shock in the whole group of countries. Nominal interest rates in Baltic countries (Estonia, Latvia, Lithuania) seem to be more responsive to the expected real interest rate shock in comparison with the rest of the group.

Comparison of the results for pre-crisis and extended periods revealed interesting differences between the periphery and the core Euro Area member countries. Despite some minor differences, the responsiveness of long-term interest rates to the shock of expected real interest rates in periphery countries during the extended period slightly increased ( the effect is clear especially during first months since the shock), while remaining countries experienced opposite trend. We suggest that investors required higher risk premium (associated with higher expected real interest rates) to hold risky government bonds of PIGS countries considering that these countries were exposed the most to the threat of default during the crises period.

Effects of the expected real interest rates shock on the long-term nominal interest rates gradually decreased with increasing time horizon and completely died out in the horizon of 2 to 4 years of the shock in the respective country. As a result, the effect of this shock is neutral in the long run that corresponds to our assumptions in the model specification and structural shocks definition. However, Expected real interest rates remain a significant driver of the long-term nominal interest rates movements in the short run.

Immediate responsiveness of long-term interest rates to the positive inflation expectations shock was generally negligible (in comparison with expected real interest rates shock) though the intensity of the shock continuously increased over time. As a result, effects of inflation expectations on long-term nominal interest rates are much stable with increasing time horizon in all Euro Area member countries. While short-term (within first twelve months since the shock) response of interest rates to the shock of inflation expectations was generally lower than in the case of expected real interest rates, it remained positive and stable with increasing time horizon and even permanent in the long run. The positive effect of the shock culminated till the end of the second year since the shock. The shock of inflation expectations clearly dominated in the medium term in determining long-term nominal interest rates and our results confirm its permanent effect on interest rates in the long run (though with reduced intensity in some countries, e.g. Greece and Italy).

Crises period affected the responsiveness of interest rate on 10-year government bonds to the shock of inflations expectations in both groups of countries. While the vulnerability of long-term nominal interest rates to the shock of inflation expectations in periphery countries decreased, the rest of the Euro Area experienced opposite scenario. Economies of GIIPS countries suffered the most during the crisis period. We suggest that the reasonable risk of deflation and deflationary spiral reduced the role of inflation expectations in the nominal interest rates determination.

Examined differences in the responsiveness of the long-term interest rates to the inflation expectations shock between periphery and core countries of the Euro Area reveals many opened questions associated with suitability of monetary policy conducted by ECB in the single currency area consisting of significantly heterogeneous countries. Implications of quantitative easing accompanied by near-zero levels of the key interest rates aiming to boost the inflation may be biased due to existing differences in the inflation expectations between North and South of the Euro Area.

### 6.4.4. Decomposition of Long-term Nominal Interest Rates

In this section, we provide a decomposition of long-term nominal interest rates into inflation expectations and expected real interest rates components. Stationary and permanent components of the long-term interest rates are calculated by the accumulation of the effect of both structural shocks. Estimation of expected real interest rates is calculated by adding the stationary components to the mean of the difference between observed long-term interest rates and contemporaneous rate of inflation[23] (St-Amant, 1996). Estimation of inflation expectations is calculated by subtracting already

23 Mean of difference between observed long-term interest rates and contemporaneous rate of inflation: AT (1.636%), BE (1.815%), CY (3.431%), DE (1.815%), EE (3.023%), ES (1.884%), FI (1.783%), FR (2.062%), GR (5.010%), IE (2.465%), IT (2.390%), LT (2.931%), LU (1.141%), LV (1.501%), MT (2.279%), NE (1.516%), PT (3.126%), SI (1.132%), SK (0.473%).

calculated expected real interest rates from the nominal long-term interest rates.

**Figure 6.2 Decomposition of Long-term Interest Rates on Government Bonds[24]**

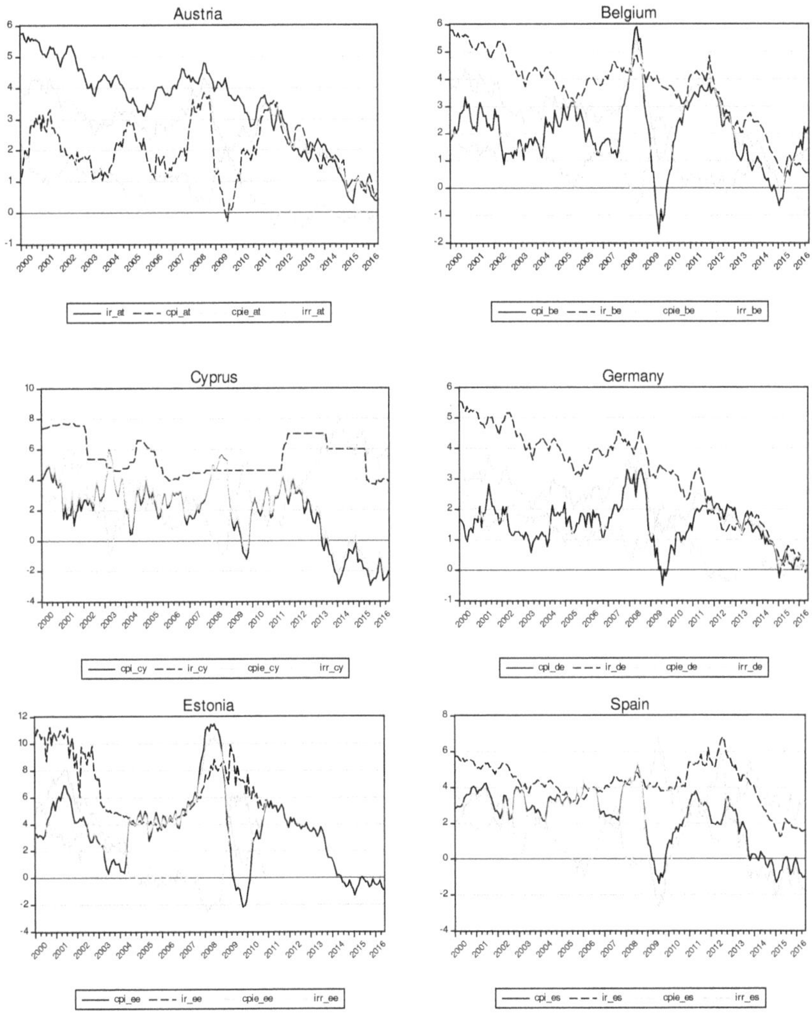


24 Since 2011 there are no Estonian sovereign debt securities that comply with the definition of long-run interest rates for convergence purposes according to ECB. No suitable proxy indicator has been identified.

Finland
cpi_fi
ir_fi
cpie_fi
irr_fi

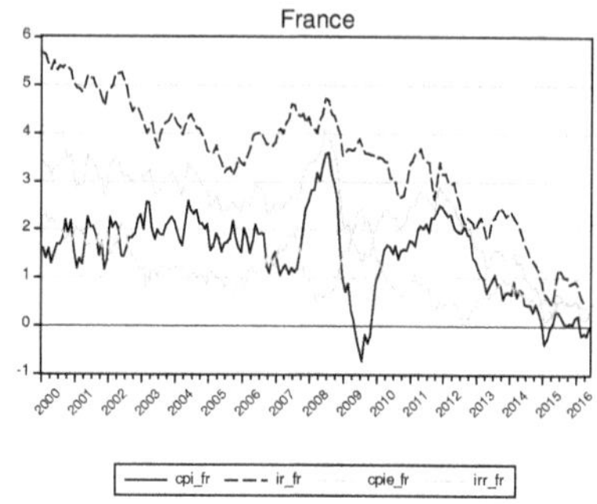
France
cpi_fr
ir_fr
cpie_fr
irr_fr

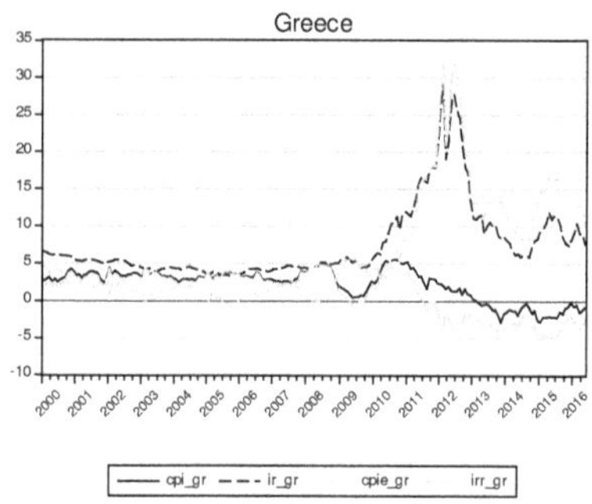
Greece
cpi_gr
ir_gr
cpie_gr
irr_gr

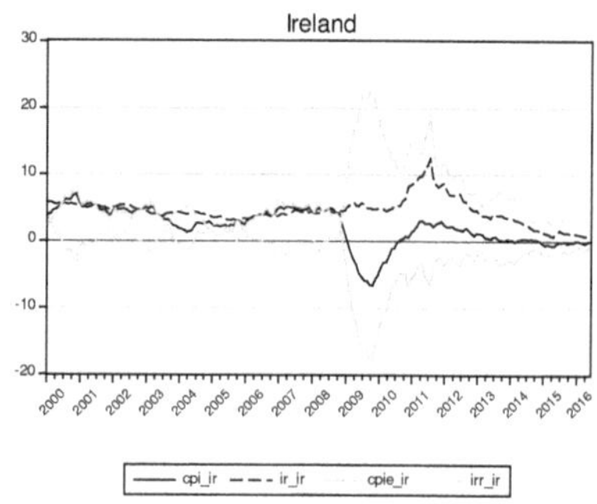
Ireland
cpi_ir
ir_ir
cpie_ir
irr_ir

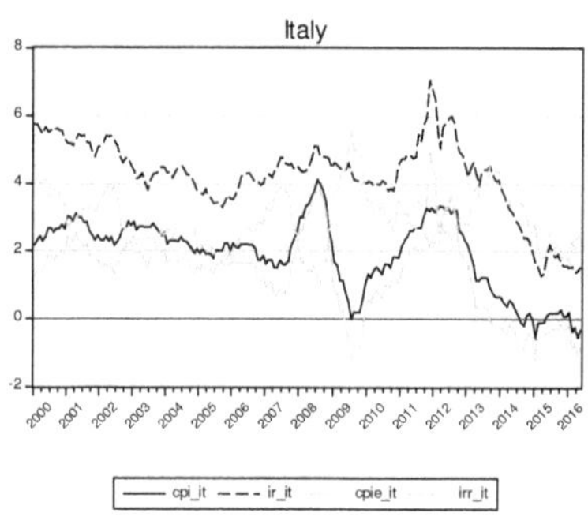
Italy
cpi_it
ir_it
cpie_it
irr_it

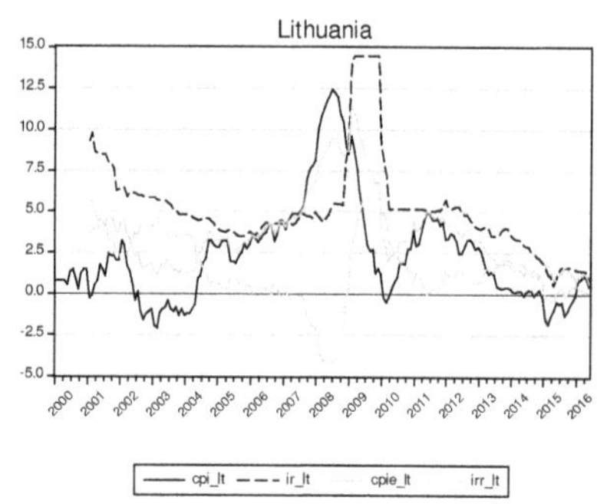
Lithuania
cpi_lt
ir_lt
cpie_lt
irr_lt

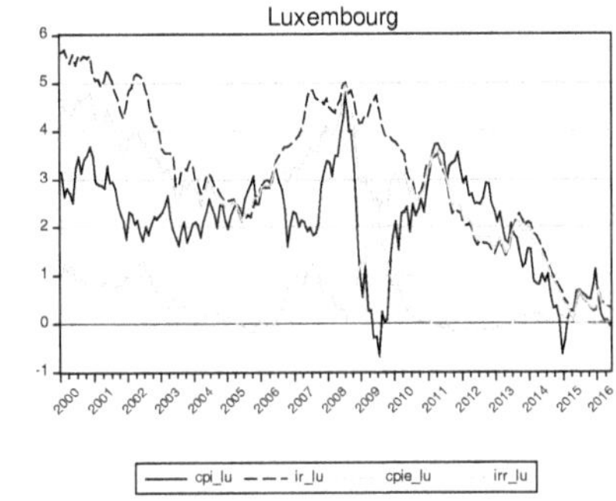
Luxembourg
cpi_lu
ir_lu
cpie_lu
irr_lu

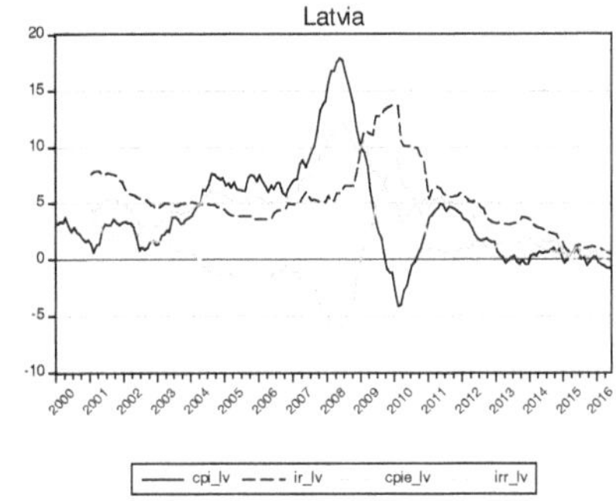
Latvia
cpi_lv
ir_lv
cpie_lv
irr_lv

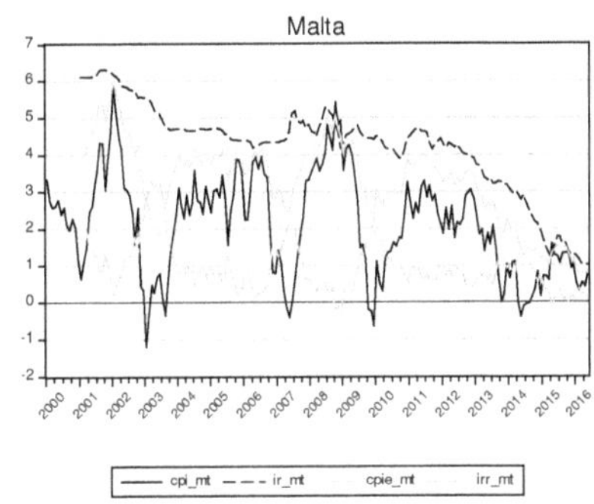
Malta
cpi_mt
ir_mt
cpie_mt
irr_mt

Netherlands
cpi_ne
ir_ne
cpie_ne
irr_ne

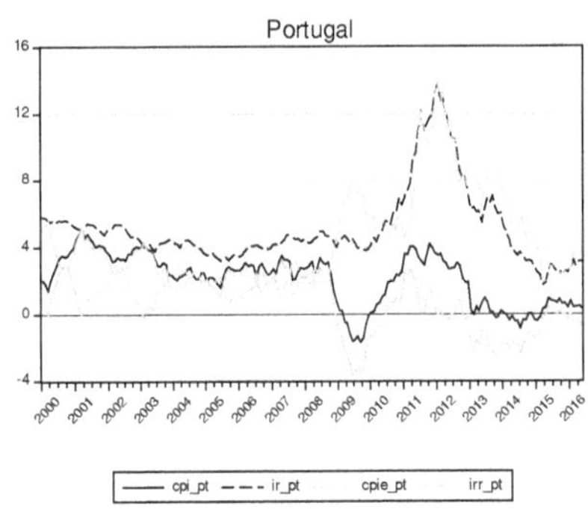
Portugal
cpi_pt
ir_pt
cpie_pt
irr_pt

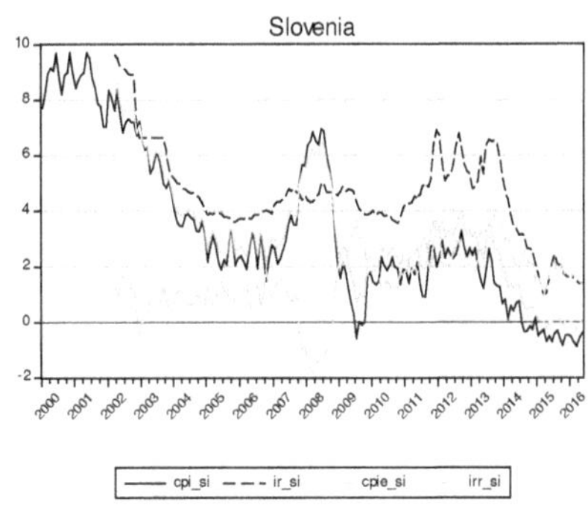
Slovenia
cpi_si
ir_si
cpie_si
irr_si

***Note:*** Curves represent the development of nominal interest rate on 10-year government bonds (IRR), inflation measured by CPI (CPI) and estimated components of long-term nominal interest rates represented by inflation expectations (CPIE) and expected real interest rates (IRR) during the period 2000-2016.

***Source:*** Author's calculations.

Decomposition of long-term interest rates on 10-year government bonds in both the periphery and core member countries of the Euro Area revealed interesting differences in the (a) relative contributions of inflation expectations and expected real interest rates into nominal interest rates leading path since the establishment of the Euro Area as well as (b) relationship between inflation rates and inflation expectations in the above mentioned countries (Figure 6.2). The downward trend in long-term interest rates in the Euro Area member countries and related convergence in their development between North and South of EU during the most of the pre-crisis period was associated with a drop in inflation expectations while expected real interest rates remained relatively stable at 0-2 per cent corridor on average. However, expected real interest rates were generally higher in Ireland, Italy, Portugal and Spain or more volatile in Cyprus, Baltic countries, and Slovakia. At the same time, inflation expectations experienced increasing trend during the last 2-3 years of a pre-crisis period when long-term interest rates tend to increase in most of the Euro Area member countries.

First crucial implication resulted from our estimations is represented by clear differences between inflation and inflation expectations derived from long-term interest rates between periphery economies and the core of the Euro Area. Inflation expectations in GIIPS countries tend to undershoot a trajectory of inflation path during the whole pre-crisis period. Moreover, this trend was even intensified during the crisis period. We suggest that increased uncertainty on the markets together with crisis-related problems (recession, the risk of default, fiscal unsustainability, etc.) clearly reduced inflation expectations below recent rates of inflation. As a result, the risk of deflation during the periods of decreasing inflation expectations that even undershoot low inflation target generally increased. Moreover, low inflation expectations that undershot inflation in periphery countries of the Euro Area induced higher expected real interest rates in comparison with their true levels. Similarly to our results from the impulse-response analysis, we suggest that undershooting patterns in inflation expectations result from increased fear of deflation and slumping real economy in light of tightening financial conditions that shifted expected real interest rates upward.

Decomposition of interest rates on government bonds in the core of the Euro Area revealed different picture about the relative importance of inflation expectations and expected real interest rates in long-term interest rates determination. Inflation expectations tend to overshoot the long-term path of inflation in both countries during the whole period. This pattern is more significant during the pre-crisis period. Higher inflation expectations than recent inflation that did not induce excessive inflation pressures are a good signal for the central bank in good times though during periods of persisting deflationary pressures combined with the recession it may decrease the chance to boost inflation up and possibly worsen the deflationary spiral. However, the mismatch between inflation expectations and recent inflation decreased during the crisis period. On the other hand, lower expected real interest rates, as a component of nominal long-term interest rates, may improve the liquidity of government bonds in the core of the Euro Area and soften the conditions on their sovereign debt markets.

## 6.5. Conclusion

Examination of the relative importance of inflation expectations and expected real interest rates in determining long-term nominal interest rates on 10-year government bonds in the periphery and core countries of the Euro Area revealed interesting implications of existing economic differences between both groups of countries. Increased contributions of expected real interest rates to the development of long-term nominal interest rates, undershooting patterns in inflation expectations according to the inflation rates together with strong positive correlation between inflation and inflation expectations in periphery countries of the Euro Area represent clear signal of markets to policy makers and possible scenarios of boosting inflation (ECB) and economic growth (national governments) in the Euro Area.

Higher expected real interest rates than actual real interest rates together with increased exposure of holding risky government bonds of periphery countries of the Euro area may force governments to undertake internal devaluation (with all risks associated with deflationary spiral) or to increase nominal interest rates on government bonds (with negative implications on costs of sovereign debt). We suggest that more dynamic convergence of periphery Euro Area member countries to the core countries together with the strengthening of fiscal sustainability would help to reduce perceived the risk of periphery countries followed by a reduction in expected real interest rates from government bonds.

### 6.7. References


ACHARYA, V.V., STEFFEN, S. (2015). *The "Greatest" Carry Trade Ever? Understanding Eurozone Bank Risks,* Journal of Financial Economics, 115(2): 215-236

AROUBA, S.B. (2014). *Term Structures of Inflation Expectations and Real Interest Rates: The Effects of Unconventional Monetary Policy, [Federal Reserve Bank of Minneapolis, Staff Report No.502/2014],* Minneapolis, Federal Reserve Bank of Minneapolis, 51 p.

BLANCHARD, O.J., QUAH, D. (1988). *The Dynamic Effects of Aggregate Demand and Aggregate Supply Disturbances, [National Bureau of Economic Research Working Paper No. 4637]* New York, National Bureau of Economic Research, 39 p.

BUSSIERE, M. (2013) EXCHANGE RATE PASS -THROUGH TO TRADE PRICES: THE ROLE OF NONLINEARITIES AND ASYMMETRIES, OXFORD BULLETIN OF ECONOMICS AND STATISTICS, 75(5): 731-758

Campa J.M., Goldberg L.S., González-Mínguez J.M. (2005). Exchange-Rate Pass-Through to Import Prices in the Euro Area, NBER Working Paper No. 11632 September 2005

CHERNOV, M., MUELLER, P. (2012). *The Term Structure of Inflation Expectations,* Journal of Financial Economics, 106(2): 367-394

CHRISTENSEN, J.H.E., GILLAN, J.M. (2015) Does Quantitative Easing Affect Market Liquidity?, Federal Reserve Bank of San Francisco Working Paper

EIJFFINGER, M HOEBERICHTS, E SCHALING (2000) WHY MONEY TALKS AND WEALTH WHISPERS: MONETARY UNCERTAINTY AND MYSTIQUE JOURNAL OF MONEY, CREDIT AND BANKING, PP. 218-235

CHRISTENSEN, J.H.E., LOPEZ, J.A., RUDEBUSCH, G.D. (2008). *Inflation Expectations and Risk Premiums in an Arbitrage-Free Model of Nominal and Real Bond Yields, [Federal Reserve Bank of San Francisco, Working Paper No.34/2008],* San Francisco, Federal Reserve Bank of San Francisco, 39 p.

COCHRANE, J.H., PIAZZESI, M. (2005). *Bond Risk Premia,* American Economic Review, 95(1): 138-160

CROWDER, W.J., HOFFMAN, D.L. (1996). *The Long-Run Relationship between Nominal Interest Rates and Inflation: The Fisher Equation Revisited,* Journal of Money, Credit and Banking, 28(1): 102-118

DE GRAUWE, P. (2013). *Design Failures in the Eurozone: Can they be fixed?, [LSE "Europe in Question" Discussion Paper, no. 57],* London, London School of Economics, 61 p.

DEACON, M., DERRY, A. (1994). *Estimating Market Interest Rate and Inflation Expectations from the Prices of UK Government Bonds,* Bank of England Quarterly Bulletin, 34: 232-240

DEN HAAN, W.J. (1995). *The Term Structure of Interest Rates in Real and Monetary Economics,* Journal of Economic Dynamics and Control, 19(5-7): 909-940

EMIRIS, M. (2006). *The Term Structure of Interest Rates in a DSGE Model, [National Bank of Belgium, Working Paper Research No. 88]* Brussels, National Bank of Belgium, 55 p.

ENGSTED, T. (1995). *Does the Long-Term Interest Rate Predict Future Inflation? A Multi-Country Analysis,* The Review of Economics and Statistics, 77(1): 42-54

EVANS, M.D.D. (1998). *Real Rates, Expected Inflation, And Inflation Risk Premia,* Journal Of Finance, 53(1): 187-218

FENDEL, R. (2009). *Note on Taylor Rules and the Term Structure,* Applied Economics Letters, 16(11): 1097-1101

GARCIA, R., PERRON, P. (1996). *An Analysis of the Real Interest Rate under Regime Shifts,* Review of Economics and Statistics, 78(1): 111-125

GERLACH-KRISTEN, P., RUDOLF, B. (2010). *Macroeconomic and Interest Rate Volatility under Alternative Monetary Operating Procedures, [Swiss National Bank, Working Paper No. 2010-12]* Zurich, Swiss National Bank, 40 p.

*Hetzel, R.L. (2015) Should Greece Remain in the Eurozone?, [FRB of Richmond, Working Paper no. 15-04R], Richmond, Federal Reserve Bank of Richmond, 30 p.*

KULISH, M. (2007). *Should Monetary Policy Use Long-term Rates?* B.E. Journal of Macroeconomics, 7(1): 1-26

LABADIE, P. (1994). *The Term Structure of Interest Rates over the Business Cycle.* Journal of Economic Dynamics and Control, 18(3-4): 671-697

LAI, K.S. (2004). *On Structural Shifts and Stationarity of the Ex Ante Real Interest Rate,* International Review of Economics and Finance, 13(2): 217-228

LANNE, M. (2001). *Near Unit Root and the Relationship between Inflation and Interest rates: A Reexamination of the Fisher Effect,* Empirical Economics, 26(2): 357-366

MCGOUGH, B., RUDEBUSCH, G., WILLIAMS, J.C. (2005). *Using a Long-term Interest Rates as the Monetary Policy Instrument,* Journal of Monetary Economics 52(5): 855-879

MICOSSI, S. (2015) THE MONETARY POLICY OF THE EUROPEAN CENTRAL BANK (2002 - 2015),

[CEPS SPECIAL REPORT, NO. 109], BRUSSELS, CENTRE FOR EUROPEAN POLICY STUDIES, 37 P.

MICHAUD, F.-L., UPPER, CH. (2008*). What Drives Interbank Rates? Evidence from the Libor Panel, [BIS Quarterly Review, March 2008],* Basel, Bank for International Settlements, p. 47-58

NEELY, CH.J., RAPACH, D.E. (2008). *Real Interest Rates Persistence: Evidence and Implications, [Federal Reserve Bank of St. Louis, Review No. 6/2008]* St. Louis, Federal Reserve Bank of St. Louis, 90(6): 609-641

PEERSMAN, G. (2011) *Macroeconomic Effects of Unconventional Monetary Policy in the Euro Area, [ECB Working Paper, no. 1397],* Frankfurt am Main, European Central Bank, 33 p.

RAGAN, C. (1995). *Deriving Agents' Inflation Forecasts from the Term Structure of Interest Rates. [Bank of Canada, Working Paper, No. 1/1995]* Ottawa, Bank of Canada, 41 p.

RUDEBUSCH, G.D., SACK, B.P., SWANSON, E.T. (2006). *Macroeconomic Implications of Changes in the Term Premium, [Federal Reserve Bank of San Francisco, Working Paper No.46/2006],* San Francisco, Federal Reserve Bank of San Francisco, 48 p.

RUDEBUSCH, G., SWANSON, E. (2012). *The Bond Premium in a DSGE Model with Long-run Real and Nominal Risks,* American Economic Journal: Macroeconomics, 4(1): 105-143

ST-AMANT, P. (1996). *Decomposing U.S. Nominal Interest Rates into Expected Inflation and Ex Ante Real Interest Rates Using Structural VAR Methodology, [Bank of Canada, Working Paper No. 2/1996]* Ottawa, Bank of Canada, 28 p.

Chapter 7

# Social Market Economy Leading the EU out of the Gridlock?

Václav Šmejkal, Stanislav Šaroch

## 7.1. Introduction - Why this Question?

The question in the title of the chapter has at least two reasons. From a legal perspective, it is clear that the Lisbon EU Treaty (TEU), where in Art. 3 (3) the aim of "highly competitive social market economy aiming at full employment and social progress" appeared for the first time in the history of European integration, opened the possibility for a more social EU. Even if the principle of *ius ad finem dat ius ad media* does not apply to such Treaty goals, there is no doubt that they represent direct guidelines of constitutional importance. Their impact was supposed to be further strengthened by the newly inserted "Horizontal Social clause" of Article 9 of the Treaty on Functioning of the EU (TFEU) and also by the Charter of Fundamental Rights of the European Union (comprising Title IV "Solidarity") that became legally binding together with the Lisbon Treaty. Moreover, the term "social" was repeated 167-times in the text of TEU and TFEU. Therefore, a certain potential for changes could have been expected, for changes that would entail a certain re-balancing between the economic and monetary integration on the one hand and the social rights and welfare on the other.

From a practical standpoint, however, there's the fact that, neither this enhancement of social integration objectives in the Lisbon Treaty nor the financial, economic and debt crisis after 2008, have brought about any significant social re-orientation of the integration project. Rather the opposite happened as the crisis solutions adopted at the EU level were inspired by the neoliberal doctrine of fiscal discipline, budgetary austerity, and labour market flexibility. The European left who has not failed to criticize them repeatedly, however, has not been able to offer another sufficiently effective and acceptable paradigm that would change the parameters of the measures taken to rescue and stabilize the Eurozone (EMU) (Bruun and Lorcher and Schömann, 2014). The European Commission President, J.-C. Juncker, a politician of Christian-social orientation, in his first speech to the European Parliament, recognized, that "there was a lack of social fairness" in the measures taken during the crisis (Barnard, 2015).

From the centre to the left side of the political spectrum in the EU, it is thus believed that the strengthening of the social dimension of integration is necessary to compensate for the effects of economic integration which especially after the capital movements' and services' liberalization as well as with the imposition of the single currency budgetary discipline, affected in a negative manner the nation-based social welfare systems. Some would even argue that the new EU's social dimension "is supposed to regulate freedom of movement and curb the dominance of the Single Market integration" while almost everyone who believes that the EU integration project as such should continue would agree that the enhanced social dimension is necessary for the political backing of the project by the general population (Schellinger, 2015:3).

The contradiction between the social accents of the Lisbon Treaty and the socially problematic impact of the internal market freedoms and the fiscal coordination applied within the EMU has, of course, its explanation, which is beyond the scope of this chapter. In brief, it can only be recalled that on the separation of the market integration, carried out at the EU level, from the social compensation measures, retained by the Member States within their competence, the founding compromise of European integration had been built in the 50s of the past century. This distribution of roles in the style of "Smith abroad, Keynes at home" lasted until the 90s, when the completion of the internal market for the first time threatened the political capacity of the Member States to impose their social policy norms (de Witte, 2015:46; Micossi and Tosato, 2009:46). At that time, the EU responded - within the powers conferred upon it – with an effort to harmonize certain standards (health and safety at work, maximum working hours, protection of employees in cases of collective redundancy or the sale of a company or employer's inability to pay etc.), which had to prevent the regulatory race to the bottom between EU countries.

With the outbreak of the current crisis, however, it became clear that the diversity of social welfare systems, stemming from the national regulatory autonomy, could destabilize the EMU. Social considerations have been then subjected to the need to solve the critical situation in the most indebted countries. Tools such as the Excessive Deficit Procedure (EDP), Macroeconomic Imbalance Procedure (MIP) and the Memoranda of Understanding (for "bail-out" countries) had been used to impose cuts in social benefits and to enhance labour market flexibility (Bruun and Lorcher and Schömann, 2014:39). It looks as if the EU has started pushing towards a stronger social coordination and harmonization, albeit guided mostly by monetary orthodoxy and thus, despite all social accents of the Lisbon Treaty, not very socially friendly at all. Can a certain revival of the social market economy goal lead the EU out of this unsustainable situation? And how can the EU law and policies contribute to it? The rest of this chapter tries to provide plausible answers from both a legal and an economic point of view.

### 7.2. Social Market Economy as the Right Solution to the Problem?

Such question cannot be answered without uncertainty because of two groups of reasons.

First, the primary law of the EU as the key fundament to any discussion of EU goals and competencies, offers in the current version no specific hints. The Lisbon Treaty does not mention the social market economy anywhere else than in Art. 3(3) TEU. This paragraph 3 seems more a "wish list" as it features a total of 18 internal EU market “goals” (House of Lords, 2008:21). A wide range of socio-cultural and environmental objectives dominate among them; however, there are also references to the liberal-market values (price stability, high competitiveness). It is therefore difficult to distillate out of it any coherent economic and social model. Precisely measurable objectives (growth, stability, competitiveness) and those that can be regulated by law (equality, non-discrimination, the rights of the child) find themselves in line with the appeals to the general well-being (social progress and solidarity, solidarity between generations and the Member States, the full employment). To such a list of incongruent goals, the notion of the social market economy - in itself, a rather complex concept of social and economic processes' regulation, is associated without any differentiation.

The Lisbon Treaty neither changes nor expands the concept and scope of EU competences in the social sphere (Title X "Social Policy"). Moreover, in its other parts, it contains provisions based on the neo-liberal foundations (especially in Title VIII Economic and Monetary Policy, which includes repeated references to “open economy with free competition”). It is therefore not clear at all how strongly, through which ways and with what tools, should the EU carry out – not in words but in deeds - its turn towards some socially acceptable model, especially if in the social sector it can only "support and complement" the measures adopted by the Member States and any EU harmonization is either subjected to unanimity vote or even remains forbidden regarding the key issues of pay and collective rights of workers.

Secondly, the European Commission as the initiator of the new measures at EU level, refers to the concept of social market economy (namely in the speeches and documents of DG Employment, Social Affairs and Inclusion) quite often, but without defining it more precisely as the model of a mixed economy that avoids both extremes of the *laisssez-faire* and the socialization of economy. The Commission, therefore, understands the social market economy as something that has traditionally existed in Western Europe and particularly in Scandinavia and Germany it has been so far successfully adapted to today's challenges (Andor, 2011:13-15). It is thus not clear whether the EU should contribute to the achievement of the social market economy goal by anything more than using better its limited competencies plus by encouraging the sharing of best practices and other actions that may lead to a spontaneous convergence of social standards and their enforcement tools at a national level.

The EU Court of Justice (CJEU), which is called to provide the authoritative interpretation of the legal terms of the Treaty, has not yet provided any clear guidance to the meaning of the highly competitive social market economy goal. It even seems that until very recently (until the judgment C-201/15 from December 21st, 2016) the CJEU has been consciously avoiding any reference to this goal in its reasoning, apparently because the Member States, as “masters of the Treaty”, did not agree to give any normative content to it (Šmejkal, Šaroch and Svoboda, 2016:70-71).

In general, one cannot expect much from the EU institutions in this respect, for the basic reason that even in the second decade of the 21st century the EU remains a "Stateless market" or a "Stateless monetary union". There is still a Treaty and not a Constitution, the EMU has economic governance instead of a government, and the EU on its own can develop several specific policies but not a common comprehensive social and economic development policy. Going even deeper, one has to acknowledge that the EU not only lacks competencies in the social field but, even more importantly, it has neither the capacity nor the possibility to socially and culturally embed any long-standing democratic consensus on a single model of a society and on the way its social imbalances should be adjusted (Šmejkal, Šaroch, and Svoboda, 2016:58-62). The social market economy goal can hardly change it, and it would be naive to expect that it could automatically drive the EU towards a full-fledged economic and social Constitution.

These two groups of reasons create uncertainty as to whether the social market economy could have been understood by the drafters of the Treaty as a distinct model that should be achieved by the EU and through the instruments conferred to it. This makes the interpretation of the social market economy goal difficult but at the same time necessary if any proposal on how to achieve it is to be formulated.

It is clear that the EU's goal of the social market economy cannot mean a direct copy of the concept of the economic and social policy of post-war West Germany at the time of Ludwig Erhard and Alfred Müller-Armack (Joerges, 2015:82). First, their policy had been a compromise made of Ordoliberal, Social-Christian, and Social Democratic elements, hence a specific product of social consensus in one particular EU country during the 50s and 60s of the 20th century (Hasse and Schneider and Wigelt, 2002). Moreover, it is clear that the former perception of the social needs of citizens, and their effective social rights, cannot be compared to the present time when the standard of consumption, housing, education, leisure, etc. is completely different. Due to its blended origin, however, the social market economy concept is fortunately not embedded in any clear-cut ideology and thus remains open to modern interpretations that reflect on the state of markets and of the social needs of the 21st century (van Suntum and Böhm and Oelgemöller, 2011:2). On the other hand, none of the current interpreters of social market economy can deny that this concept has a distinct Ordo-liberal pedigree because, only thanks to it, all discussions about what this concept means for the current EU could find a certain common ground and save the social market economy from degenerating into a meaningless catchword.

First, it is obvious that such a goal will push neither for socialist or social-democratic dominance of politics over the market nor for any outright prevalence of social rights over the EU freedoms of movement. An open market with free competition must remain the basis of not only economic but generally of human freedom as such (Joerges and Rödl, 2004). It, however, needs to be subjected to a strict framework of rules designed to ensure that the market is not destroyed either by excessive concentration of economic power or by the social inequalities that market economy has a tendency to create as its externalities. A model of the social market economy will thus prefer market-sensitive and not corporatist or protectionist measures.

Secondly, it is clear that the sought-after framework of rules will give priority to rule-based and not outcome-based solutions wherever possible, as it is supposed to rely rather on directing independent energies of responsible individuals than on the wisdom of a State as an omnipotent manager. This means that the key principles that are forming the constitutional rules of the social market economy should not be either numerous or very detailed. A significant role in their interpretation and application will be played by an independent judiciary.

Third, it is clear that due to the first two principles and also with regard to the principle of subsidiarity, enshrined both in the EU construction and in the concept of the social market economy, the principles to be adopted and enforced uniformly by the EU authorities should represent only a small part of what the maintenance of a functional social market economy would require in everyday practice. In order to give to the EU's concept of the social market economy the necessary democratic legitimacy, political support and thus also the practical effectiveness, no "one-size-fits-all" model promoted by the multinational institution through a single set of technocratic rules can ever be contemplated.

At the same time, it has to be stressed that the economic part of the constitutive and regulative principles of the Ordoliberal order, had been historically built into the EU foundations. Price stability, open markets, private property, freedom of contract, individual liability and protection of competition are traditionally written in either the Treaty provisions or general principles of the EU law. EU-embedding of social principles of the social market economy, e.g. income policy, social inclusion, effective labour markets, correction of (social) externalities, has been so far much less clear given the historical division of tasks and responsibilities between the EU and the Member States. Should the EU move closer to the model of the social market economy, it will have to strive for a certain rebalance for being granted, in accordance with the outlined principles, greater powers, and duties in the social field.

The purpose of further questioning therefore, would be whether and where the EU law and policies should undergo changes, so that the EU, while keeping with the principle of subsidiarity, and with the basic framework of the division of powers between the EU and the Member States, could change its image of liberalizing, deregulating, socially insensitive entity alienated to ordinary people, enhancing at the same time its potential for competitiveness and growth by reducing social inequality and exclusion (Ostry and Tsangarides, 2014). Within such a limited assignment, the attention will be paid just to the measures whose implementation at the EU level would fit the concept of the social market economy and at the same time would help to remedy the perceived "lack of social fairness" of the European integration.

### 7.3. Social Market Economy Goals as a Balancing Clause

The least controversial hypothesis would be to perceive the social market economy as a general commandment to consistently balance the social and the economic impact of each act or measure of the EU (Costamagna, 2011:7). This assumption seems to reflect the ideas of the Treaty drafters best. Retrospective analysis of how this objective got into the Lisbon Treaty demonstrates that this goal was transposed into TEU from the draft Constitutional Treaty (CT) of 2004 without any noteworthy discussion (Convention, 2003). At the time of drafting CT, it was obvious that without emphasizing the social aspect of the EU the new Treaty would be unacceptable to the voters scared by the impact of the EU enlargement and global competition. As the CT's Working Group XI - *Social Europe* had neither been able to agree on strengthening of the EU powers in the social field nor to emphasize the necessity of “Social Europe”, it had introduced "the Highly competitive social market economy" as a generally acceptable compromise, as nothing more than an appeal to mediate between market freedoms and social welfare (Joerges and Rödl, 2004:21).

The insertion of the „Horizontal Social clause“ into Article 9 of TFEU shows the same direction: in defining and implementing its policies and activities, the Union shall take into account several social goals such as high level of employment, adequate social protection, fight against social exclusion, etc. Needless to stress that the policies the EU can develop and implement on its own are, according to Article 3 TFEU, first of all, customs union and common trade policy, protection of economic competition on the internal market and currency policy of the EMU, hence policies of economic nature. Among the so-called shared-powers' policies, the completion and further development of the internal market come first (Art 4(2)a TFEU). Therefore, the social clause is called to integrate the social considerations into traditional economic policies conducted by the EU, e.g. to re-balance their content so that their impact does not compromise the achievement of the enumerated social goals.

Nowadays, we can see that while immediately after the introduction of an innovative system of governance, which is referred to as the "European semester"[1] emphasis on measures important for macroeconomic stabilization and fiscal consolidation was prevailing, later, more assertive sub-

---

[1] The European semester is the umbrella name for the annual cycle for the coordination of budgetary and economic policies in the EU. The focus is on two main objectives: Creating a consistent framework which in a single integrated unit connects the various levels of coordination processes in the EU and euro area. Closer link between the decision-making processes at the level of EU member states with a view of the Union's institutions. The first round of the European Semester was launched at the beginning of the year 2011. His form subsequently underwent some incremental changes and stabilized on schedule, with the following nodes: European Semester cycle is initiated by the Commission, which in November publishes two materials. The first of these is the Annual Growth Survey (Annual Growth Survey, AGS), whose task is to identify the main issues and challenges facing the EU and the Eurozone next year. Within the framework of macroeconomic surveillance Alert Mechanism Report (AMR) is simultaneously published. By the end of November, the Commission also will examine draft budgets of Eurozone member states for next year, from the point of view of their compliance with the obligations of the Stability and Growth Pact. If it comes to a serious breach of the rules of European budgetary discipline, the Commission may request a reworking of the budget proposal. Two more months are reserved for AGS discussion in the EU Council to adopt conclusions and in the European Parliament which issues an opinion. In March, the spring meeting of the European Council takes place. On the basis of the Commission's analysis, this supreme authority issues political guidance (policy orientation), which determine the direction in which member countries should focus in designing their budgetary and economic policies. March is also reserved for the publication of in-depth reviews of countries in which the Commission found signs of macroeconomic imbalances. With the knowledge of the policy orientation guidance the Member States submit two documents the Commission in April. First, there are stability programs (Eurozone members) and convergence programs (non-members of the Eurozone), which present the medium-term budgetary strategy. Furthermore, the national reform programs, which inform on the envisaged structural measures. In May, the Commission will examine the documents submitted and for each member country of the EU develops one integrated set of proposals for action, e.g. Country-specific recommendations (CSR). This is the term for specific, direct and controllable suggestions on the creation of budgetary and economic policies, which the Commission believes member states should implement. CSR is not issued for countries in the correctional program, which itself involves strict supervision of the fulfillment of program conditions. CSR are subsequently discussed in the Council, which shall give its conclusions. Their final version is approved by the European Council. In the second half of the year national parliaments discuss and approve their draft budgets for next year, including accompanying legislation. At that time the view of the EU institutions to the required measure of budgetary and economic policies is already available. The Commission continuously monitors the performance of CSR.

measures, that focus attention precisely on better monitoring and evaluating indicators of social development, began to gain importance in the framework of the procedures of the European Semester. The latest examples are the new indicators incorporated into the MIP Scoreboard; for 2014 as a subsidiary, in 2015 already as part of the set of headline indicators.[2] A similar trend can be seen in the context of the formulation of the annual CSR (Country Specific Recommendations), which is also included in the European Semester process (see footnote). Zeitlin and Vanhercke (2014) explain comprehensively and convincingly the institutional reasons for this shift in preferences and emphases. CSR recommend a series of structural reforms aimed at labor markets, education system and the creation or strengthening of social inclusion and eradicating poverty and thus have an undeniable Ordo-liberal feature in terms of institution building. In terms of enforcement measures in the framework of the European semester, within the so-called open coordination method, it is but obvious that this method has its limits. Despite the formal strengthening of coercive power thanks to the RQMV (reverse qualified majority voting procedure in the Council) procedure in compliance with fiscal rules, it is becoming obvious that the momentary interests of the big players - at the time of this text, particularly France and Italy - again will lead to substantive disrespect of the rules. Just as toothless, this procedure proves to be the MIP in the case of German external imbalances. It is therefore questionable whether and, if so, to what timescale, is the OCM the way to strengthen the social dimension of the EU in the spirit of the SME concept based on the Ordoliberal spirit of respecting the rules.

Then, unavoidably emerges the subsequent question, whether by the EU-prescribed austerity should be partially compensated by direct financing of selected social measures by EU budget. (We deal in more in detail with this problem in section 5).

---

The annual cycle of the European Semester is concluded at the end of the year, when the new Annual Growth Survey the Commission assesses how Member States took into account the recommendations addressed to them. (European Commission 2016b)

2 Specifically, the following changes are considered: 3 years change in pp of the activity rate, with a threshold of -0.2%, 3 year change in pp of the long-term unemployment rate, with a threshold of + 0.5% and 3 year change in pp of the youth unemployment rate, with a threshold of + 2%. (European Commission, 2015b)

### 7.4. EU Court of Justice as a Rather Reluctant Balancer

Legally speaking, however, the final word in such balancing between the social and the economic aspects, should belong to none other than the CJEU. At least since its judgment of 1973 *Continental Can*, the target provisions of the Treaties should not be read as if they "merely contain a general program devoid of legal effect", but as being "indispensable for the achievement of the Community tasks" and due to this, the EU authorities are kept to implement them in practice (CJEU C-6/72, 1973). In the event of any dispute as to whether the acts of EU institutions sufficiently respect the balance between the economic and the social, the CJEU should be the key body to decide on the invalidation of any measure going against this or the key value or goal of the EU (see Article 263 TFEU).

It is however symptomatic for the CJEU today that while in cases of conflict of social measures with provisions on competition protection, where it consistently recognizes the social limits of the application of competition rules (or allows for extensive exemptions from their prohibitions), it does not take the same position in the conflicts of social measures with the freedoms of movement of the internal market (Šmejkal, Šaroch and Svoboda, 2016:96-98). Here, the CJEU still upholds its well-known pre-Lisbon stance taken in the cases of the so-called "*Laval* quartet" (CJEU C-438/05, 2007; C-341/05, 2007; C-346/06, 2008; C-319/06, 2008). In these precedents, it has recognized that the Community "has not just economic but also a social purpose" hence the rights of the free movement must be balanced against the objectives pursued by social policy. However, it applied its traditional "breach-proportionality-justification" test. It means that the CJEU treated the rights of workers as a possible exception from the general free movement rule. Such exception must not only be kept proportionate in size but also needs to be objectively justified. Thus, in the eyes of the CJEU judges, the right to enjoy the freedom of movement does not necessitate any justification as the motivation of those who move is irrelevant; however, the exercise of social rights is dependent on their justification by pursuance of an objective public interest.

In the post-Lisbon period, the CJEU has repeatedly been called upon by Advocates General (AG) to adjust its approach to the new social accents of the Lisbon Treaty. AG Trstenjak in the Opinion in case *Commission v. Germany* (CJEU C-271/08, 2010) and very similarly AG Cruz Villalon in the Opinion in case *Santos Palhota* (CJEU C-515/08, 2010), suggested to the CJEU that when deciding on the conflict of social rights and economic freedoms, it should satisfy itself with the test of proportionality, e.g. the CJEU should seek their fair balance instead of keeping the *de facto* hierarchy between the general rule and a duly justified *ad hoc* exception to it. However, the CJEU has not moved that way so far, on the contrary, it has stressed in particular that the collective rights of workers must be exercised in accordance with the EU law, therefore not in conflict with the requirements of the freedoms protected by the Treaty. The CJEU has also expressly rejected parallels between its approach to the conflict between competition rules and social rights and the one it adopts in the cases of clashes between fundamental market freedoms and social rights (CJEU C-271/08, 2010). This does not mean, of course, that the CJEU adjudicates programmatically to the detriment of the rights of workers and their trade unions (see, e.g., its friendly decision on defence of rights of posted workers in case C-396/13, 2015), but it seems that the changes made by the Lisbon Treaty (2009) have not been a strong enough impetus for the CJEU to reverse its precedential stance.

In the wave of criticism of the CJEU decisions in "*Laval* quartet" and similar cases the European Trade Union Confederation (ETUC) proposed in 2008, a so-called Social Progress Protocol was attached to the Treaties. There the trade unions suggested that "Nothing in the Treaties, and in particular neither economic freedoms nor competition rules shall have priority over fundamental social rights and social progress... In case of conflict, fundamental social rights shall take precedence." (ETUC, 2008). Such a reversal of the current hierarchy would maybe correspond to the ideal of "Social Europe" but not to the concept of social market economy because the performance of market freedoms would be radically subordinated to the interests of social protection instead of their fair balance that does not allow for permanent dominance of one or the other principle.

In terms of the social market economy, it would, therefore, be better if the CJEU began to weigh the fundamental market freedoms against the protection of social rights and welfare on a strictly equal footing. It has to be acknowledged here that the CJEU has been, at last from 2015, gradually adapting its approach to cases involving sensitive social issues. In a series of judgments on the so-called „benefit tourism" of EU citizens from poorer Member States the CJEU abandoned its traditional case law insisting on the priority of the EU citizen´s rights to move to another EU country over the concerns of the host countries about the cost of such intra-EU migration for their social systems (CJEU C-333/13, 2014; C-67/14, 2015; C-299/14, 2016; C-308/14, 2016). At the very end of 2016 the CJEU, in a seminal judgment on the legality of a Member State´s decision denying prior authorization to collective redundancies from a company in economic difficulties, strongly stressed the necessary balance between free movements and social policy goals (CJEU C-201/15, 2016). The Grand Chamber of the CJEU even referred to social market economy goal of Art 3(3) TEU and the horizontal social clause of Art 9 TEU. Contrary to what had been suggested by the Advocate General, the judges found that the protection of employees and employment against collective redundancies would not, under certain circumstances, contravene the freedom of establishment and the freedom to conduct business protected by EU law.

To strengthen and stabilize this new tendency in the CJEU case law it would be desirable to amend the Treaty provision of key importance for the purpose. The natural way would be to change the Horizontal Social clause so that social values in the latter gained the unquestioned status of the values of the Union. This change can be inspired by Article 14 TFEU, which classifies the services of general economic interest as "the shared values of the Union." Thanks to this, they enjoy a sufficiently accommodating treatment from the EU law under the protection of competition, state aid control, and the internal market. The new wording of Article 9 TFEU should therefore be:

„In defining and implementing its policies and activities, the Union shall take into account the requirements linked to the promotion of a high level of employment, the guarantee of adequate social protection, the fight against social exclusion, and a high level of education, training and protection of human health, *as they hold the status of fundamental values of the Union.*"

The signal from the legislature could not be understood by the CJEU otherwise than as a command to a definite, fully equivalent treatment of market freedoms and social rights, e.g. to the abandonment of the requirement of justification and for maintenance of only the proportionality test when assessing their conflict. Of course, an addition to a Treaty article means an amendment to the EU primary law, which requires unanimity and ratification by all Member States. Unlike the solution proposed by the Social Progress Protocol of ETUC, it is impartial towards social rights and market freedoms and could, therefore, receive a more consensual acceptance, being finally also in accordance with the principles of the social market economy.

## 7.5. Social Market Economy Goals as an Appeal to Certain Redistribution

A better wording of the Horizontal Social clause of TFEU can "ease the pressure" exerted by the market freedoms on social rights. In itself, however, it would not give to the EU any effective tool for independent implementation of any of the social measures that traditionally form the part of the concept of social market economy. Although these measures are not "carved in stone", as it was pointed out above, all authors commenting on the social market economy of today include in this concept the correction of income distribution, measures of social compensation, regulation of (social) externalities or intervention in cases of "legitimate poverty" (Hasse and Schneider and Weidelt, 2002; van Suntum and Böhm and Oelgemöller, 2011; Franke and Gregozs, 2013). Surely, the EU is already providing some funds from its budget on social cohesion, in particular through the European Social Fund, and thus tries to promote active employment policy measures. Its main problem here, however, lies in the lack of competences and resources for a greater autonomous activity.

The EU may not intervene in income distribution or in balancing of the relations on labour markets in any way that would harmonize the minimum wage or the scope of trade union rights to collective action. Even there, where certain measures may be promoted by the EU, they cannot restrict the Member States in defining their own principles of social security systems or significantly affect the financial equilibrium of these systems (Article 153 (4)(5) TFEU). Should the EU itself want to invest socially, or to provide directly certain types of social benefits (as it is nowadays recommended from many sides), the existing financial provisions of the TFEU, which regulate the establishment and use of the EU budget, would represent a straight jacket for any expansion (Vandenbroucke, 2014:18).

To demonstrate clearly the existing limits, it is enough to compare the current EU budget in terms of size and structure of expenditure with the national budgets of EU member states. The EU budget is fixed at 1% of EU GNI and the tendency of the major states "donors" is to downsize it even further (Cipriani, 2014:88). Cohesion funds drain from it slightly more than one-third, and about 25% of this goes to the European Social Fund (ESF). This fund disposes of for a seven-year period from 2014 to 2020 of a sum in the order of EUR 80 billion. In contrast, the national budgets represent on average 49% of the GDP of member countries, of which about 21% goes to social purposes (in the case of countries such as France, Finland, Belgium and Denmark even over 30%). A sum of the annual budgets of the 28 Member States is roughly 45 times larger than the EU's annual budget, and annual budgets of medium-sized EU countries such as Austria or Belgium exceed in their absolute size that of the EU budget (European Commission, 2015a). In the current situation, the EU has no possibility to strengthen the bond between itself and the EU citizens by providing them with some complementary benefits. In the same vein, it cannot support measures proposed under the European semesters by its own social investment of any considerable size. Increased fiscal capacity of the EU, therefore, looks like a necessity for both the stabilization of the EU and for the strengthening of its legitimacy in the eyes of citizens.

Unfortunately, for such reasonable arguments, any new own resources for the EU can be created according to Article 311 of TFEU only by unanimous approval in the Council and a subsequent ratification by each Member State. However unlikely any quick and easy approval of such increase in the EU budget for social purposes is, it certainly would be useful, and it would correspond to the objective of the social market economy. In this part of the chapter, it is needed to emphasize that the openness and ability to integrate knowledge of other directions of economic theory can be counted to the advantages of the Ordoliberal doctrine that eventually gave rise to the concept of the social market economy (Herzog, 2010:147-169). From this point of view, especially the OCA (Optimum Currency Area) theory and the New Political Economy (NPE) are legitimate parts of economic theory. Within the OCA theory, it needs to be dealt especially with the argument of the so-called omitted integration. A common fiscal policy is the undisputed feature of the optimal currency area, including the so-called implicit transfers – e.g. pre-defined transfers between different areas of the monetary zone, helping to compensate for the consequences of asymmetric shocks. In the field of NPE, the approach of Jeffrey Freiden (1991) especially, is a challenge. His approach of identifying the "Winners and Losers" of a policy measure is based on the provision of compensation from winners to losers which should be initiated and negotiated by the "policymaker" ideally at the time of enforcing the measure. Thus, if the losers are the unemployed and low-income social groups - and so it should be, because the advantage of the single currency is a more efficient allocation of capital - then it is, in the spirit of the above approaches, fully legitimate to think about:

a) The common additional fiscal capacity

b) Redeeming transfers to "losers"

c) Where the source of these transfers is the taxation of winners

Several new tools that would of that kind have already been proposed in the literature treating the topic (e.g. Complementary European unemployment insurance) as well as the sources of which they could be financed without increasing the Member States' contributions (redirecting of the existing agricultural and structural subsidies (Mau, 2014), using the interest generated by the ECB (Natali, 2014), through the introduction of a financial transaction tax (FTT) or carbon tax (Ponzano, 2014)). Some of them have already appeared as drafts or legislative projects, as for instance the FTT proposed by the European Commission to the enhanced cooperation of 11 EMU countries (European Commission, 2013) or new sources proposed pursuant to Article 11 TEU by the European citizens' initiative called *New Deal 4 Europe* (2013).

The logic of these proposals is compelling. If the Member States observe the fiscal discipline they are prescribed to within the EMU, and should the EMU be able to deal effectively with social consequences of future asymmetric shocks in some of its parts, it cannot suppose that long-term and immediate social costs will be satisfactorily ensured by the concerned Member States. This is largely a matter of self-preservation of the EU to secure enough resources for social purposes. In this respect an agreement of the Member States to increase the EU budget by just 1 percentage point, e.g. to make it equivalent to 2% of EU GNI, would bring to the EU budget each year EUR 140-150 billion more, which would easily allow to multiply the current size of the European Social Fund by ten.

The proposed new EU instruments such as the EU or Eurozone unemployment scheme (Kadidlo and Lacina, 2015), or for instance a scheme for the payment of certain benefits to the unemployed who decide to look for a job in another Member State, would undoubtedly help to better balance the economic and social elements of the EU's activities, while not changing the distribution of roles and powers of the EU and Member States in the social field. The EU would not receive any of the social powers that the Lisbon Treaty under Article 153 TFEU does not want to confer to it. Conversely, however, it can get equipped with an additional tool for the correction of the burning social problems in a situation when a concerned Member State would not be capable of doing so. The EU citizens would gain direct EU contribution to maintain their social welfare without having to pay any direct EU-tax. At this point one can only speculate whether the inability of the EU-28 (or EU-27 in the near future) to reach an agreement, would push forward an EMU-alone solution or that of several key states, acting through an enhanced cooperation, or through a by-pass of the Treaty by another international "Pact".

## 7.6. Social Market Economy Goal as an Impetus for Further Harmonization Measures

Socially critical authors propose to the EU a wide variety of other measures, including e.g. introduction of the EU-harmonized minimum wage as a percentage of the median wage in each member state or even of the EU-guaranteed minimum income (Natali, 2014:21-22 and 98-108). While it is possible that such measures could contribute to the social well-being of EU citizens, to the popularity of the EU, as well as to higher labour mobility, in terms of the social market economy they would represent a significantly restrictive harmonization towards market freedoms and thus going beyond the minimum necessary for balancing the market and social elements in the policies of the EU.

On the contrary, the proposals for further harmonization of minimum social and labour standards are welcome, especially if they revive the trend of the 90s, when the EU adopted most of the directives on health and safety at the workplace, protection of employees rights in cases of collective redundancies, transfer of undertakings, insolvency of their employer and even converted into binding directives the agreements reached within the European social dialogue (on parental leave, part-time work, fixed-term contracts) (Vandenbroucke, 2014:11-12; Guibonni, 2015:18; Voss, 2011:18). The secondary EU law should maximally utilize there the limits of the powers already conferred to the EU in order to prevent the sinister race to the bottom between the Member States at the expense of social welfare. It seems that the European Commission by its initiative on the European Pillar of Social Rights from March 2016 points just in that direction: no challenge to the existing division of tasks between the EU and the Member States´ levels, no re-statement or modification of the existing social rights but first of all better and more active use of the competencies that the EU already possesses (European Commission, 2016).

For the needs of this chapter, it is sufficient to point out that such measures of a secondary EU law could definitely bring the EU closer to the concept of social market economy, even though they would not be radical enough for socially frustrated part of European voters.

## 7.7. Conclusion

The EU's social market economy objective must be seen not as a call for building a Social Europe in the meaning of the primacy of social policy over the free market, but rather as a "mere" correction of the free market by dumping its anti-social impacts. Only in this way, the EU can get the social market economy that would strengthen its competitiveness and secure high employment and social progress at the same time.

While the Lisbon Treaty created a number of new constitutional options for genuine fulfilling of this goal, the consequences of the way in which single currency was introduced according to the Maastricht Treaty and the reaction to the debt and financial crisis makes meeting this goal more difficult.

From the economist's point of view, European Semester, as a reaction to the crisis, brought a formal strengthening of coordination between member states and the Commission. However, this entire process is still grounded in the so-called Open Method of Coordination and solutions continue to depend on the political will of member states. It is rather improbable, that member states will be thorough in introducing social reforms recommended in European Semester procedures (for example by Country Specific Recommendation), which could strengthen institutions leading to sustainability and improvement of the shape of SME. It is already apparent today, that predominantly big member states do not (again!) keep to the original intention of short-term obligations which stem from modified fiscal stability rules (France, Italy) or Macroeconomic Imbalance Procedure recommendations (external balance of Germany).

Thus, for an economist, for the proper solution of how to sustain and strengthen social market economy characteristics, it is, in the EU case, crucial to remove the systemic flaw called "omitted integration", especially in the fiscal policy field. Strengthened common fiscal policy, in this case, means - according to OCA theory - a common body of policymaking, its clearly defined income (equivalent to some type of federal tax) and common transfers for selected purposes in the social policy area.

It was shown and argued that certain changes in primary and secondary law would be desirable, and perhaps even possible.

From the lawyer´s point of view, this analysis was focused primarily on two key amendments to the Lisbon Treaty, one completing the Horizontal Social clause, another proposing new size, and role of the EU budget and therefore it pleaded for changes affecting the EU primary law and requiring unanimous support of Member States. Nevertheless, the proposed amendments are not radical changes that would alter the existing character of the EU or deprive the Member States of their decisive say in ensuring social rights and welfare of their citizens. The implementation of the proposed measures could eliminate the historical problem of the weaker position of social and employment rights compared to the strength of the internal market freedoms. In the same manner, the EU could be enabled by them to bring solutions to situations of asymmetric social shocks. Rather minimal changes can give there a major signal to the general public that the goal of a social market economy is not just another declaration that would never have any positive impact on the EU and its citizens' future.

The social market economy goal of Article 3(3) TEU is therefore definitely a task for the EU law and policies, but it requires neither substantive changes in the current EU setting nor any „legislative storm“ of dozens of acts of newly harmonized social legislation. On the contrary, the beneficial balance of social and market aspects of the EU can be achieved without any "social revolution". It seems that the inclusion of this objective in the Treaty was a wise compromise that the EU should actively use in the current fight for its survival.

### 7.8. Acknowledgement

This chapter was created within the project GA CR. Project registration number 14-23623S.

## 7.9. References

ANDOR, LÁSZLÓ (2011). Building *a social market economy in the European Union. SPEECH/11/695 of the EU Commissioner for Employment,* Social Affairs and Inclusion. Manchester, October 20th.

BARNARD CATHERINE (2015). *How to Make EU Social Policy Live Up to its Name.* Social Europe, October 8th.

BRUUN, NIKLAS, LORCHER, KLAUS, SCHÖMANN, ISABELLE EDS. (2014). *The Economic and Financial Crisis and Collective Labour Law in Europe.* Oxford: Hart Publishing.

CIPRIANI, GABRIELLE (2014). *Financing the EU Budget. Moving Forward or Backwards?* Brussels: Centre for European Policy Studies.

CONVENTION (2003). *Final Report of Working Group XI on Social Europe.* CONV 516/1/03. Brussels 4/02/2003.

COSTAMAGNA, FRANCESCO (2011). *The Internal Market and the Welfare State after the Lisbon Treaty.* Research Paper – Observatoire Social Européen, N. 4 April.

COURT OF JUSTICE OF THE EU (1973). *C-6/72 Europemballage Corporation and Continental Can Company Inc. v Commission of the European Communities.* EU:C:1973:22.

COURT OF JUSTICE OF THE EU (2007). *C-341/05 Laval un Partneri Ltd v Svenska Byggnadsarbetareförbundet, Svenska Byggnadsarbetareförbundets avdelning 1, Byggettan and Svenska Elektrikerförbundet.* EU:C:2007:809.

COURT OF JUSTICE OF THE EU (2007). *C-438/05 International Transport Workers' Federation and Finnish Seamen's Union v Viking Line ABP and OÜ Viking Line Eesti.* EU:C:2007:772.

COURT OF JUSTICE OF THE EU (2008). *C-346/06 Dirk Rüffert v Land Niedersachsen.* EU:C:2008:189.

COURT OF JUSTICE OF THE EU (2008). C-*319/06 Commission of the European Communities v Grand Duchy of Luxemburg.* EU:C:2008:350.

COURT OF JUSTICE OF THE EU (2010). *C-271/08. European Commission v Federal Republic of Germany. EU:C:2010:183.* Opinion of Advocate General Trstenjak.

COURT OF JUSTICE OF THE EU (2010). *C-515/08 Santos Palhota and Others. EU:C:2010:245.* Opinion of Advocate General Cruz Villalón.

COURT OF JUSTICE OF THE EU (2014). *C-333/13 Elisabeta Dano and Florin Dano v. Jobcenter Leipzig* EU:C:2014:2358.

COURT OF JUSTICE OF THE EU (2015). C-67/14 *Jobcenter Berlin Neukölln v Nazifa Alimanovic and Others* EU:C:2015:597.

COURT OF JUSTICE OF THE EU (2015). *C-396/13 Sähköalojen ammattiliitto ry v Elektrobudowa Spolka Akcyjna* EU:C:2015:86

COURT OF JUSTICE OF THE EU (2016). *C-299/14 Vestische Arbeit Jobcenter Kreis Recklinghausen v Jovanna García-Nieto and Others* EU:C: 2016:114.

COURT OF JUSTICE OF THE EU (2016). *C-308/14 Commission v. United Kingdom* EU:C:2016:436.

COURT OF JUSTICE OF THE EU (2016). *C-201/15 Anonymi Geniki Etairia Tsimenton Iraklis (AGET Iraklis) v. Ypourgos Ergasias, Koinonikis Asfalisis kai Koinonikis Allilengyis.* EU:C:2016:972.

DE WITTE, FLORIS (2015). *The Architecture of a "Social Market Economy"*. LSE Law, Society and Economy Working Papers N. 13/2015.

ETUC (2008). *Proposal for a Social Progress Protocol.* Brussels, 18/03/2008. [online]. [8. 12. 2016] Available at: https://www.etuc.org/proposal-social-progress-protocol

EUROPEAN COMMISSION (2013). *Proposal for a Council directive implementing enhanced cooperation in the area of financial transaction tax.* COM(2013) 71 final. Brussels, 14/02/2013.

EUROPEAN COMMISSION (2015A). *Budget. Myths and Facts.* [online]. [8. 12. 2016] Available at: http://ec.europa.eu/budget/explained/myths/myths_en.cfm

EUROPEAN COMMISSION (2015B). *MIP Scoreboard.* [online]. [8. 12. 2016] Available at: http://ec.europa.eu/economy_finance/economic_governance/macroeconomic_imbalance_procedure/mip_scoreboard/index_en.htm

EUROPEAN COMMISSION (2016A). *Communication from the Commission to the European Parliament, the Council, the European Economic and Social Committee and the Committee of the Regions Launching a consultation on a European Pillar of Social Rights.* COM(2016) 127 final. Strasbourg, 8/3/2016.

EUROPEAN COMMISSION (2016B). *Making it happen: the European Semester* [online]. [16. 11. 2016] Available at: http://ec.europa.eu/europe2020/making-it-happen/index_en.htm

FRANKE, SIEGFRIED F., GREGOSZ, DAVID (2013). *The Social Market Economy. What Does It Really Means.* Berlin: Konrad Adenauer Stiftung.

FREIDEN, JEFFREY (1991). *Invested Interests: The Politics of National Economic Policies in a World of Global Finance.* International Organization, Vol. 45 Issue 4 (Autumn) p. 425-451.

GIUBONNI, STEFANO (2015). *Europe´s Crisis-Law and the welfare state: A Critique.* European Labour Law Journal, Vol. 6, No 1, p. 5-19.

HASSE, ROLF H., SCHNEIDER, HERMANN, WEIDELT, KLAUS (2002). *Social Market Economy. History, Principles and Implementation From A to Z.* Johannesburg: Konrad Adenauer Stiftung.

HERZOG, BODO (2010). *Old wine in new skins? Economic Policy Challenges for the Social Market Economy in a Globalized World. In Glossner and Gregosz, 60 Years of Social Market Economy – Formating,* Development and Perspective of a Peacemaking Formula, p. 147 - 169

HOUSE OF LORDS (2008). *The Treaty of Lisbon: An Impact Assessment. European Union Committee Report Vol. I.* HL Paper 62-I. London: The Stationery Office Limited.

JOERGES, CHRISTIAN, RÖDL, FLORIAN (2004). *Social Market Economy as Europe´s Social Model?* EUI Working Paper LAW, N. 2004/8.

JOERGES, CHRISTIAN (2015). *The Legitimacy Problématique of Economic Governance in the EU. The Governance Report 2015.* Oxford: Oxford University Press, p. 69-94.

KADIDLO, LUKÁŠ., LACINA, LUBOR (2015). *Why Would Eurozone Need an Own Budget?* Policy Paper Series of Mendel European Centre, Vol. 6 N. 4/2015.

MAU, STEFFEN (2014). *European integration – with or without social policy?* Eutopia-Ideas for Europe magazine, May 20th.

MICOSSI, STEFANO, TOSATO, GIAN LUIGI EDS. (2009). *The European Union in the 21st Century. Perspectives from the Lisbon Treaty.* Brussels: Centre for European Policy Studies.

NATALI, DAVID ED. (2013). *Social development in the European Union 2013.* Brussels: ETUI.

NEW DEAL 4 EUROPE (2013). *For A European Special Plan For Sustainable Development And Employment.* [online]. [8. 12. 2016] Available at: http://www.newdeal4europe.eu/en/

OSTRY, JONATHAN D., BERG, ANDREW, TSANGARIDES, CHARALAMBOS (2014). *Redistribution, Inequality and Growth.* IMF Staff Discussion Note, SDN 14/02 February.

PONZANO, PAOLO (2014). *Réorienter l´Europe vers la croissance et l´emploi : l´initiative citoyenne pour un plan européen extraordinaire.* Revue du Droit de l´Union Eurupéenne, N. 2/2014 Juillet, p. 287-297.

SCHELLINGER, ALEXANDER (2015). *Giving Teeth to the EU´s Social Dimension. Dismail Failure and Promising Potential.* Berlin: Friedrich Ebert Stiftung.

ŠMEJKAL, VÁCLAV, ŠAROCH, STANISLAV, SVOBODA, PAVEL (2016). *European Union as a Highly Competitive Social Market Economy. Legal and Economic Analysis.* Waldkirchen: rw&w Science&New Media Passau-Berlin-Prague.

VAN SUNTUM, ULRICH, BÖHM, TOBIAS, OELGEMÖLLER, JENS, ILGMANN, CORNELIUS (2011). *Walter Eucken´s Principles of Economic Policy Today.* CAWM Discussion Paper No. 49 August.

VANDENBROUCKE, FRANK (2014). *The Case for a European Social Union. From Muddling Through to a Sense of Common Purpose.* KU Leuven EUROFORUM, September 2014.

VOSS, ECKHARD ET AL. (2011). *European Social Dialogue: Achievements and Challenges Ahead: Results of the stock-taking survey amongst national social partners in the EU Member States and candidate countries. Final Synthesis Report – May 2011.* Project of the European Social Partners with the financial support of the European Commission.

ZEITLIN, JONATHAN, VANHERCKE, BART (2014). *Socializing the European Semester? Economic Governance and Social Policy Coordination in Europe 2020.* Swedish Institute for European Policy Studies.

Chapter 8

# Revisiting Baumol's "Growth Disease"

Roman Stöllinger

## 8.1. Introduction

This contribution has two objectives. Firstly, it tests a variant of one of the predictions implied by an unbalanced growth scenario (Baumol, 1967) which Nordhaus (2008) labelled "Baumol's growth disease". As in the case of the more famous cost disease, the origin of the growth disease is the fact that productivity advances typically differ across industries while wage increases tend to progress more uniformly. As a result, the employment share in total GDP of fast growing industries – the *progressive* industries in Baumol's terminology – will decline over time while the opposite is true for low-growth industries – or *non-progressive* industries. This changing composition of output in favour of the non-progressive industries acts as a drag on overall productivity growth. This phenomenon is going to be referred to as "Baumol's growth disease." I investigate a variant of this growth disease hypothesis according to which the relatively more tradable industries are the more progressive sectors of the economy while the less tradable industries are rather non-progressive. The implication is that countries which specialise in the production of more tradable output will grow faster than countries producing predominantly non-tradable output. Making use of a recently developed tradability index (Stöllinger, 2017), which reflects the extent to which a country is geared towards the production of tradable output, I test the tradability-based Baumolian growth disease hypothesis in a standard growth model for a set of mainly European OECD and non-OECD countries. To this, I add the hypothesis that countries' initial capabilities as revealed by their export complexity (Hidalgo and Hausman, 2009), which itself was found to be a predictor of economic growth (Hausmann et al., 2007), reinforces the growth enhancing the effect of countries' specialisation in more tradable output.

The second objective is to demonstrate that the tradability index is a more intuitive and appropriate measure for economic openness than conventional measures of openness. Openness measures such as the share of exports in

GDP are often included in growth regressions which are considered either as a proxy for the impact of free trade policy on growth or it is used as a structural indicator. The former seems inappropriate because trade openness is an output measure and not a policy measure. Therefore associating the coefficient of the openness variable with trade policy is flawed as a high openness ratio is typically the result of a successful open market policy. Consequently, a positive coefficient would only suggest that a successful open market trade policy is associated with higher growth which provides little insights. More interesting is the interpretation of the trade openness measure as a readily available indicator for the trade orientation of a country with regards to its output structure. The problem with the openness measure is, however, that it is highly endogenous as it reflects the country's own exports and its trade policy. I suggest that a more appropriate structural measure is the tradability index which is a country's *predicted* trade openness given it production structure. A key advantage of the tradability index is that by definition it does not reflect a country's own exports as it is constructed on the basis of global export flows.

Baumol's growth disease and the hypothesis that countries specialised in the production of tradable output grow faster coincide as long more tradable industries are indeed the *progressive* ones, while the less tradable industries are the *non-progressive* ones. Of course, this is what Baumol had in mind because he considered manufacturing to the sector with higher productivity growth while (most) services would be a stagnant industry. Figure 8.1 shows that for European countries this is a valid assumption. In all countries for which information on total factor productivity (TFP) is available from the 2016 update of the EU KLEMS database (Jäger, 2016), TFP in the manufacturing sector exceeds that of the market economy. In Germany, for example, TFP increased by 22% between 2001 and 2014, while the corresponding rate in the market economy was about 5%. Even in more services-oriented economies such as the United Kingdom, TFP growth in manufacturing is much higher than in the market-related sector of the economy in general. The same is true for Italy which actually recorded negative TFP growth over that period but also in this case manufacturing less was less affected by the unfavourable development.

**Figure 8.1. Total factor productivity (TFP) growth in selected European countries, 2001-2014**

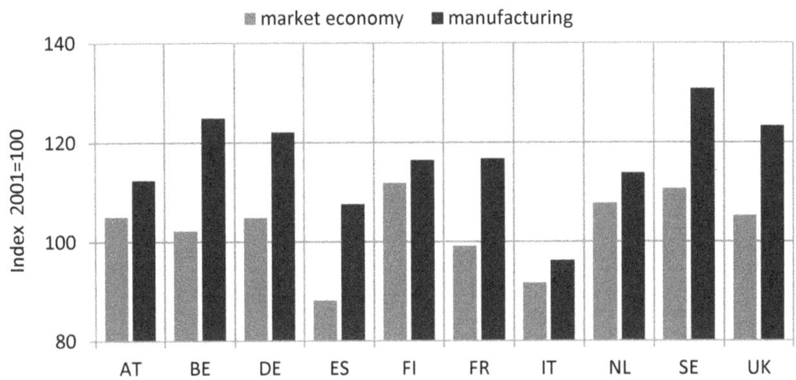


**Notes:** Market economy comprises the industry total excluding the NACE Rev.2 industries L, O, P, Q, T, and U. Belgium: Comparison is with total economy instead of the market economy. Italy: numbers refer to the year 2013. TFP expressed as an index using 2001 as the base year.

**Source:** EU KLEMS database, version 2016

The described variant of Baumol's "growth disease" prediction which puts centre stage the tradability of goods and services (instead of the differentiation between manufacturing and non-manufacturing) can be tested empirically making use of the newly developed tradability index. This index is a comprehensive measure for the tradability of an economy's output which is highly appropriate to test the hypothesis that higher tradability is conducive for growth.

While the scope of the empirical analysis is in principal global in scope, the European countries are overrepresented in the sample. While the availability of a larger sample would be preferable, the European bias in the sample means that the obtained results are reflecting the situation of European countries very much. Therefore they can be more directly linked to the ongoing debate about "de-industrialisation" in Europe. For this reason, I will relate the findings also to the divergence debate in the Euro Area focusing on the differences in economic structures and performance between Germany on the one hand and the crisis-stricken Euro Area members of the Southern periphery (Greece, Spain, Portugal, Italy) and France.

The remainder of the chapter is structured as follows. Section 2 discusses some of the related literature. Section 3 presents the growth model to be estimated. Section 4 explains the construction of the tradability index and its relationship with the conventional openness measures. Section 5 provides information on the main data sources, and Section 6 contains the econometric results. Section 7 concludes.

## 8.2. Related Literature

The importance of the economic structure for the growth prospects of an economy has long been realised. Though largely ignored by many growth models (Harvey, 1998), growth differentials between industries and the role of particular industries, especially manufacturing, as the driver of economic growth and development have been studied extensively. Baumol's (1967) famous cost disease is derived from the observation that productivity advances are larger in manufacturing (or in progressive sectors) than in services industries (non-progressive sectors). The key point is that in the case of unbalanced growth, e.g. if productivity growth differs across industries, but wage progression is uniform across industries (for institutional reasons), the non-progressive sectors will experience an increase in unit costs. If the price elasticity of demand is low or the income elasticity of demand in the non-progressive sector is high, the non-progressive sector will attract additional resources[1]. Szirmai and Verspagen (2015) present data which shows that the share of services increased in both developed and developing countries since the 1950s. This structural development is presumably due to the high-income elasticity of demand for services. A rising share of the non-progressive industries in nominal output implies that it will act as a drag on aggregate productivity and aggregate output growth as it will command an ever-increasing share of the input factors (Nordhaus, 2008). Nordhaus (2008) calls such a slowdown in economic growth due to the composition of output "Baumol's growth disease". Testing this growth disease for 67 US-industries over the period 1948-2001, he finds as a summary estimate that the composition effect decreased aggregate annual productivity growth by approximately 0.5 percentage points. This result is in line with the finding in Syrquin (1988) that the impact of resource reallocation on total factor productivity growth (TFP) is less important for developed than for developing countries and that a *"different – and probably negative – allocation effect may become important as labour continues to shift into services"* (p. 258). This

---

[1] In the opposite case, if price elasticity of demand is not highly inelastic, the share of non-progressive sectors in real output is bound to shrink, though Bradford (1969) showed that this does not need to be the case.

statement illustrates that the development literature associates manufacturing with modern economic growth. Smirzai and Verspagen (2015) discuss several reasons why the manufacturing sector can be expected to be the engine of growth. Apart from the stylised fact that TFP growth is higher in manufacturing than in the rest of the economy (see Figure 8.1), the most important argument has to do with demand effects. Given that the income elasticity of demand if typically low for agricultural products, specialisation in agriculture may lead impediments to growth due to demand constraints. In contrast, by fostering manufacturing production, a country can avoid such limitations and profit from growing world markets for manufactured goods (Smirzai and Verspagen, 2015). More recently, this argument has been made in the context of services because of the sector's high-income elasticity of demand. However, Smirzai and Verspagen (2015) argue that since most services are not traded internationally, the growing demand for services is a consequence rather than the cause of economic growth. In their cross-country analysis, these authors find a modest growth-enhancing effect of the share of manufacturing which turns out to be stronger for developing countries. When splitting their sample into sub-periods, they also find that this growth-enhancing effect is detectable only in the period 1970-1990. From this, they conclude that manufacturing has become a more difficult route to growth than it used to be in previous decades.

A variant of the engine of growth argument in favour of manufacturing is made in Rodrik (2010) who argues that what matters for growth, at least in developing countries, is the output of non-traditional trades. In this narrative, the growth in developing countries depends on the world economy absorbing a growing supply of tradable goods.

The approach in this chapter is very close to that in Rodrik (2010) in the sense that the emphasis is more on tradability as the main characteristic of the goods or services produced than whether they are manufacturing products. However, in contrast to Rodrik, I do not proxy the tradable sector by the industrial sector but use the tradability index which reflects the tradability of an economy's entire output. In addition, instead of putting the proxy for tradable output in competition with a measure of export openness in one regression to see whether the "*tradables-are-special*" - story or the *"spillovers-from-exporting"* - *the* story is empirically more relevant, I test them in separate regressions. The main point in this context is that, while used in many growth regressions, including in the work of Smirzai and Verspagen (2015), conventional measures of trade openness are impossible to interpret – besides the fact that only occasionally they turn out to be statistically significant.

## 8.3. Growth Model

The starting point for the empirical growth model into which the modified growth disease hypothesis is incorporated is a standard Cobb-Douglas production function. By taking logs and first differences one gets:

$$\Delta ln\, Y_i = \alpha \cdot \Delta ln\, K_i + \beta \cdot \Delta ln\, L_i + \Delta lnA_i + \varepsilon_i \quad (1)$$

where $\Delta lnY_i$ is the growth rate of real GDP of country $i$ from 1995 to 2014, $\Delta lnK_i$ is the growth rate of the physical capital stock, $\Delta lnL_i$ is the growth rate of labour and $\Delta lnA_i$ is total productivity growth. $\varepsilon_i$ denotes the error term.

Different strands of the growth literature have suggested various factors as the driving force for productivity growth. For example, one strand of the literature emphasizes the (mainly indirect) role of human capital in the growth process through the impact on productivity growth (e.g. Benhabib and Spiegel, 1994). Mirroring such a set-up, this chapter focuses on the degree of specialisation in the production of tradable output as the engine of productivity growth. In the context of unbalanced growth, the reason why the tradability of output feeds into aggregate productivity growth is twofold. Firstly, TFP growth is assumed to be higher in more tradable sectors. Secondly, specialisation in highly tradable goods reduces the risk of facing demand constraints given that the output can be sold on the world market. Taking into account that initially, more backward countries may have higher productivity growth the following law of motion for productivity growth is modelled:

$$\Delta ln\, A_i = \rho + \theta \cdot TI_i^{ini} + \xi \cdot GAP_i^{ini} \quad (2)$$

where $TI_i^{ini}$ is the level of the tradability index of country $i$ at the beginning of the period and $GAP_i^{ini}$ is country $i$'s gap in terms of GDP per capita vis-à-vis the leading country at the beginning of the period. Following the approach pioneered by Nelson and Phelps (1966) this income gap is calculated as $\frac{GAP_{max}-GAP_i}{GAP_{max}}$.

The main implication of equation (2) is that countries with a production structure geared towards tradable output will enjoy higher productivity growth which feeds into higher GDP growth.

According to Rodrik (2010, 2013) growth in developing countries, e.g. countries with a high-income gap, is to a larger extent dependent on foreign markets and hence on the tradability of output. I take this possibility into account by formulating a variant of the law of motion which includes an interaction term between the gap variable and the tradability index.

$$\Delta ln\, A_i = \rho + \theta \cdot TI_i^{ini} + \lambda \cdot \left(TI_i^{ini} \times GAP_i^{ini}\right) + \xi \cdot GAP_i^{ini} \qquad (2')$$

Another extension of the law of motion for productivity growth is that the advantage of a country specialising in the production of tradable goods is larger, the larger is its capabilities base. In other words, countries with higher capabilities should benefit more from shifting its production structure towards tradables. As a proxy for capabilities, I use the export complexity index (ECI) developed by Hidalgo and Hausmann (2009). The ECI has two dimensions, diversity and ubiquity. The former refers to how strong a country's production structure is connected to other products. The latter indicates the exclusiveness of its production structure. More diversity allows countries to move more easily into new products. Low ubiquity means that only a few other countries are able to produce the same good which, ceteris paribus, means less competition and potentially higher price-cost markups and therefore higher productivity. Keeping the assumption that initially more backward countries have higher productivity growth, the law of motion for productivity growth has the following form:

$$\Delta ln\, A_i = \rho + \theta \cdot TI_i^{ini} + \varphi \cdot (TI_i^{ini} \times ln\, ECI_i^{ini}) + \omega \cdot lnECI_i^{ini} + \xi \cdot GAP_i^{ini} \qquad (3)$$

where $ln\, ECI_i$ is the log-level of country $i$'s export complexity index at the beginning of the period.

Inserting (2') into equation (1) yields the basic regression equation:

$$\Delta ln\, Y_i = \rho + \alpha \cdot \Delta ln\, K_i + \beta \cdot \Delta ln\, L_i + \theta \cdot TI_i^{ini} + \lambda \cdot \left(TI_i^{ini} \times GAP_i^{ini}\right) + \xi \cdot GAP_i^{ini} + \varepsilon_i \qquad (4)$$

Likewise, the export complexity augmented version of the model has the following form:

$$\Delta ln\, Y_i = \rho + \alpha \cdot \Delta lnK_i + \beta \cdot \Delta ln\, L_i + \theta \cdot TI_i^{ini} + \varphi \cdot \left(TI_i^{ini} \times ECI_i^{ini}\right) + \omega \cdot ECI_i^{ini} + \xi \cdot GAP_i^{ini} + \varepsilon_i \qquad (5)$$

Note that the complexity augmented version in equation (5), in some sense, runs counter the expectation that producing tradable output matters more for backward countries, insofar as countries with lower per capita income tend to have less complex export structures and hence lower ECIs.

## 8.4. Tradability and Openness

This section illustrates the construction of the tradability index *(TI)* which is at the same time the predicted openness given a country's production structure. Furthermore, the relationship and the differences between the TI and the export to GDP ratio, the conventional measure of export openness in growth regressions, are explored.

### 8.4.1. Calculation of the Tradability Index

A natural benchmark for the tradability of goods and services is how much they are actually traded (De Gregorio et al., 1994)[2]. De Gregorio et al. (1994) classify sectors either as tradable or non-tradable with a sector being considered as tradable if more than 10 percent of its output is exported. Here I depart from this dichotomous classification and switch to a continuous measure of sectors' tradability. Hence, all goods and services produced in the different sectors are considered to be potentially tradable, though to different degrees. This way the dual distinction between tradable sectors and non-tradable sectors is replaced with a continuous "tradability score" specific to each sector.

The tradability scores (TS) are the first component required for the calculation of the tradability index (TI). The TS are defined as the ratio between the industry-specific, a global value-added exports (Johnson and Noguera, 2012) and industry-specific global value added. Therefore the value added exports at the industry-country level need to be calculated. For this, we follow the trade in value-added concept in Johnson and Noguera (2012) and the expositions in Stehrer (2012). Intuitively, the value added exports of a

---

[2] An alternative approach to capture the tradability of goods (or sectors) is to look at tariffs or trade barriers more generally. The difficulty is that the magnitude of such trade barriers is hard to identify. While the trade costs for merchandise can be estimated with gravity models (see e.g. Anderson and Wincoop, 2004), this approach is harder to implement for services.

particular industry and country is the part of the value added created by that country that is absorbed by other countries.[3]

The tradability scores are calculated for 14 broad sectors of the economy[4]. Since I interpret the tradability as characteristic reflecting various technical and physical features of a good or a service, the TI is constructed in a way that keeps the tradability scores constant over time. For this reason, country and time-specific value added and VAX data is aggregated over countries and over time to arrive at global, industry-specific TS that represent average values over the sample period (1995-2011). Formally, the global tradability score ($TS_i$) is calculated as the ratio between the global sector-level value added exports ($VAX_i$) and the sector-level value added ($VA_i$).

$$TS_i = \frac{\sum_{t=1995}^{T}\sum_{j=1}^{J} VAX_{i,t}^{j}}{\sum_{t=1995}^{T}\sum_{j=1}^{J} VA_{i,t}^{j}} = \frac{VAX_i^{global}}{VA_i^{global}} \quad (6)$$

where the subscript $t$ is the time index, $i$ is the sector index, and $j$ is the country index.

The resulting tradability scores for the 14 sectors are shown in Figure 8.2 which reveals a very intuitive ranking. Mining and manufacturing emerge as the sectors producing by far the highest share of output that is exported resulting in tradability scores of 0.51 and 0.41 respectively. They are followed by the transport and communication sector and the agricultural sector. At the bottom of the ranking are the services sectors health and public administration which are both characterised by a very low tradability, associated with a TS of 0.006 and 0.014 respectively. This ranking also confirms the conventional wisdom that goods are still much more tradable than services.

---

[3] See Appendix for the methodological details of calculating the value added exports.

[4] For the list of sectors see Appendix 2.

**Figure 8.2. Global tradability scores (TS) of sectors**

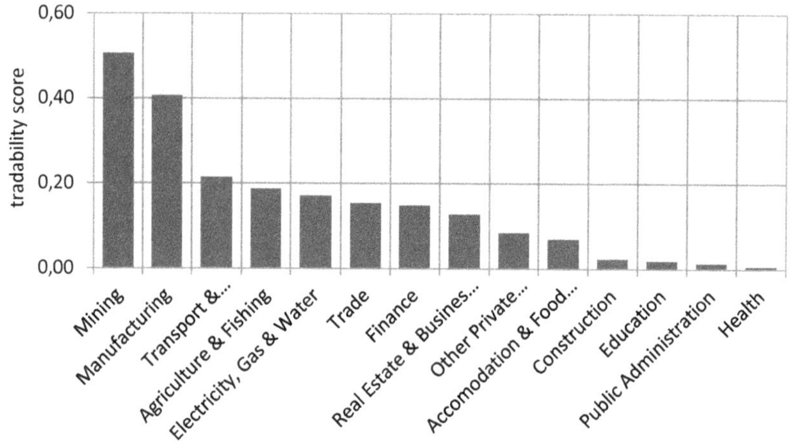


**Note**: TSvax = tradability score based on value added exports.

**Source**: wiiw Tradability Dataset.

The second component of the TI is the countries' value added shares. More precisely, to obtain the TI the TS are weighted with each country's sectoral value added shares, e.g. the sector-specific value added ($VA_{i,t}^{j}$) over total value added ($\sum_i VA_{i,t}^{j}$). Note that the value added shares vary over time and over countries. The tradability index is retrieved by summing up the weigthed tradability scores over all industries *i*. Formally, the *TI* of country *j* in any year *t* is calculated as:

$$TI_t^j = \sum_i \frac{VAX_i^{global}}{VA_i^{global}} \cdot \frac{VA_{i,t}^j}{\sum_i VA_{i,t}^j} \qquad (7)$$

The advantage of the tradability index is that it reflects the entire composition of production of each country. This makes it an interesting summary variable for an investigation of the nexus between the tradability of output and economic growth. Note that the tradability index, $TI_t^j$, is country and time specific and that the variance over time is coming uniquely from the changes in the respective country's sector composition of value added. This is because we chose the tradability scores to be time invariant[5]. As mentioned above, intuitively the tradability index can be interpreted as the expected export openness given a country's production structure.

Figure 8.3 shows the development of the TI over time in selected Euro Area members. More precisely, Germany, France and the countries of the Southern Euro Area periphery are displayed in order to illustrate the emerging divergence across these countries up to the Great Recession of 2008/2009.

**Figure 8.3. Tradability index: development in Germany, France and the Southern periphery of the Euro Area, 1995-2014**

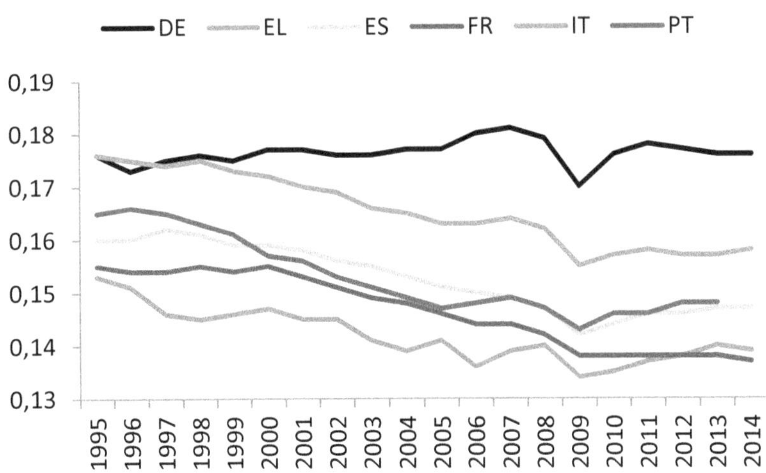


**Note**: TSvax = tradability score based on value added exports.

**Source**: wiiw Tradability Dataset

Typically, the divergence between Germany and the Southern periphery in terms of international competitiveness is illustrated using different trends in unit labour costs (see for example Gaulier and Vicard (2012). Figure 8.3 reveals that a similar story can be told by looking at the structural

---

[5] For details on the construction of the tradability index see Bykova and Stöllinger (2017).

development of this set of countries[6]. At least two facts are worth stressing in this context. First, the tradability index of Germany was rising modestly but steadily between 1995 and the beginning of the crisis in 2008. In contrast, in France and the Southern periphery countries, the trend in the tradability index was clearly negative. Secondly, with the exception of Italy, the tradability score was already markedly higher in Germany than in the other countries in Figure 8.3. For example, the differential in the tradability index between Germany and France was two percentage points in 1995 with the gap widened to 4 percentage points until 2014. According to the tradability-based Baumolian growth disease hypothesis, this should inflict a "structural change burden" (Timmer and Szirmai, 2000; Peneder, 2003; Szirmai and Verspagen, 2015) on the peripheral countries resulting in lower economic growth.

### 8.4.2. Predicted Openness and Actual Openness

As explained in the previous sub-section, the tradability index is the openness of a country that can be expected given its economic structure. Due to the construction of the measure, it is obvious, that the tradability index and the conventional export openness, e.g. the ratio of exports to GDP, are very different statistics. One of the key features differentiating the two measures is the fact that the export openness is strongly influenced by country size as for small countries the international market is relatively more important compared to larger economies. In contrast, the tradability index is by construction independent of country size. The independence of country size is one advantage of the tradability index as a structural indicator. Another advantage is that it is to a large extent independent of trade policy such as tariffs or export subsidies. Indirectly, trade policy may affect the tradability score due to the resulting specialisation in production. But the latter is a structural feature which is exactly what I intend to capture with the tradability index. Importantly, this indicator is not influenced by the country's exports. Since exports are also a part of GDP, letting exports entering the openness measure causes a reverse causality problem in a growth regression. This issue

[6] It should be stressed, however, that the structural developments do not simply reflect changes in relative prices. This is shown in Stöllinger (2017) in the context of the relationship between the tradability index and the current account.

does not arise in the case of the tradability index because it reflects only global exports[7].

**Figure 8.4. Tradability index and actual trade openness across countries, 2014**

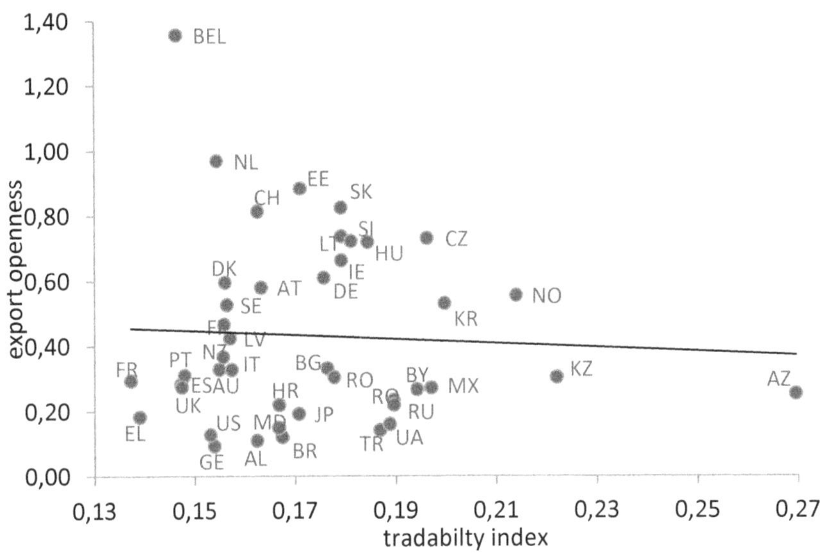


**Note**: Graph shows value added exports based tradability and export openness based on gross exports.

**Source**: PWT 9, WIOD, own calculations.

To demonstrate how distinct the two measures are, Figure 8.4 shows the correlations between the tradability index and the export openness. As can be seen, there is only a rather weak relationship between the actual openness of countries and the tradability index which is, if anything, negative.

---

[7] One may argue that the tradability index reflects changes in the global stance to trade policy because it includes the global value added exports to vale added ratio. However, since we take the average over time of this ratio, only a long term average of the world's stance towards "globalisation" all that is included in the tradability score.

## 8.5. Data

The sample comprises 43 mainly European OECD and non-OECD countries for which the industry value added data to construct industry shares are readily available. The sample period covers the years 1995 to 2014. Therefore the initial conditions refer to the year 1995. For most countries, the data for the tradability index is taken directly from the wiiw Tradability Dataset[8]. For the non-European countries, the value added data needed for the construction of the tradability index comes from the OECD SNA database.

The inter-country input-output data needed to calculate the value added exports is obtained from the World Input-Output Database (WIOD), 2013 Release[9], which is available for the years 1995-2014. The WIOD database (2013 Release) comprises 40 countries plus the rest of the world and 35 industries (see also Timmer et al., 2015). The VAX are calculated at this more detailed industry-level and then aggregated to the broader 14 sectors on which the tradability index is based[10].

Data for real GDP growth rates, capital stock, and employment is taken from the Penn World Tables, Version 9 (Feenstra et al., 2015)[11]. The same is true for expenditure sidereal GDP and population which is used for calculating the income gaps. Finally, the export complexity index (ECI) is retrieved from the Atlas of Economic Complexity Database[12] which is explained in detail in Hausmann et al. (2013).

## 8.6. Results

### 8.6.1 The tradability-Based Baumolian Growth-disease Hypothesis

This section reports the results of the empirical growth models stipulated in equations (4) and (5). In addition to the models that test the tradability-based Baumolian growth-disease with the tradability index – the results of which are reported in Table 8.1 – the second set of results with the conventional export openness as the structural indicator is presented (Table 8.2).

---

8 The data is available at: http://wiiw.ac.at/wiiw-tradability-dataset-ds-1.html.

9 The data is available at: http://www.wiod.org/release13.

10 For the list of the resulting 14 sectors and the corresponding NACE Rev.1 and NACE Rev.2 industry codes see Appendix 2.

11 The data is available at http://www.rug.nl/ggdc/productivity/pwt/.

12 The data is available at http://atlas.cid.harvard.edu.

Table 8.1 provides the results for the basic model (specification 1); the basic model but allowing for country-specific growth effects of the tradability index depending on their stage of development (specification 2); and the capabilities-augmented model (specifications 3 and 4).

**Table 8.1 Tradability of output and economic growth, regression results, 1995-2014**

| Dependent variable: | Δln Y | | | |
|---|---|---|---|---|
| | (1) | (2) | (3) | (4) |
| | basic model | | capabilities-augmented model | |
| Δln K | 0.3574 | 0.3726 | 0.3670 | 0.3662 |
| | (0.2317) | (0.2259) | (0.2404) | (0.2394) |
| Δln L | 0.2814 | 0.2995 | 0.2867 | 0.2714 |
| | (0.2502) | (0.2490) | (0.2556) | (0.2538) |
| GAP | 0.5137*** | 0.5943*** | 0.5615** | 0.5758** |
| | (0.1759) | (0.1617) | (0.2323) | (0.2264) |
| TI | 4.6486** | -4.2618 | 4.5912** | 3.1757* |
| | (1.9019) | (4.3025) | (1.9060) | (1.6343) |
| TI x GAP | | 12.5083* | | |
| | | (6.9273) | | |
| ln ECI | | | 0.0717 | 0.0059 |
| | | | (0.1606) | (0.1874) |
| TI x ln ECI | | | | -10.7010 |
| | | | | (9.7936) |
| Obs. | 43 | 43 | 43 | 43 |
| R-squared | 0.5960 | 0.6232 | 0.5973 | 0.6090 |
| R-squared adj. | 0.553 | 0.572 | 0.543 | 0.544 |
| F test | 8.256 | 10.67 | 6.999 | 7.168 |

**Note: TI** = tradability index. Robust standard errors in parentheses. ***, **, and * indicate statistical significant at the 1%, 5% and 10% level respectively. All regressions include a constant. GAP, TI, and lnECI refer to initial values in 1995. TI, and lnECI are centred in regressions with interaction terms.

Starting with the control variables, a first result is that the initial income gap of a country to the lead country is a key determinant of GDP growth. The positive coefficient is evidence for the famous catch-up effect which is well documented in the growth literature. In this growth framework, initially, more backward countries grow faster because they benefit from knowledge spillovers originating from more advanced countries (Nelson and Phelps, 1966). In the tradability-growth context, however, the most important result is the statistically significant and positive coefficient of the *TI*. The magnitude of the coefficient suggests that a one unit increase in the tradability index, e.g. from 0.18 to 0.19, would increase real GDP growth by 0.0465 log growth points (the sample average being 0.55). This rather large effect seems rather large but can be explained by the fact that a one unit change in the tradability index is a significant structural shift in the production structure. Assume for example that the tradability index increases from 0.18 to 0.19 due to a shift of production towards manufacturing. The question is how much the manufacturing sector must expand in order to arrive at this one percentage point change in the TI. The tradability score of the manufacturing sector is about 0.4. If one further assumes that the initial share of the manufacturing sector in GDP was 20% and that resources were shifted out of a sector with a tradability score of about 0.18 (e.g. agriculture), the share of the manufacturing sector needs to increases by approximately 5 percentage points (≈(0.40-0.19) x ((0.20+0.25)/2) to 25% of GDP. This is obviously a significant structural shift that is required to lift the *TI* by one unit, in this example from 0.18 to 0.19.

Specification 2 explores further the impact of the *TI* on growth by introducing an interaction term between the *TI* and the initial income gap *(GAP)*. This is one way of taking into account that gearing economic activity towards tradables sectors may be particularly important for developing countries as is often claimed, e.g. by Rodrik (2010, 2013). The regression result in Specification 2 provides some support for this claim as the positive coefficient of this interaction term, which is statistically significant at least at the 10 percent level.

Figure 8.5 shows the estimated marginal effect obtained in specification 2 for each country where this effect obviously depends on countries' initial income gap. About a third of the countries are estimated to have growth effects larger than estimated in the linear model. About two-thirds of the countries in the sample derive positive effects from specialising in tradables. This leaves almost a third of the countries, ranging from the UK to the US, where according to specification (2) specialising in the production of tradables actually acts as a structural burden. This is not in line with the expectations of the manufacturing sector as the main tradable-producing sector is characterised by higher productivity growth than the rest of the economy also in high-income countries. One explanation would be that high-income countries tend to have comparative advantages in specific services industries like information and communication services which are less tradable than for example manufacturing (tradability score of 0.21) but at the same time are characterised by comparatively high productivity growth.

**Figure 8.5 Marginal effects of the initial TI on the log-growth rate of GDP (1995-2014)**

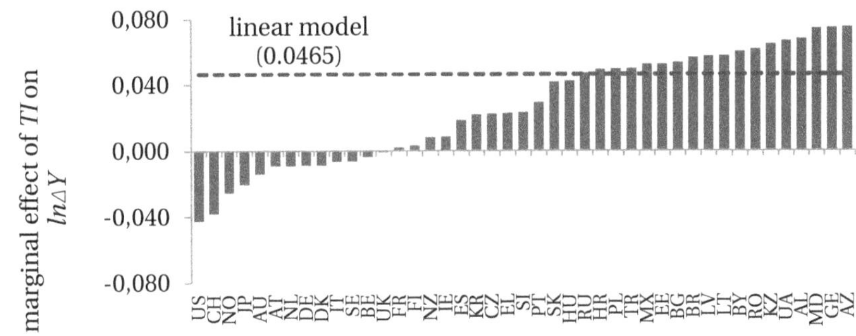


**Note**: Marginal effects based on the point estimates of specification (2) in Table 8.1.

Note that while these results in favour of a growth-enhancing effect of tradables confirms a long-established hypothesis, it is new empirical evidence because to my knowledge it is the first time that this hypothesis has been tested using a comprehensive measure for the tradability of the output a country produces (instead of relying on the manufacturing sector as proxy for the tradability of the entire economy).

To illustrate the quantitative implications of the results, Table 8.2 presents the structural change burdens associated with differences in the tradability index for France and the Southern peripheral countries of the Euro Area. Since the marginal effects were obtained from cross-country regressions, the hypothetical scenario assumes that the above-mentioned countries had the same tradability index as Germany in 1995. This difference is shown in the first column in Table 8.2. The resulting structural change bonus from such an increase in the tradability index is shown for both the linear and the non-linear model. As can be seen, the effect is largest in Greece, where such a structural bonus would add between 5 (non-linear model) to 11 (linear model) percentage points to the log growth rate. Given Greece's real (log) GDP growth rate for the period 1995-2014, the assumed structural shift towards tradables would boost economic growth by two-thirds in the linear model and by one-third in the non-linear model. The effects are smaller for Spain and Portugal but still sizeable. In France, there is also a particularly large difference in the hypothetical structural bonus depending on whether the linear or the non-linear model is considered. This is due to the fact that the marginal effect of France in the non-linear model is estimated to be small. In the case of Italy, there is no structural change bonus in this hypothetical scenario because Italy's tradability index in 1995 was basically identical to that of Germany.

**Table 8.2 Structural change bonus in selected Europe Area members assuming the German TI level of 1995**

| country | ΔTI to DE level | hypothetical "structural bonus" | | real (log) GDP growth | hypothetical real (log) GDP growth | | hypothetical 'structural bonus' in % of growth rate | |
|---|---|---|---|---|---|---|---|---|
| | linear | linear | non-linear | | linear | non-linear | linear | non-linear |
| IT | 0.000 | 0.000 | 0.000 | 0.085 | 0.085 | 0.085 | 0.0% | 0.0% |
| FR | 0.021 | 0.098 | 0.004 | 0.295 | 0.392 | 0.299 | 33.1% | 1.4% |
| ES | 0.016 | 0.074 | 0.030 | 0.380 | 0.454 | 0.409 | 19.6% | 7.8% |
| EL | 0.023 | 0.107 | 0.051 | 0.156 | 0.263 | 0.207 | 68.7% | 32.9% |
| PT | 0.011 | 0.051 | 0.032 | 0.212 | 0.263 | 0.244 | 24.2% | 15.1% |

**Note**: Structural bonuses and growth effects based on marginal effects based on the point estimates of specification (1) and (2) in Table 8.1. The structural change assumed is a shift to the level of the tradability index of Germany in 1995.

The hypothetical exercise illustrated in Table 8.2 shows that the growth implications of varying economic structures are sizeable. One issue, which at this stage is left to be addressed by future research, is that the range of the implied structural bonus is sizeable because of the large differences in the estimated marginal effects in the linear model and in the non-linear model.

The capabilities-augmented model in Table 8.3 (specifications 3 and 4) adds the initial value of countries' export complexity index (in log form) as an explanatory variable (*lnECI*). The capabilities-augmented framework hypothesises that specialisation in highly tradable, complex goods should be associated with higher economic growth. This effect may be direct (specification 3), but in addition, it may also work indirectly, via the tradability of output (specification 4). Indeed, the coefficient of the export complexity index (*lnECI*) has the expected positive sign, but in contrast to the results reported in Hausmann et al. (2007), it is not statistically significant (specification 3). This result does not change when the *TI* interacts with the export complexity index. This implies that the empirical growth model in equation (5) provides no evidence for the role of the complexity of exports (as measured by the *ECI*). On the one hand, this result is disappointing because having a production structure geared towards tradable and exporting complex and sophisticated products should yield a double advantage. On the other hand, it is reassuring that the tradability index remains statistically significant even after controlling for export complexity, which after all, is what matters for the tradability-growth nexus. Also, given the strong results obtained for the catch-up effect, it is not all that surprising that the export complexity does not alter the effect of the *TI* on growth. Since high-income countries tend to have higher export complexity than developing countries (though of course income and export complexity do not coincide) it would be surprising to find that countries with higher income gaps benefit more from producing tradable output while simultaneously also countries with more complex export structures benefit more strongly from a high initial *TI*. It seems that in the specifications above, the catch-up effect dominates a potential export complexity effect. So possibly, an alternative measure of the capabilities of a country may lead to a different result.

### 8.6.2. Tradability Index versus Export Openness

The second objective of this contribution is to demonstrate that the TI, which is the expected openness of a country given its economic structure, is both a more appropriate structural indicator and a more relevant driver of future growth than the conventional measure of export openness, e.g. exports over GDP. The latter suffers from the drawback that they depend strongly on the country size and also that they are highly endogenous as they include a country's own exports.

Repeating the estimation of the regression models from above but replacing the *TI* with the export openness allows demonstrating that the actual export openness (calculated as exports over GDP) is indeed less relevant for economic growth than the tradability index. Table 8.3 presents the results showing that across all four specifications, the actual export openness is not a relevant predictor for economic growth.

**Table 8.3 Export openness and economic growth, regression results**

| Dependent variable: | $\Delta$ln Y | | | |
|---|---|---|---|---|
| | (1) | (2) | (3) | (4) |
| | basic model | | capabilities-augmented model | |
| $\Delta$ln K | 0.3633 | 0.3560 | 0.3761 | 0.3707 |
| | (0.2390) | (0.2370) | (0.2483) | (0.2473) |
| $\Delta$ln L | 0.3167 | 0.3174 | 0.3263 | 0.3274 |
| | (0.2737) | (0.2838) | (0.2829) | (0.2874) |
| GAP | 0.7446*** | 0.6290*** | 0.8019*** | 0.7935*** |
| | (0.2040) | (0.2102) | (0.2586) | (0.2630) |
| OPEN | 0.0383 | 0.5094 | 0.0198 | -0.0420 |
| | (0.1631) | (0.4157) | (0.1707) | (0.2120) |
| OPEN x GAP | | -1.2514 | | |
| | | (1.0065) | | |
| ln ECI | | | 0.1027 | 0.1392 |
| | | | (0.1818) | (0.2064) |
| OPEN x ln ECI | | | | 0.5215 |
| | | | | (0.8375) |
| Obs. | 43 | 43 | 43 | 43 |
| R-squared | 0.5425 | 0.5630 | 0.5451 | 0.5477 |
| R-squared adj. | 0.494 | 0.504 | 0.484 | 0.472 |
| F test | 5.860 | 5.825 | 5.483 | 4.755 |

**Note: TI** = tradability index. Robust standard errors in parentheses. ***, **, and * indicate statistical significant at the 1%, 5% and 10% level respectively. All regressions include a constant. GAP, OPEN, and lnECI refer to initial values in 1995. OPEN and lnECI are centred in regressions with interaction terms.

To some extent, this is surprising because export openness – in contrast to what is often claimed – does not measure open market-oriented trade policy. Rather it reflects successful open market policy. Therefore one should expect a positive correlation between economic growth and the exports-to-GDP ratio because higher exports should also feed into higher economic growth. However, the result is in line with several other contributions to the growth literature which regularly fails to find a positive effect of openness in growth regressions (e.g. Szirmai and Verspagen, 2015 or Rodrik, 2010[13]). In any case the comparison between the results in Table 8.1 with those in Table 8.2 confirms that the tradability index, which can be interpreted as the predicted openness given the production structure of a country, is a more reliable determinant of economic growth than the actual openness which was the main point to be shown in this section.

## 8.7. Conclusion

This chapter provides new additional empirical evidence for what Rodrik calls the *"tradables-are-special"*-story. According to this view, specialisation in the production of tradable goods and services may entail a "structural growth bonus". In contrast to other contributions in this literature, I use an aggregate measure of the extent to which an economy's production structure is geared towards tradables instead of using the simple value added a share of industry or the manufacturing sector as a proxy for tradable output. This aggregate tradability measure – the tradability index – turns out to be positively associated with economic growth in a cross-country regression framework that controls for both changes in factor inputs and initial income. I consider this result as evidence for the existence of a tradability-based growth disease which results from a lack of a sufficient manufacturing base, endowments with natural resource or other tradable sectors (e.g. tourism). The results suggest that this tradability-growth nexus is stronger for countries with larger income gaps. This implies that these countries can reap a "structural change bonus" by specialising in the production of tradables. For the most advanced countries, the situation may be different insofar as there seem to be a potential to specialise successfully in less tradable sectors that nevertheless impact economic growth positively.

These results regarding the tradability-growth nexus entail two central policy implications. Firstly, international markets represent a huge opportunity, especially for emerging economies, to foster economic growth by specialising in tradable output where the risks of demand constraints are strongly reduced. Secondly, it means that countries that integrate into the global economy are well advised to manage their integration process carefully. This is necessary because the dynamics of such an integration process are much more complex than suggested by standard (static) trade models. A pure

---

[13] In the case of Rodrik (2010) this is at least true for the post-1990 sample period. See Table 7.2 (p. 137) therein.

laissez-faire approach to globalisation with a full reliance on existing comparative advantage may lead to an unfavourable specialisation pattern with a too strong reliance on relatively less tradable sectors. Due to the tradability-based Baumolian growth disease, this has a detrimental effect on growth prospects. Note, that this is not a call for protectionism. It should rather be understood as a reminder that a well-designed industrial policy that in certain circumstances chooses to "defy current comparative advantages" (as recommended by Ha-Joon Chang in Chang and Lin, 2009) has its merits. Given the evidence presented in this chapter, interventions aiming at a more growth-oriented economic structure which ensures a certain average tradability of output are advisable from a dynamic perspective. Hence, while more research on this issue is needed, the preliminary policy conclusion to be drawn from the results is that for most countries a targeted approach to increase the value added in tradable-producing industries would be one way to foster growth. As illustrated by the hypothetical scenario in which the tradability index of the Southern periphery countries of the Euro Area was shifted to the German level, the growth-enhancing potential of a higher tradability of output is sizeable. These findings are in line with an unbalanced growth framework à la Baumol as long as productivity growth is higher in highly tradable industries than in less tradable industries.

## 8.8. Acknowledgement

The author would like to thank the participants of the 9th FIW Research conference, Vienna, for very useful comments and suggestions. The author is particularly indebted to Alexandra Bykova for very valuable research assistance.

## 8.9. References

BAUMOL, W.J., (1967). *Macroeconomics of Unbalanced Growth: The Anatomy of Urban Crisis,* American Economic Review, 57(3), pp. 415-426.

BENHABIB, J. & SPIEGEL, M. M. (1994). *The role of human capital in economic development. Evidence from aggregate cross-country data,* Journal of Monetary Economics, 34, 143-173.

BRADFORD, D.F. (1969). *Balance on Unbalanced Growth,* Zeitschrift für Nationalökonomie, 29, pp. 291-304.

BYKOVA, A., STÖLLINGER, R. (2017). *Tradability Index: A Comprehensive Measure for the Tradability of Output. Technical Paper on the wiiw Tradability Dataset,* wiiw Statistical Reports, No. 6, January 2017.

DE GREGORIO, J., GIOVANNINI, A., WOLF, H.C. (1994). *International Evidence on Tradables and Nontradables Inflation,* European Economic Review, 38, pp. 1225-1244.

FEENSTRA, R.C., INKLAAR, R., TIMMER, M.P (2015). *The Next Generation of the Penn World Table, American Economic Review,* 105(10), pp. 3150-3182.

GAULIER, G. AND V. VICARD (2012). *"Current account imbalances in the Euro Area: competitiveness or demand shock?",* Quarterly selection of articles – Bulletin de la Banque de France, 27, pp. 5–26.

HARVEY, M.C., (1998). *Ecarts de productivité et "maladie des coûts". Apports et limites du modèle de croissance déséquilibrée de William J. Baumol,* Revue Économique, 49(2), pp. 437-467.

HAUSMANN, R., HWANG, J., RODRIK, D. (2007). *What you export matters,* Journal of Economic Growth, 12(1), pp 1–25.

HAUSMANN, R., HIDALGO, C.A., BUSTOS, S., COSCIA, M., SIMOES, A., YILDIRIM, M.A. (2013). *The Atlas of Economic Complexity: Mapping Paths to Prosperity.* http://atlas.cid.harvard.edu/media/atlas/pdf/HarvardMIT_AtlasOfEconomicComplexity.pdf

HIDALGO C. A., HAUSMANN R. (2009). *The building blocks of economic complexity,* Proceedings of the National Academy of Sciences of the United States of America, 106(26), pp. 10570–10575.

JÄGER, K. (2016). EU KLEMS *Growth and Productivity Accounts 2016* release - Description of Methodology and General Notes, December 2016.

JOHNSON, R.C., NOGUERA, G., (2012). *Accounting for Intermediates: Production Sharing and Trade in Value Added,* Journal of International Economics, 86(2), 224-236.

LIN, J., CHANG, H.-J. (2009). *Should Industrial Policy in Developing Countries Conform to Comparative Advantage or Defy it?* A Debate Between Justin Lin and Ha-Joon Chang, Development Policy Review, 27 (5), pp. 483-502.

NELSON, R., PHELPS, E. (1966). *Investment in humans, technological diffusion, and economic growth,* American Economic Review: Papers and Proceedings, 51 (2), 69-75.

NORDHAUS, W.D. (2008). *Baumol's Diseases: A Macroeconomic Perspective,* B.E. Journal of Macroeconomics, 8(1), pp. 1935-1690

PENEDER, M. (2003). *Industrial structure and aggregate growth,* Structural Change and Economic Dynamics, 14, pp. 427-448.

RODRIK (2010). *"Growth after the Crisis", in: Spence, M., Leipziger, D. (eds.) Globalization and Growth - Implications for a Post-Crisis World: Commission on Growth and Development, Chapter 7)* Commission on Growth and Development. World Bank, pp. 125-150. https://openknowledge.worldbank.org/handle/10986/2440.

RODRIK, D. (2013). *Unconditional Convergence in Manufacturing,* Quarterly Journal of Economics, 128(1), pp. 165-204.

STÖLLINGER, R. (2017). *Tradability of Output and the Current Account: An Empirical Investigation for Europe,* wiiw Working Paper, No. 134, January.

SYRQUIN, M. (1988). *"Patterns of Structural Change", in: Chenery, H.B., Srinivasan, T.N. (eds),* Handbook of Development Economics, Amsterdam. North-Holland, pp. 203-273.

SZIRMAI, A., VERSPAGEN, B. (2015). *Manufacturing and economic growth in developing countries, 1950–2005,* Structural Change and Economic Dynamics, 34(C), pp. 46-59.

TIMMER, M.P., DIETZENBACHER, E., LOS, B., STEHRER, R., DE VRIES, G.J. (2015). *An Illustrated User Guide to the World Input–Output Database: the Case of Global Automotive Production,* Review of International Economics, 23, pp. 575–605, available for download at www.wiod.org/new_site/database/wiots.htm.

TIMMER, M.P., SZIRMAI, A. (2000). *Productivity growth in Asian manufacturing: the structural bonus hypothesis examined,* Structural Change and Economic Dynamics, 11, pp. 371-392.

## 8.10. Appendix 1: List of Countries

| Abbreviation | Country | Country Category |
|---|---|---|
| AL | Albania | Non-OECD |
| AU | Australia | OECD |
| AT | Austria | OECD |
| AZ | Azerbaijan | Non-OECD |
| BY | Belarus | Non-OECD |
| BE | Belgium | OECD |
| BR | Brazil | Non-OECD |
| BG | Bulgaria | Non-OECD |
| HR | Croatia | Non-OECD |
| CZ | Czech Republic | OECD |
| DK | Denmark | OECD |
| EE | Estonia | OECD |
| FI | Finland | OECD |
| FR | France | OECD |
| GE | Georgia | Non-OECD |
| DE | Germany | OECD |
| EL | Greece | OECD |
| HU | Hungary | OECD |
| IE | Ireland | OECD |
| IT | Italy | OECD |
| JP | Japan | OECD |
| KR | Korea | OECD |
| KZ | Kazakhstan | Non-OECD |
| LV | Latvia | OECD |
| LT | Lithuania | Non-OECD |
| MD | Moldova | Emerging |
| MX | Mexico | OECD |
| NL | Netherlands | Developed |
| NO | Norway | Developed |
| PL | Poland | Emerging |
| NZ | New Zealand | OECD |
| PT | Portugal | OECD |
| RO | Romania | Non-OECD |

| | | |
|---|---|---|
| RU | Russia | Non-OECD |
| SK | Slovakia | OECD |
| SI | Slovenia | OECD |
| ES | Spain | OECD |
| SE | Sweden | OECD |
| CH | Switzerland | OECD |
| TR | Turkey | OECD |
| UA | Ukraine | Non-OECD |
| UK | United Kingdom | OECD |
| US | United States | OECD |

## 8.11. Appendix 2: List of Sectors for the Calculation of the Tradability Index

| Number | Sector | NACE Rev. 1 | NACE Rev. 2 |
|---|---|---|---|
| 1 | Agriculture, hunting, and forestry + Fishing | A+B | A |
| 2 | Mining and quarrying | C | B |
| 3 | Manufacturing | D | C |
| 4 | Electricity, gas and water supply | E | D+E |
| 5 | Construction | F | F |
| 6 | Wholesale, retail trade, repair of motor vehicles, etc. | G | G |
| 7 | Hotels and restaurants | H | I |
| 8 | Transport, storage + Communication | I | H + J |
| 9 | Financial intermediation | J | K |
| 10 | Real estate, renting and business activities | K | L+M+N |
| 11 | Public administration, defence, compuls.soc.security | L | O |
| 12 | Education | M | P |
| 13 | Health and social work | N | Q |
| 14 | Other community, social and personal services + Private households with employed persons | O+P | R+S+T |

## Appendix 3: Methodology for Calculating Value Added Exports and the Tradability Scores

Deriving the tradability score requires the calculation of the value-added exports (VAX) at the industry-country level. This appendix illustrates the basic input-output methodology to calculate the VAX, including a 3-country, 2-sector example.

Following the trade in value-added concept in Johnson and Noguera (2012) and the expositions in Stehrer (2012), we require three components in order to calculate the value added exports. For any country *r*, these components are the value added requirements per unit of gross output, $v_i^r$; the Leontief inverse of the global input-output matrix, ***L***; and the final consumption vector, $c_i^r$. Both vectors as well as the Leontief inverse have an industry dimension $i$. The industry index is omitted in order to facilitate the exposition.

Country *r*'s value added coefficients are defined as $v_i^r = \frac{value\ added_r}{gross\ output_r}$. The value added coefficients are arranged in a diagonal matrix of dimension 1435 x 1 (41 countries x 35 industries). This matrix contains the value added coefficients of country *r* for all industries along the diagonals. The remaining entries of the matrix are zero because the interest here is with the value added created in country *r*.

The second element is the Leontief inverse of the global input-output matrix, $\boldsymbol{L} = (\boldsymbol{I} - \boldsymbol{A})^{-1}$ where $\boldsymbol{A}$ denotes the coefficient matrix. In the World Input-Output Database (WIOD) the coefficient matrix (and hence the Leontief matrix) is of dimension 1435 × 1435 which contains the technological input coefficients of country *r* in the diagonal elements and the technological input coefficients of country *r's* imports (from a column perspective) and exports (from a row perspective) in the off-diagonal elements.

The final building block is the global final consumption vector. This vector is also industry-specific and is of dimension 1435 × 1. Most importantly, for our purposes, final consumption must be split into separate blocks indication the origin of the consumed goods though within the elements in the column vector. As usual, each row is associated with one source of the final demand. The full final demand vector, $f_i^J$, in the 3-country, 2-sector case, with $m$ (for manufacturing) and $s$ (for services) indicating the sector, then has the following form:

$$f_i^J = \begin{pmatrix} f_m^{r,r} + f_m^{r,2} + f_m^{r,3} \\ f_s^{r,r} + f_s^{r,2} + f_s^{r,3} \\ f_m^{2,r} + f_m^{2,2} + f_m^{2,3} \\ f_s^{2,r} + f_s^{2,2} + f_s^{2,3} \\ f_m^{3,r} + f_m^{3,2} + f_m^{3,3} \\ f_s^{3,r} + f_s^{3,2} + f_s^{3,3} \end{pmatrix}$$

where the subscript $J$ indicates that the vector comprises the consumption of all countries $j \in J$. The typical element of this vector contains the final consumption from all possible sources. For example, the element $f_m^{r,3}$ captures the value of final goods that country 3 demands from the manufacturing sector in country $r$. Since the idea of value added exports is that they comprise only value added that is created in one country but absorbed in another, the final demand from country $r$ itself needs to be eliminated for the calculation of country $r$'s VAX. Therefore an adjusted final demand vector, $f_i^{j \neq r}$, is used in which country $r$'s final demand (e.g. the first column in the above matrix) is set to zero. Country $r$'s value added exports can then be calculated as

$$VAX_i^{r,*} = \boldsymbol{v}_i^r \cdot \boldsymbol{L} \cdot f_i^{j \neq r} \qquad (8)$$

where $VAX^{r,*}$ are the sector-specific value added exports of country $r$ to all partner countries.

To illustrate this, the detailed matrices in the three countries, 2-sector case, where country $r$ acts as the model countries are shown. Equation (8) then has the following form:

$$\begin{pmatrix} VAX_{m,*}^{r,*} \\ VAX_{s,*}^{r,*} \\ 0 \\ 0 \\ 0 \\ 0 \end{pmatrix} = \begin{pmatrix} v_m^r & 0 & 0 & 0 & 0 & 0 \\ 0 & v_s^r & 0 & 0 & 0 & 0 \\ 0 & 0 & 0 & 0 & 0 & 0 \\ 0 & 0 & 0 & 0 & 0 & 0 \\ 0 & 0 & 0 & 0 & 0 & 0 \\ 0 & 0 & 0 & 0 & 0 & 0 \end{pmatrix} \cdot \begin{pmatrix} l_{m,m}^{r,r} & l_{m,s}^{r,r} & l_{m,m}^{r,2} & l_{m,s}^{r,2} & l_{m,m}^{r,3} & l_{m,s}^{r,3} \\ l_{s,m}^{r,r} & l_{s,s}^{r,r} & l_{s,m}^{r,2} & l_{s,s}^{r,2} & l_{s,m}^{r,3} & l_{s,s}^{r,3} \\ l_{m,m}^{2,r} & l_{m,s}^{2,r} & l_{m,m}^{2,2} & l_{m,s}^{2,2} & l_{m,m}^{2,3} & l_{m,s}^{2,3} \\ l_{s,m}^{2,r} & l_{s,s}^{2,r} & l_{s,m}^{2,2} & l_{s,s}^{2,2} & l_{s,m}^{2,3} & l_{s,s}^{2,3} \\ l_{m,m}^{3,r} & l_{m,s}^{3,r} & l_{m,m}^{3,2} & l_{m,s}^{3,2} & l_{m,m}^{3,3} & l_{m,s}^{3,3} \\ l_{s,m}^{3,r} & l_{s,s}^{3,r} & l_{s,m}^{3,2} & l_{s,s}^{3,2} & l_{s,m}^{3,3} & s_{s,s}^{r,3} \end{pmatrix}$$

$$\cdot \begin{pmatrix} 0 + f_m^{r,2} + f_m^{r,3} \\ 0 + f_s^{r,2} + f_s^{r,3} \\ 0 + f_m^{2,2} + f_m^{2,3} \\ 0 + f_s^{2,2} + f_s^{2,3} \\ 0 + f_m^{3,2} + f_m^{3,3} \\ 0 + f_s^{3,2} + f_s^{3,3} \end{pmatrix}$$

The coefficients in the Leontief matrix represent the total direct and indirect input requirements of any country in order to produce one dollar worth of output for final demand. For example, the coefficient $l_{m,s}^{r,r}$ indicates the input requirement of country *r*'s services sector from country *r*'s manufacturing sector for producing one unit of output. Likewise, the coefficient $l_{m,m}^{r,3}$ indicates country *r*'s input requirement in the manufacturing sector supplied by country 3's manufacturing sector.

The resulting elements in this example, $VAX_{m,*}^{r,*}$ and $VAX_{s,*}^{r,*}$, are the total value added exports of country *r*'s manufacturing and services sectors, respectively, to all other sectors of all partner countries.

The VAX are not only calculated for country *r* but for all 40 countries plus the rest of the world. Hence, the final step needed to arrive at the global industry-level VAX is to sum up the VAX of all countries for each individual sector *i*. Dividing the global industry-specific VAX by the corresponding industry-specific value added yields the tradability score by sector. In that process, also the more detailed industry structure (35 industries) is aggregated to the 14 broad sectors on which the tradability index is based.

Chapter 9

# Are Fiscal Rules Really Omnipotent? The Case of the EU

István Benczes

## 9.1. Introduction

The European Economic and Monetary Union (EMU) has an unprecedented institutional set-up for several reasons. Never before in modern history – in times of peace – have countries surrendered their sovereignty on monetary policy. No regional integration has succeeded ever before in reaching such a high level of complexity, with a supranational monetary authority at the centre. And never before has monetary policy been given up without the simultaneous introduction of a federal system of spending and taxation. No one has ever debated the fact that the design of the EMU is unique. By now, however, more and more commentators claim that its design was flawed or even that it was a total failure by institutionalising an asymmetry in the conduct of economic policy.

On the positive side, the EMU project did revitalise the European integration process to a substantial degree. The euro became the symbol of how countries can *voluntarily* withdraw a part of their national sovereignty and delegate it to a supranational level, without fully giving up their sovereignty in economic policy – a phenomenon that was most welcomed by neofunctionalists. On the negative side, the unusual structure made the EMU and the whole EU vulnerable to external shocks. The global economic and financial crisis made it painfully overt how weak and fragile economic governance was in the European Union.[1]

---

[1] There are different definitions for economic governance. According to the most widely used interpretation by Dixit (2009:5), governance is defined as "the structure and functioning of the legal and social institutions that support economic activity and economic transactions by protecting property rights, enforcing contracts, and taking collective action to provide physical and organizational infrastructure". With regard to the EU, the European Parliament (2013) suggested the following

It was only in the autumn of 2008, right after the collapse of Lehmann Brothers, when proponents of the single currency had to admit that the EMU had fallen short on economic governance. With the European financial-cum-sovereign-debt-crisis, it has become clear that the original design of European economic governance was not feasible any longer (Benczes 2013). Until 2010, economic governance (mostly in the form of policy coordination) was mainly based on (mutual) consensus. From the adoption of the Maastricht Treaty onwards, the EU tried to widen the scope of economic coordination significantly. Coordination stretched through cooperation by exchange of information (e.g. the macroeconomic dialogue), the open method of coordination (by setting benchmarks and identifying best practices), and the delegation of policies (e.g. monetary policy or competition policy) (Thomas 2012). The (in)famous exception to this trend was the adoption of the Stability and Growth Pact, which called for binding rules and procedures. From the start of the Greek debt crisis, e.g., from late 2009 onwards, the EU has devoted, therefore, quite substantial attention to the reform of the economic governance of the Eurozone and the EU itself. The aim of these reforms was twofold: to work out a detailed framework and schedule for crisis management and resolution,[2] and to strengthen the prevention pillar of economic governance. While most scholarly studies addressed the former, this piece attempts to provide a critical reflection on the latter, the preventive arm of the new regime. Following the introduction, section two gives a short overview of the preventive part of the newly designed European architecture. Section three and four turn to the main element of the new regime, fiscal rules. Accordingly, the effectiveness of domestic fiscal rules will be analysed first, which will be then followed by contrasting the results with the main points of the fiscal compact, an intergovernmental treaty that was adopted in order to restore fiscal discipline EU-wide. Section five concludes.

---

instead: "the system of institutions and procedures established in view of achieving the European Union objectives in the economic area, namely the coordination of economic policies for the promotion of economic and social progress for EU peoples".

2 Europeans first managed to launch a three-pillar financial rescue programme, comprising the *European Financial Stabilisation Mechanism* (EFSM), the *European Financial Stability Facility* (EFSF) and the IMF's financial assistance. Since the three-pillar system was designed for a temporary period only, the EU decided to activate its own bail-out fund, the *European Stability Mechanism*, a permanent rescue facility, from 2013 onwards.

### 9.2. Six-pack, Two-pack...

Monetary policy was in fact delegated to the supranational level in the EMU, but fiscal policy has remained under the sole authority of governments with the aim of providing tools for stabilisation in case of asymmetric shocks. In order to preserve the stability of the whole euro-zone, in the original design of the EMU, worked out in detail in the Maastricht Treaty (1991) and the Stability and Growth Pact (1997 and reformed in 2005), member states were asked to regard their fiscal policies as a matter of common concern (Article 120, TFEU) and avoid excessive deficit (Article 126, TFEU). They were also provided guidance (in terms of broad economic policy guidelines) in order to enhance fiscal sustainability (Article 121, TFEU). Each year member states were requested to specify all the relevant measures needed to achieve the medium-term budgetary objectives (MTO) in their stability or convergence programmes.

Following the crisis, the EU initiated a revision of the Stability and Growth Pact with the definitive aim of giving teeth to the pact by ensuring compliance and enforceability. As opposed to the earlier reform of the Pact in 2005, this time member states were not reluctant to endorse a more rigorous monitoring and sanctioning mechanism. In the so-called "six-pack" and "two-pack" legislations, enforceability has become the main objective; thus, sanctions would automatically be imposed on countries which violated the new fiscal rules. Moreover, the EU went beyond fiscal policy and called for actions in the fields of macroeconomic imbalances, too, especially in case of a deterioration in the external balance and the loss of competitiveness of member states.

One of the most obvious results of the reform was that fiscal rules have become stronger than ever. Instead of abandoning them and moving towards a fiscal union, the EU clearly insisted on the usefulness of fiscal rules as one of the main devices in creating and maintaining fiscal discipline in the EU. The European Commission, in fact, claimed that domestic fiscal rules should have become an indispensable part of the new economic governance structure of the Economic and Monetary Union as early as 2010 (European Commission 2010). Accordingly, the six-pack was created with two major objectives in mind. First, it aimed at strengthening the preventive and corrective arms of the Stability Pact in order to achieve long-term sustainability of public finances. Second, by creating a totally new mechanism, it aimed at reducing macroeconomic imbalances and enhancing competitiveness by enacting both preventive and corrective measures beyond the realm of public finances.

In more concrete terms, the excessive deficit procedure (EDP) was modified in order to adopt stricter rules on the one hand and to improve enforcement on the other hand. Fiscal sustainability was given an operationalised meaning by enforcing strict debt rules in the future. More importantly, following the recommendation of the Commission, a decision to impose sanctions on the countries violating the new regulations was to be adopted by the Council unless a qualified majority of member states voted against it – the so-called reverse qualified majority voting procedure. In case of non-compliance, a non-interest-bearing deposit would be converted into a fine. The fine increases as a member state neglects the recommendations yet again.

In addition, the six-pack also called for actions in order to reduce macroeconomic imbalances and promote competitiveness. One of the most often cited weaknesses of the European Union has been the lack of competitiveness of some of its member states. Even worse, relative competitiveness did not recover in the worst-performing countries as a response to the single market or the single currency; instead, the gap between good performers and bad performers widened significantly in the last two decades or so. Competitiveness is a serious issue, however, not just because it is the ultimate driver for economic growth and development (and as such for the catching up the process at the periphery), but also because it can be responsible for major macroeconomic imbalances within the E(M)U. Therefore, a completely new surveillance and enforcement mechanism was set up in order for the EU to be able to identify and correct macroeconomic deteriorations at the earliest phase possible.[3]

Most importantly, similarly to the EDP, a new excessive imbalance procedure (EIP) has been created, based on Article 121(6) of the TFEU. The EIP allows the Commission and the Council to adopt preventive recommendations under Article 121.2 of the TFEU at a relatively early stage in order to prevent the macroeconomic imbalance to fully develop. Member states are obliged to submit a corrective action plan, indicating the roadmap and deadlines for implementing the corrective measures. Non-compliance

[3] Its main elements are the following: an early warning system has been launched in the form of a scoreboard, which brings together a large number of macroeconomic indicators. With the help of the scoreboard, the EU wants to engage in in-depth studies in order to identify the signs for imbalances in member states. Importantly, the new regulation makes it possible for the Commission to pay a visit together with the ECB to the troubled nation and to conduct additional on-the-spot investigations.

can also be penalised by a fine. An interest-bearing deposit is expected to be imposed on the member state in case of one non-compliance. After, however, a second compliance failure, this interest-bearing deposit can be converted into a fine (up to 0.1% of GDP). Sanctions can also be imposed for failing twice to submit a sufficient corrective action plan. The EIP adopts the reverse qualified majority voting in order to speed up the procedure and to give teeth to enforcement.

The two-pack went even further than the six-pack. The Treaty on the Stability, Cooperation and Governance of the EMU (TSCG), or as more commonly known the "fiscal compact", aimed at strengthening the economic pillar of the EMU by adopting tougher fiscal rules than ever before (Article 1 TSCG). It is strict in the sense that "the budgetary position of the general government of the Contracting Parties shall be balanced or in surplus" (Article 3 (1a) of TSCG). Similarly to the earlier regulations, the annual deficit cannot be higher than 3 percent, but the so-called structural deficit should not exceed 0.5 per cent of the GDP (Article 3 (2a) TSCG).[4] Additionally, if the general government debt ratio exceeds 60 percent, the contracting party has to achieve an annual decline of one-twentieth of the part that exceeds the 60 percent limit (see also the Six-pack legislations).

In principle, the new rules can perform rather well in terms of effectiveness, since they are more or less well-defined, strictly binding and automatically enforceable – a three-point-benchmark that was set up by the ECB (2013). What really can add teeth to the fiscal compact is the conditionality of getting access to financial rescue. The EU's own rescue fund, the European Stability Mechanism (ESM), can be tapped by troubled countries only if the TSCG is fully respected.

The treaty also required member countries to transpose the balanced budget rules into their national law "through provisions of binding force and permanent character, preferably constitutional, or otherwise guaranteed to be fully respected and adhered to throughout the national budgetary process" (Article 3 (2) TSCG).

---

4 The structural balance adjusted for the cyclical component and the one-off and temporary measures.

## 9.3. Are Fiscal Rules Effective Enough?

As it has been shown in the previous section, a strong belief in the usefulness of fiscal rules was not washed away by the crisis; in fact, this conviction was further strengthened by the deteriorated public finance performances of some member states. By now, fiscal rules have become the major disciplining forces in the EU. The fiscal compact has made it evident that the EU wants to circumvent another crisis with the help of strict and all-encompassing fiscal rules. But are the rules really so effective? Can they become the cure-all in the post-crisis era of the EU?

In our earlier study (Benczes 2014), a comprehensive data set was compiled on domestic fiscal rules that were used by EU nations during the pre-crisis period (Croatia was not part of the analysis due to the unavailability of data). It was shown that, except for Greece, each member state had been eager to create its own fiscal responsibility framework by establishing new rules or even a new fiscal council.

The data set concentrated on the pre-crisis period, e.g. from 1990 to 2007. The following sources were used for the data compilation: the European Commission's fiscal rules data collection, the European Commission's AMECO database, and the OECD's country data sets. For the purpose of the analysis, only the most typical fiscal rules were selected, such as debt rules, balanced budget rules, and expenditure rules. Rules targeted the national/federal level, the regional/state level and the social security system. With the data at hand, the following question was put forward: how did the adoption of a specific fiscal rule (or a set of rules) in year "t" affect the debt dynamics of EU countries? More specifically, how did the debt-to-GDP ratio react to the adoption of rules in the first year (t+1) and in the third year (t+3)?

Even a simple stylised facts analysis can reveal that fiscal rules do matter. Table 9.1 displays the debt dynamics of the EU27 on average. By adopting a fiscal rule, EU countries managed to reduce the debt-to-GDP ratio of their GDP by 0.8% on average by year t+1, when a new rule was adopted. The three-year-long cumulative effect was even stronger, 3.9%. Nevertheless, if these results are put into a wider context, it can be shown that the EU27 embarked on a rather substantial consolidation process in the years under investigation independently from the fact whether a rule was adopted or not: the debt ratio dropped by 0.5 percentage point every year (see the data on the entire population in Table 9.1). By and large, it can be claimed that EU countries were determined to downsize their debt mountains throughout the nineties and the early years of the new millennium – rules, though, could make a difference in terms of pace and the magnitude of reduction.

**Table 9.1 Debt dynamics in the EU27**

| | Annual change in the debt-to-GDP ratio | Cumulative change (3 years) in the debt-to-GDP ratio |
|---|---|---|
| A rule (or set of rules) was adopted n=33 | -0.8 (3.3) | -3.9 (6.7) |
| The whole period N=364 | -0.5 (4.0) | -1.4 (9.7) |

**Source**: own construction.

**Notes**: Changes are as percent of the GDP. Standard deviation in brackets.

The data set allows us to conduct a simple regression analysis (using OLS), so the effectiveness of domestic fiscal rules can be tested against evidence. Following Roubini and Sachs (1989) and Hallerberg, Strauch and von Hagen (2007) in particular, the change in public debt (as percent of the GDP) as the dependent variable (from year t to year t+1) was measured against two groups of explanatory variables: institutional variables, that is, fiscal rule(s) in our case, and control variables.[5] Accordingly, the regression model had the following specification:

$$\Delta(\text{Debt-to-GDP ratio})_{i,t+1} = {}_{0} + {}_{1}(FR)_{i,t} + {}_{2}(CAPB)_{i,t} + {}_{3}(OG)_{i,t} + {}_{4}(LTR)_{i,t} + {}_{5}(MT)_{i,t} \; {}_{i,t} \qquad (1)$$

Two different fiscal rule (FR) variables were used in our analysis. First, a so-called rule dummy was introduced in order to check if adopting a fiscal rule

[5] The analysis was redone by checking the effects of the independent variables on the debt ratio in year t+3, too. The effects were the same, so only the results of the first test are discussed in length.

(or a set of fiscal rules) in year t could have any impact on the first difference of public debt ratio. In the second round, a composite index, measuring the 'strength' of the adopted fiscal rule(s) was used in order to test the relevance of rules on the change of public debt. The index of strength, designed by the European Commission, was developed with the aim of capturing a wide array of qualitative and quantitative aspects of fiscal rules, including their coverage, format, enforceability, etc. Our hypothesis was that both measures could have a negative impact on the change of the debt-to-GDP ratio, as the imposition of rules on formerly discretionary fiscal policy might have induced discipline in terms of reduced debt ratios.

The control variables were comprised of basically four different factors:

1. the cyclically adjusted primary balance (CAPB), assuming that any recovery in CAPB implied a drop in the debt-to-GDP ratio;
2. output gap (OG), assuming that any increase in the output gap, the difference between the actual GDP growth rate and the potential growth rate, could result in a decline in the debt ratio;
3. long-term interest rates (LTR), proxied by 10-year government bond yields, which were expected to have a positive effect on debt dynamics (lower rates induced lower debt ratio); and last but not least
4. a so-called Maastricht dummy (MT), which was used for segmenting the period under investigation into two. If a rule was adopted between 1990 and 1997, the dummy variable had the value of 1, otherwise 0. The Maastricht dummy was supposed to test the relevance of timing. The first eleven countries to become EMU members were selected in 1998, that is, the Maastricht dummy tried to capture political commitment of incumbents to exert fiscal discipline as a condition for EMU membership.

Results are reported in Table 9.2.

**Table 9.2 Results of the regression analysis (OLS)**

| Variables | (1) | (2) | (3) | (4) | (5) |
|---|---|---|---|---|---|
| Constant | -0.25<br>(0.29) | -0.17<br>(0.26) | -1.75**<br>(0.52) | -1.67**<br>(0.51) | -1.44**<br>(0.51) |
| Rule dummy | -0.57<br>(0.87) | | 0.46<br>(0.73) | 0.58<br>(0.72) | |
| Rule index | | -1.1**<br>(0.25) | | | -0.32<br>(1.40) |

| | | | | | |
|---|---|---|---|---|---|
| CAPB | | | -0.74** (0.10) | -0.76** (0.09) | -0.72** (0.10) |
| Long-term interest rates | | | 0.72** (0.11) | 0.89** (0.13) | 0.84** (0.13) |
| Output gap | | | -0.05 (0.14) | -0.21 (0.15) | -0.21 (0.15) |
| Maastricht dummy | | | | -1.79** (0.62) | -1.84** (0.62) |
| $R^2$ | 0.002 | 0.07 | 0.32 | 0.34 | 0.35 |

**Source**: own calculations using the data set of Benczes (2014).

Contrary to our expectations, the rule dummy (introducing a fiscal rule or a set of fiscal rules in a given year) did not have any impact on the change in the debt ratio. It explained only 0.2% of the variance, that is, nothing at all; in fact, it even had the wrong sign in some instances. Fortunately, the rule index, measuring the strength of a rule, did show the correct (negative) sign and had a statistically significant effect at a 5% level instead of other (control) variables. That is, the stronger a fiscal rule was, the more substantial the reduction of public debt was next year. Nevertheless, $R^2$ remained still negligible, at only 7%. Moreover, as soon as control variables were plugged into our baseline model, the rule index did not deliver the expected effect any longer (the sign was at least still the correct one).

It is not surprising that any recovery in the cyclically adjusted primary balance evoked a statistically significant drop in the debt ratio: a one per cent decline in CAPB revoked an at least 0.72 percentage point decline in the debt ratio. Importantly, since CAPB captures non-cyclical changes in primary balance, it can essentially grasp and measure the discretionary impulses initiated by incumbents on public spending and/or on taxes. Also, CAPB is calculated without interest payments; it concentrates, therefore, on politically sensitive budget items. As a corollary, CAPB may also mirror the political will of governments to embark on real adjustments in the general government.

As far as the long-term yields on government bonds are concerned, the analysis reiterated the general conviction: lower rates make financing the state (and its debt in particular) cheaper. A drop in interest rates can quite significantly reduce the debt ratio as well: a 100 basis point reduction generates a drop of 0.8-0.9 percentage points in the debt ratio. The two effects, e.g., recovery in CAPB and lower interest rates, can, of course, mutually reinforce each other. Any convincing improvement in the CAPB puts downward pressure on long-term yields as well, making interest payments, normally a substantial part of annual budgetary spending and headline deficit, to decline. (On this combined effect, see especially Feldstein 1982).

On the other hand, while the output gap had the right sign in our analysis, it did not deliver statistically significant reactions on public debt. The message is quite straightforward: no government can outgrow its public debt by artificially boosting aggregate demand in order to have actual growth exceed the potential growth rate. Success in terms of reduced public debt can be assured only if the cabinet is dedicated to measures downsizing deficit *over* the cycle. This finding simply upholds the significance of political commitment to reduce the primary deficit.

The single most surprising result that our OLS analysis has revealed was, nevertheless, the statistically significant effect of timing itself. If a fiscal rule was adopted in the years of the run-up to the EMU, e.g., between 1990 and 1997, it was definitely followed by a substantial drop in the debt-to-GDP ratio (the size being rather substantial: 1.8% of the GDP). The relevance of the Maastricht dummy reiterates the suspicion that only dedicated governments can make a difference in terms of fiscal discipline. It surely does not mean that rules adopted after 1997 could not exert any impact on fiscal performance; the observations, instead, highlight that political will is probably a more determining factor in success than anything else. One of the manifestations of political determinacy could be the adoption of fiscal rules themselves, as this action is possibly the most straightforward and transparent way to send a signal to the market about the willingness and capability of incumbents to initiate lasting fiscal reforms.

All in all, fiscal rules can have an impact on fiscal performance, but they normally exert such an effect only indirectly. Quantifying the impact of rules is, therefore, not an easy and unambiguous endeavour. What matters in case of the introduction of rules is the wider economic and political context. From this perspective, the fiscal compact may perform rather weakly in the future. It does endow rules with strength but remains largely indebted with the clarification of the circumstances (context). It is still up to the individual countries whether they follow their rules or not.

Fortunately, there is unambiguous evidence for the willingness of crisis-hit economies to engage in the adoption of new sets of rules enshrined in the national constitution or other, higher level law. The Spanish fiscal rules were undeniably the most rigorous ones, accepted well before the crisis. Nevertheless, the country decided to adopt an even stricter set of rules in 2011-12 (by adopting a complex set of balanced budget rule, debt rule, and expenditure rule). Fiscal rules now cover all layers of the general government from the central government to local authorities. Its strength index is the highest in the whole EU28. One of the specialties of the new rules is that if the social security system faced a deficit, the central government should cut its own budget by the same amount without hesitation and it would also have to adopt a reform plan to remedy the deterioration in the social security system. Even the 60 percent debt limit has been cut into three to signal the determinacy of the Spanish to provide transparency and accountability of each of the three levels of the government. The central government is now limited to 44% (of the GDP), the regions are allowed to accumulate a total of 13%, while local governments cannot have more than 3%. The new rules have been enshrined in the Spanish constitution, specifying also the mechanism for sanctioning. Additionally, a new and independent fiscal council was created in 2013.

Ireland managed to implement the most successful consolidation package amongst the programme countries in the last couple of years. Its headline deficit fell from 23.3% in 2010 to just below 3% in 2015. Its public debt ratio, which jumped by ca. 100 per cent points in just 3 years thanks to the cleaning off of its banks' balance sheets, has declined to 110% by now. The recovery was due to the improvement in the international environment, along with substantial cuts in public expenditures (IMF 2015). In line with the fiscal compact, the country enacted first a fiscal responsibility act inclusive of new fiscal rules and a new fiscal council in 2012; additionally, a new medium-term fiscal budgeting framework was adopted (Kopits 2014).

Italy introduced its own strict rules, enshrined in the constitution in 2012, just before the fiscal compact came into force. Besides the pact's debt and deficit criteria, Italy also enacted a new expenditure rule. For the regional and local authorities, the Italians hammered out a golden rule as well (allowing to run a deficit in case of investment expenditures only). Obedience to the rules is safeguarded by a new fiscal council.

Greece was the only old member state which did not have any national fiscal rule before the crisis. One of the conditionalities of the 2010 rescue package was the introduction of fiscal rules on the national level, but Greece was not in a hurry to meet the request. It did ratify the fiscal compact in May 2012, but it did not show too much interest in elaborating on how the country wanted to make the compact a full-fledged success. In fact, there was even no debate in the parliament in Athens about the pact or the rules themselves (Marketou, 2015), strongly questioning the effectiveness of the Greek rules. On the other hand, Portugal managed to adopt new rules in accordance with the fiscal compact, but it did not succeed to ensure wide political support for the new incentives. The constitutional amendment would have required a solid two-thirds majority in the parliament, but the cabinet failed to convince the opposition to join.

## 9.4. Evaluating the Fiscal Compact

It is often claimed that the fiscal compact is simply a reinforcement of existing rules; it only restates the ones adopted by the six-pack – enough to mention the balanced budget rule, the focus on debt sustainability or the escape clauses attached to the treaty (ECB 2012). Others, however, argue that because the new treaty is much tougher than the previous EU framework, the current rules will arrange themselves in a clear hierarchy. Supremacy will be given to the new structural balance rule of the compact, and the EU rules (the Lisbon Treaty and the six-pack in particular) would provide a sort of safety net to the balanced budget rule (Blizkovsky 2012, Verhelst 2012).

Originally, the EU was built around a "dual constitution, supranational in the single market's policies and intergovernmental in (among others) economic and financial policies" Fabbrini 2013: 1003). Accordingly, policies related to the single market have been conducted with the robust involvement of supranational institutions such as the European Commission and the Court of Justice of the European Union. In the case of financial and economic policies, however, an intergovernmental mentality has prevailed since the signing of the Maastricht Treaty. In consequence, the Council and the European Council, in particular, have been solidly involved in both crisis management and crisis prevention, e.g., laying down the foundations of the future economic governance of the EU. The fiscal compact is, in fact, the result of such intergovernmental mentality, supported especially by Germany.

The new intergovernmental treaty wanted to break away with the past for once and for all. The Lisbon Treaty, along with the Stability and Growth Pact, were evidently lacking real rigour and sanctioning. When the foundations of the EMU were laid down in the early nineties, no actor involved in the negotiations wanted to restrict sovereignty beyond the surrendering of monetary policy. The Maastricht Treaty, back in 1992, was a sort of compromise, therefore. The Court of Justice of the EU, for instance, did not have a role at all in the EDP. Even the role of the Commission was substantially limited in the process (TFEU 126). The consequence was the total negligence of the Stability Pact as early as 2003. The fiscal compact, therefore, intended to sign the end of that particular era. It called for the active and effective involvement of both the European Commission and the

Court of Justice.[6] Strangely enough, it was an intergovernmental treaty which nevertheless managed to restore the authority of these two supranational institutions in the field of economic policies.

It has been noticed long ago in the scholarly works of political economy that rational politicians are reluctant to delegate authority over issues which can redistribute rents to their constituencies (for instance see Drazen 2000). Since direct access to distributional resources makes the government capable of organising a winning coalition in election times, no rational incumbent has the incentive to weaken its own sovereignty. Alesina and Tabellini (2007) have demonstrated that politicians delegate only those tasks to bureaucrats and (supranational) institutions which require technical knowledge on the hand and provide little direct benefit to incumbents on the other hand. Monetary policy has become an ideal policy area for delegation since it assumes special skills and it is difficult to communicate its direct benefits. The situation is rather different, however, with regard to fiscal policy: both taxation and spending can provide ample room for politically motivated actions, which are easy to target and communicate.

While European politicians agreed on the establishing of an independent central bank, they have remained very reluctant to give up national authority over fiscal policy. Member states have not shown too much interest in authorising the Commission to act on behalf of member states in times of an economic crisis, either. Heads of states and governments have anxiously tried to keep their hands on every single detail of crisis management, thereby reflecting a strong inclination toward intergovernmentalism. Though the fiscal compact is, in fact, an intergovernmental treaty, it did make a strong leap forward to a more supranational supervision of economic policies of member states. The compact is about acknowledging that neither the ECOFIN nor the European Council, possesses the capacity and skills to enforce compliance with fiscal rules. In turn, the preamble of the treaty calls for the integration of the compact into EU legislation as soon as possible.

---

[6] According to Article 8 of the Treaty on Stability, Coordination and Governance of the EMU, any member state can take another contracting party to the Court of Justice of the European Union if the latter happened to ignore the claim of transposing the balanced budget rule along with the correction mechanism into national law, possibly into the constitution. The decision of the Court of Justice is binding. The Court may impose a penalty on the non-complying country which shall not exceed 0.1 per cent of GDP.

Besides the involvement of able supranational authorities, the fiscal compact also wanted the signatory parties to commit themselves to the new regime as firmly as possible. The fiscal compact required countries to introduce the new fiscal rules into domestic law "through provisions of binding force and permanent character, preferably constitutional, or otherwise guaranteed to be fully respected and adhered to throughout the national budgetary process" (Article 3 (2) TSCG). Since one of the major shortcomings of the Stability Pact and its rules was the lack of enforcement, the fiscal compact made it compulsory for countries to enshrine domestic fiscal rules in national law, possibly in the constitution or as basic law. However, some of the most recent studies on fiscal unions (see especially Bordo et al. 2011, and Henning and Kessler 2012) have shown that successful fiscal rules cannot be imposed on member countries from above. The firm ownership of fiscal rules is a precondition for effectiveness.

The single most important problem with the fiscal compact could be though the fact that the crisis itself was not triggered by the lack of discipline of incumbents. It is well-known by now that except for Greece, EU countries did refrain from fiscal laxity before the crisis; they did not accumulate huge deficits or debts. Ireland had a debt-to-GDP ratio less than half of that of the 60% limit. But Spain and Portugal also managed to keep their debt dynamics within constraints. Fiscal deficits in these countries jumped to unlikely high levels only as a consequence of cleaning off commercial banks' balance sheets. The contagious effect of the banking crisis was transmitted onto the sovereigns, ending up in public debt crisis. De Grauwe (2013) referred to the intimate relationship between banks and sovereigns as "the deadly embrace".

Bailing out banks was officially left to the national government after the decision of the European Council in October 2008, just one month after the collapse of Lehmann Brothers. However, the banking sector had grown incredibly large, thanks to the success of the single market project. At the extreme, total banking assets were eight times that of the GDP in Ireland. The ratio was four in Austria and France, three in Spain and two and a half in Portugal (ECB 2014.) Recapitalising the banks meant a huge burden on taxpayers in the crisis-hit economies. Consequently, the debt-to-GDP ratio was elevated by ca. 100% of the GDP in Ireland. What is now called as the European debt crisis, therefore, emerged not as a result of the mismanagement of public finances. It was an unintended consequence of tackling the first wave of the 2008 global *financial* crisis. It was the private sector, and not the public sector, which triggered the crisis. Consequently, it is highly unlikely that a treaty like the fiscal compact could have prevented the eruption of the crisis of 2008. Since the roots of the crisis stemmed not from the public sector, a fiscal compact could not provide shelter from skyrocketing deficit and debt ratios.

It is always true in an open economy that

$$(X\text{–}M) = (S\text{–}I) + (T\text{–}G) \qquad (2)$$

where X stands for export, M is an import, S and I are the savings and investment of the private sector, whereas *T* denotes taxes and *G* governmental spending.

Equation (2) demonstrates that the external balance can deteriorate even if the public sector is in the balance (T=G). Investment exceeding savings culminates in trade deficit – as was the case in countries at the periphery. It all happened with the active involvement of the banking sector which *nomen est omen* was responsible for financial intermediation on the single market. It is thus not surprising that the six-pack enacted a new regulation on the establishment of macroeconomic imbalance procedure.

According to equation (2), if both the external position and the general government are in the balance (or close to balance), the private sector will be in a balanced position too, and no domestic savings would be exceeded by private investments. But is it reasonable to assume that both the public and the private sectors are in balanced positions at the same time? In federal states (or in a common currency union) it is not rare at all that certain regions (states) have very different positions due to both cyclical and structural factors, the latter including economic development, competitiveness, etc. In turn, the EMU can either accept that disequilibrium cannot be prevented to emerge and creates a permanent transfer mechanism in order to reduce the likeliness of the occurrence of a crisis or institutionalise such mechanisms that can guarantee the balanced position of each of the three parts of equation (2). In the current circumstances, the fiscal compact can be successful only if it is supplemented by another pact that focuses on the stability of the private sector. Mody (2013) for instance urges the adoption of a banking and a competitiveness pact besides the fiscal compact.

## 9.5. Conclusion

The adoption of tough new rules occurred in 2012, at the bottom of the second cycle of the crisis. Evidently, the adoption of the fiscal compact was supposed to severely contain the fiscal space of national governments, galvanise cooperation indirectly in terms of economic policies, and ensure the stability of the euro-zone.

Nevertheless, as most of the euro-zone countries were still under excessive deficit procedure when signing the compact, commentators were afraid that European countries would not be able to find their way back to solid growth and increased employment amidst tough conditions imposed on member states by Germany. However, as the current chapter demonstrated, the recovery from the crisis should induce countries to implement economic policies which not simply stop further deficit financing and debt accumulation, but also restore the long-term competitiveness and sustainability of the crisis-hit countries.

According to the fiscal compact, fiscal rules will play a significant role in the exit process from the crisis by re-establishing fiscal discipline and putting an end to further debt accumulation. As it has been shown in this chapter, fiscal rules may indeed contribute to the creation and maintenance of fiscal discipline, but the commitment of national governments to fiscal sustainability is probably even more important than the rules themselves. Just as the Maastricht process throughout the nineties (e.g., the qualification for euro-zone membership) helped politicians to demonstrate their willingness to refrain from unnecessary and destabilising discretionary deficit financing, the current financial and economic crisis might have provided another window of opportunity for troubled countries to engage in comprehensive reforms of their general budget and also their private sector.

## 9.6. References

Alesina, Alberto, and Guido Tabellini. 2007. "Bureaucrats or Politicians? Part I: A Single Policy Task." American Economic Review, 97(1): 169-179.

Benczes István (2013). No exit, no bail-out, no default... So what's next? In: Lubor Lacina, Peter Rozmahel, Antonin Rusek (eds.) Political economy of eurozone crisis: Reforms and their limits. Bucovice: Martin Stríz Publishing, 142-164.

Benczes István (2014). The fiscal compact and national ownership. Romanian Journal of Political Science 14(1), 87-115.

Blizkovsky, Peter (2012). Does the golden rule translate into a golden EU economic governance? Lee Kuan Yew School of Public Policy, Policy Brief Series No. 7.

Bordo, Michael, Markiewicz, Agnieszka, Jonung, Lars (2011). A fiscal union for the euro: Some lessons from history. NBER Working Paper Series, No. 17380.

De Grauwe, Paul (2013). Design failures in the eurozone: Can they be fixed? Europe in question. LSE Discussion Paper Series No. 57.

Dixit, S. (1995). Governance. In: S. N. Durlauf and L. E. Blume, The New Palgrave Dictionary of Economics, Palgrave Macmillan.

Drazen, Allen (2000). Political economy in macroeconomics. Princeton, N. J.: Princeton University Press.

ECB (2012). Montly bulletin, May. Frankfurt: ECB, 79-93.

ECB (2014). Statistic pocket book. Franfurt: ECB.

European Commission (2010). A new EU economic governance – a comprehensive Commission package of proposals. Brussels, 29 September 2010.

Fabbrini, Sergio (2013). Intergovernmentalism and its limits: Assessing the European Union's answers to the euro crisis. Comparative Political Studies, 46(9), 1003–1029.

Feldstein, Martin (1982). Government deficits and aggregate demand. Journal of Monetary Economics 9 (1), 1-20.

Hallerberg, M. – Strauch, R. –Hagen, von J. (2007). The design of fiscal rules and forms of governance in European Union countries. European Journal of Political Economy 23 (2), 338–359.

Henning, Randall, Kessler, Martin (2012). Fiscal federalism: US history for architects of Europe's fiscal union. Peterson Institute for International Economics, Working Paper No. 12–1.

IMF (2015). Ireland. Country Report, No. 15/77., Washington D.C.

Kopits, George (2014). Ireland's fiscal framework: Options for the future. The Economic and Social Review, 45(1), 135–158.

Marketou, Afroditi (2015). Constitutional change through euro crisis law: Greece. European University Institute.

Mody, Ahoka (2013). A Schuman compact for the Euro Area. Bruegel Essay and Lecture Series, Brussels: Bruegel Institute.

Roubini, N. – Sachs, J. (1989). Political and economic determinants of budget deficits in the industrial democracies. European Economic Review 33 (5), 903-933.

Thomas, G. (2012). The sovereign debt crisis: The EU's comprehensive response. Lunchtime conference, Luxembourg, 25 September.

Verhelst, Stijn (2012). How EU fiscal norms will become a safety net for the failure of national golden rules? European Policy Brief, No. 6.

Chapter 10

# Reforming the Eurozone: at Mercy of Politics

Zdenek Kudrna

## 10.1. Introduction

The Eurozone is currently stable, its economy is growing at a modest pace and unemployment is gradually decreasing to pre-crisis levels. However, this stability masks important differences among Eurozone countries as well as continued fragility caused by the incomplete institutional architecture of the single currency area. The unorthodox policies of the European Central Bank (ECB) underpin the stability, but they are insufficient for the long-term. Consequently, the Eurozone needs to adopt and implement additional reforms that ought to be complemented by structural reforms in the member states, especially those most impacted by the Euro crisis. Until the completion of such reforms, there remains a considerable risk that any major unexpected or unintended event derails the tentative stability and brings the Euro crisis back to the forefront.

There is no shortage of ideas for economic reforms necessary for completing the Eurozone architecture. The leaders of the European Union have presented a reform blueprint (Juncker et al. 2015) – so-called Five presidents' report – and there are plenty of recommendations from academic economists as well as analysts from international organizations. However, what is missing are the political compromises that would enable the EU and Eurozone member states to adopt necessary reforms. Hence, this chapter outlines three scenarios that may enable or hamper such reforms[1] and suggests some low-probability-high-impact factors (so called swans) that could catalyze them.

[1] This chapter is based on the keynote lecture delivered at the Mendel University economic conference on March 31, 2016 in Brno. The purpose of the lecture was to introduce broader political economy context before the more technical discussion of economic reforms in the Eurozone. The text has been updated to correspond to the state of affairs in early 2017.

The chapter is structured as follows. The next section argues that the most succinct way of thinking about Eurozone reforms is a political–economy game between the creditor and debtor member states that is taking place under uncertainty. The third section discusses the dominant scenario today – the muddling through – as well as its two most likely alternatives that depend on shifts of major political constraints. The subsequent section outlines several swans that can trigger any of the scenarios or some kind of cataclysmic event. The conclusion maintains that gradual and minimalist muddling through remains the most likely scenario unless some kind of external shock overcomes prevailing political constraints.

## 10.2. The Reform Agenda and Reform Scenarios

The cacophony of EMU reform proposals ranges from official blueprints (Juncker et al. 2015, Euroepan Commission 2012), through synthetic proposals (such as Enderlein et al. 2012, Stiglitz 2016) to a myriad of partial solutions and fixes that are also discussed in other chapters of this volume. There is also a widespread agreement on the broad contours of the necessary reforms, although proposals differ widely in terms of technical designs and details. The official EU documents summarize the reform agenda under the headings of economic, financial, fiscal and political unions.

The economic union focuses on measures that make national economies competitive within the monetary union. The flagship ideas include the introduction of Competitiveness Boards and other means of assessments and comparisons of performance and policy alternatives. The point is to apply the peer-pressure to induce more reforms and enhance the compliance with policy commitments, by embedding them into the governance framework of the European Semester. The economic union agenda also includes deepening of the single market in specific segments such as energy or digital services. Such consolidation of single market should support the real exchange rate channel for convergence and stability within the monetary union (see Enderlein et al. 2012).

The financial union consists of completing the banking union as well as making progress towards the Capital Markets Union. The former remains incomplete due to the absence of the European Deposit Insurance Scheme and unresolved issue of fiscal backing for the Single Resolution Fund. The Capital Markets Union is a relatively modest proposal of 33 legislative and analytic initiatives aimed at improving the financial market integration on a cross-border basis (see Kudrna 2016a).

The aim of the fiscal union is to stabilize European public finances and ensure their long-term sustainability. The Commission is proposing an independent European Fiscal Board that should act as an advisory body for the Eurozone economic coordination and monitoring. There is also a long list of various mechanisms for fiscal stabilization, ranging from some form of common unemployment insurance, through cyclical adjustment funds, to various schemes introducing Eurobills, Eurobonds, Eurobudget or Eurotreasury. Since all these measures imply some sharing of fiscal risks and resources that impinge on the budgetary sovereignty of member states, they are highly controversial.

The political union is supposed to reduce the democratic deficit that is likely to be deepened by the implementation of the above proposals. The Eurozone needs to strengthen the democratic accountability and legitimacy of its economic, financial and fiscal policies, not least to counter the growing Eurosceptic sentiments in all member states. The dominant ideas in this domain center on increasing the role of the European Parliament as well as national parliaments in economic policy coordination and reforms. The Commission is also proposing a unified representation of the Eurozone in international financial institutions such as the IMF.

**Figure 10.1 GDP growth averages**

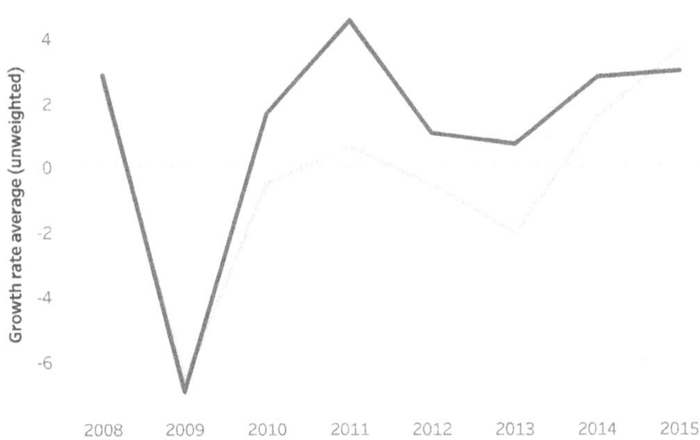


**Source**: Author's calculations based on Eurostat data. Note: Darker line depicts the "Northern" group and lighter one the "Southern" group.

The key challenge for the Eurozone is to identify those policy proposals that are politically feasible. The literature on the negotiations that have delivered recent EMU reforms such as the European Stability Mechanism (Schimmelfennig, 2014), Fiscal Compact (Tsebelis and Hahm, 2014; Bauer and Becker, 2014) or banking union (De Rynck, 2015, Howarth and Quaglia, 2013) indicates that political compromises can be found. At the same time, the Euro crisis clearly deepened political cleavages among member states. Typically, there are creditor economies such as Germany, Netherlands or Austria – generally referred to as "Northern" member states – on one side and the "Southern" states most impacted by the Euro crisis on the other.[2] The former group primarily contributes to the stabilization programs, while the latter consists of (potential) recipients, their national interests are not aligned, even though they share a common interest in the Eurozone stability. These divisions are clearly observable in the economic data (as illustrated in figure 10.1 and 10.2). They also project into policy preferences of the states with regard to Eurozone reforms (see figure 10.3) as the two groups of Eurozone members cluster in different quadrants of the relevant policy space.

**Figure 10.2 Current account deficits**

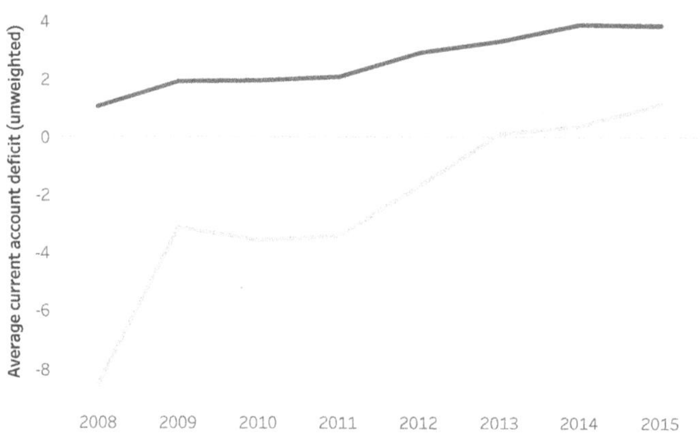


**Source**: Author's calculations based on Eurostat data. Note: Darker line depicts the "Northern" group and lighter one the "Southern" group.

---

[2] The "Northern" and "Southern" groups are empirical approximations based on prevailing economic interests. For the purposes of this chapter, the following countries are classified as "Northern" Austria, Estonia, Finland, Germany, Luxembourg, Malta, Netherlands and Slovakia, while Belgium, Cyprus, France, Greece, Ireland, Italy, Latvia, Lithuania, Portugal, Slovenia, and Spain are included in the "Southern" group. In order to indicate the tentative nature of this categorization, the group labels are presented in quotes.

Since the onset of the Euro crisis in 2009, the political interaction between the two groups of states is best characterized as muddling through. They were able to agree on Eurozone reforms including the introduction of the European Stability Mechanism (ESM) or the Banking Union, but only under the severe pressure of the crisis. Moreover, when the details of these breakthroughs agreements were specified, they converged on the most minimalist reform designs. While the muddling through is a justifiable reform strategy under highly uncertain and politically charged circumstances (see Lindblom 1959), it prolongs the time necessary for completing the Eurozone institutional architecture necessary for its long-term viability. Consequently, it induces a search for alternative scenarios and prolongs the time when reform processes are exposed to political challenge.

**Figure 10.3 Policy positions on fiscal discipline and redistribution**

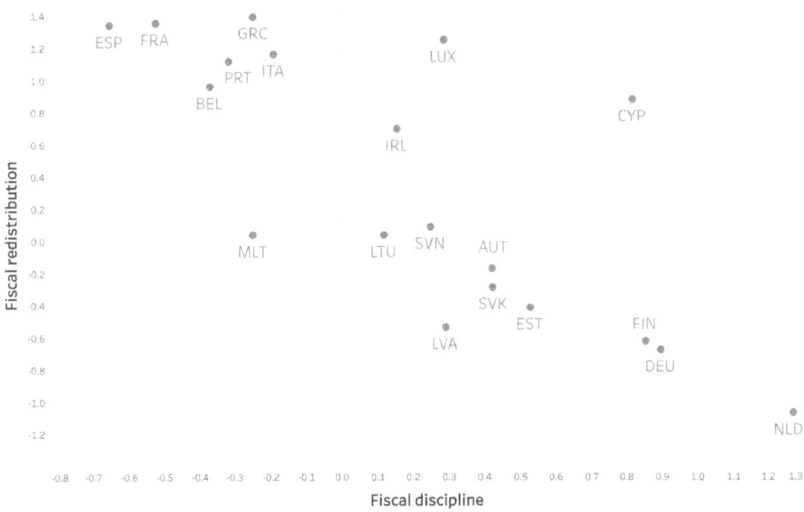


**Source**: Wasserfallen and Lehner (2017).

**Notes**: Data aggregate position scores on 44 policy issues related to the Greek programs, EFSF, ESM, Six- and Two-packs, banking union and fiscal union debated by member governments during the 2010 to 2015 period. Score are aggregated using the Bayesian procedure derived from Items Response Theory and depict member state ideal-points within the two-dimensional policy space.

The faster adoption of systematic reforms is blocked primarily by the opposition to the fiscal union in "Northern" countries. Their political leaders and electorates are not keen to introduce further risk- or fiscal-sharing measures beyond the ESM or single resolution pillar of the banking union. Moreover, the "Northern" political consensus is also weighting towards domestic fiscal austerity and current account surpluses, which deprives the "Southern" economies of indirect support from a more expansionary fiscal policy that would increase demand for their exports. At the same time, the reform stalemate combined with slow or no growth in the "Southern" group of countries make Eurozone vulnerable to political rejections of fiscal austerity. If governments or voters reject the fiscal discipline imposed by the stabilization programs and/or recent reforms of the Stability and Growth Pact (six–pack, two–pack and other changes to fiscal policy coordination), then they can trigger a full-blown crisis again. The North-South divide within the Eurozone thus generates three basic scenarios for further course of reforms: continued muddling through, the acceptance of greater solidarity in the "Northern" countries or the rejection of austerity in the "Southern" countries.

### 10.3. Continued Muddling Through

The muddling through reflects the absence of political consensus on more radical reform and has been the characteristic approach ever since the beginning of the crisis. Although it is generally criticized for keeping the Eurozone vulnerable, it has not been inconsequential. The EU in general and Eurozone, in particular, was able to stabilize the economy and implement reforms with substantial cumulative impact.

The fundamental element enabling gradualism in reforms is the policy of ECB. With the exception of the misguided increase in interest rates in 2011, the central bank adopted very accommodating monetary policy throughout the crisis. Since the interest rates were reduced practically to the zero bound, the ECB resorted to non-standard monetary policy measures. These consisted of operations supporting the liquidity of financial institutions through the long-term refinancing operations as well as several asset purchases programme designed to avoid deflation through buying of bonds and other securities. In combination with the clear commitment to maintaining the integrity of the Eurozone - epitomized by the statement of Mario Draghi that "the ECB is ready to do whatever it takes to preserve the euro. And believe me, it will be enough" (2012) - these programs stabilized financial markets from 2012 onwards. Consequently, they provided policy-makers with time to adopt and implement reforms both at the national and Eurozone levels.

The Euro crisis started in late 2009 when the extent of Greek deficits became apparent. Greece was no longer able to refinance its sovereign at the market conditions prevailing during spring 2010. In order to avoid its default, other Eurozone countries agreed to provide financial assistance. The first Greek program combined resources from bilateral loans with a loan from the International Monetary Fund. It was put together on ad hoc basis by the Eurogroup, although there was a debate whether to develop systematic support instruments. As solvency problems spread to Portugal and Ireland in

2011, the need for a sufficiently institutionalized solution became clear. Consequently, the EU has created the European Financial Stability Facility (EFSF) modeled on the pre-existing European Financial Stabilization Mechanism (EFSM), which together provided funding for the economic adjustment programs in the latter two countries (again the IMF provided co-financing).

The EFSF was the first new institution that provided the Eurozone with crisis management tool. It has been agreed in May 2010, but only as a temporary arrangement, because it lacked the basis in the EU law. Moreover, as the crisis continued, the effective lending capacity of programs for Greece, Portugal, and Ireland, proved insufficient. Eurozone governments had to increase EFSF's capital guarantees as well as broadening its portfolio of support instruments. The EFSF was upgraded in July and October 2011, in line with the preparation of the European Stability Mechanism. The new ESM overtook the EFSF's role and funded the next assistance programme - the banking sector stabilization in Spain in July 2012.

The ESM is the permanent crisis management mechanism that is fully embedded in the EU law. It was made possible when all EU member states adopted the necessary Treaty amendment and after all Eurozone states signed the ESM intergovernmental treaty. It is a major reform achievement that adds to completion of the Eurozone institutional framework. At the same time, it has not resulted from any grand reform design, but from the series of gradual reform stamps spanning from the first Greek Loan Facility, through the EFSF and its upgrades, to the permanent ESM arrangement. Hence, this reform case demonstrates the capacity of muddling through the approach to overcome political disagreements by a series of gradual, but functionally insufficient, reform steps that cumulatively transform into a major breakthrough.

The ESM is not the only achievement of the muddling through strategy. The banking union is a similarly significant reform of the Eurozone architecture. It was also achieved through a series of partial reforms starting with the introduction of the European Supervisory Authorities in 2009, followed by the decision to create the banking union in June 2012 and the subsequent development of the Single Supervisory Mechanism and Single Resolution Mechanism between 2012 and 2014 (see Kudrna 2016b). A similar argument could be made about reforms of economic and fiscal policy coordination, which has in a series of successive steps – so-called six- and two-packs - overhauled the Stability and Growth Pact in both its preventive and corrective functions.

Although the muddling through approach is capable of overcoming disputes and deliver reforms, there is a price for its gradualism: the longer it takes to complete reforms, the longer Eurozone remains vulnerable to economic and political shocks. Moreover, currently, even the gradualist muddling through seems to be losing momentum - as the urgency of the crisis dissipated after 2012, further reform measures are not even discussed. The equally significant political consequence of the muddling through approach is the deep division between "Northern" and "Southern" member states. While the Eurozone stabilization through fiscal discipline was relatively easy for the former group, it required extreme austerity in the latter states, which is still ongoing despite the return of growth. The rebalancing of economic activity within the Eurozone now relies primarily on the real effective exchange rate differentials, which is a very slow process, especially where markets are not fully integrated. Consequently, it is important to assess constraints that prevent faster and more systematic reform scenarios that could support rebalancing through the fiscal channel.

### 10.4. Northern Solidarity

The least the "Northern" group could do to stimulate economic growth and reforms in the "Southern" group, is to initiate more expansionary policies in their own economies. Given the trade interconnection within the Eurozone, any expansion in the North would support export-led growth in the South. However, the political emphasis in "Northern" countries that were constrained neither by excessive deficits nor debts was put on relative austerity and balanced budgets (see figure 10.4). This was especially pronounced in Germany, which is by far the most important economy and that kept practically balanced budget from 2012 on.

**Figure 10.4 Government deficits**

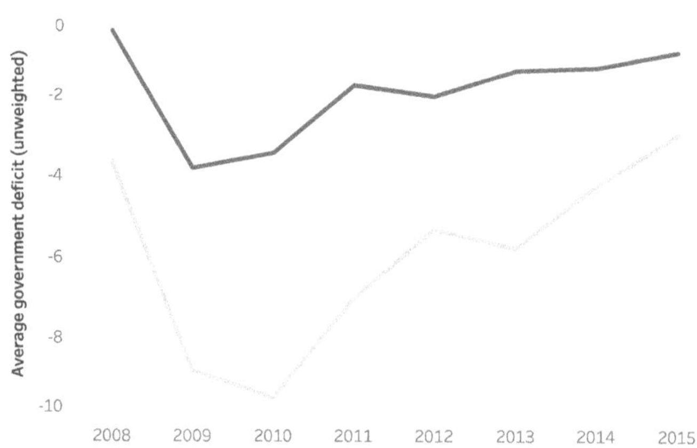


**Source**: Author's calculations based on Eurostat data.

**Note**: Darker line depicts the "Northern" group and lighter one the "Southern" group.

Beyond the coordination of national fiscal policies, the support of aggregate demand and economic reforms would be best achieved by introducing some elements of the fiscal union. In order to be able to withstand and cope with any asymmetric shocks, the Eurozone needs fiscal risk-sharing and stabilization mechanisms. While number of such mechanisms have been proposed, so far none of them was adopted. The suggested mechanisms differ in terms of potential redistribution, e.g. the percentage of GDP put at risk or temporarily transferred to Eurozone countries. At the lower end, is the idea of the cyclical adjustment insurance fund, that would transfer 1 to 2 percent of the Eurozone GDP. Guttenberg et al. (2013) outlined such an instrument and argued that the net payments from and to such a fund would be close to balance over the first decade of euro. In the early 2000s, when Germany faced an economic downturn, it would benefit from payments generated by booming "Southern" part of the Eurozone, including Greece and Spain. The flows would be reversed and broadly balanced by the onset of the Euro crisis in 2009.

Somewhat larger fiscal sharing, to the tune of 2 to 6 percent of Eurozone GDP, is implied by proposals for some kind of common unemployment insurance in the Eurozone (see Andor 2014, Dullien 2014, Beblavy and Maselli 2014). The Italian presidency initiated a Council debate on unemployment insurance based fiscal stabilizers in 2014, but there has been no progress towards some politically acceptable compromise. The same applies to even more ambitious proposals to introduce some kind of Eurobills (see Tumpel-Gugerell et al. 2014) or Eurobonds (Commission 2011, Allard et al. 2013). Myriad of these proposals put the shared fiscal resources to Eurozone GDP anywhere between single-digit percentages and 60 percent, but they were never discussed in the official fora beyond the Commission Green paper on Stability bonds (2011). Consequently, ESM/EFSF-issued bonds remain the only form of jointly guaranteed Eurobonds, while the mutualized part of the Single Resolution Fund represents the only new risk-sharing tool that has emerged from Eurozone reforms to date.[3]

The discussion of any elements of the fiscal union inevitably invokes the question of governance and political accountability. The leading idea in this domain seems to be Eurozone treasury (Enderlein and Haas 2015, Juncker et al. 2015). These proposals again range from minor changes to the current Eurogroup setup, such as introducing its permanent president, to a full-fledged ministry of finance that could oversee the ESM or even a separate

---

[3] TARGET2 payment system has also became de facto risk-sharing system, but it is not fiscal in nature.

Eurozone budget that may be created along the way to the fiscal union. Yet, this debate also failed to get any political traction.

Any element of the fiscal union requires treaty amendment that needs to be adopted with unanimous support from all member states. Therefore, any progress on this front would require a change in the political sentiment, especially in the "Northern" countries. As long as, electorates reject any new form of fiscal solidarity, the EMU reforms are unlikely to make headway over and above cumulative reforms achieved by muddling through. However, shifts in domestic politics may prevent even the muddling through and edge Eurozone towards disintegration.

### 10.5. Southern Adjustment

The Eurozone electorates have tolerated gradual reforms combined with stabilization through austerity. Voters in Greece and some other "Southern" countries have voted against this approach that increased the unemployment (see figure 10.5) and restrained growth (see figure 10.1). However, to date, none of these political challenges derailed the process of muddling through. Yet, the rejection of austerity and reforms may still come in any of the upcoming elections. Moreover, there seems to be growing sentiment that economic consequences of single-country exit from the Eurozone might be manageable. This was demonstrated by the "non-paper" of the German Ministry of Finance considering the possibility of a temporary departure from the single currency, which was presented during the charged negotiations of the third Greek support package in summer 2015 (Steinhauser 2015).

**Figure 10.5 Unemployment rates**

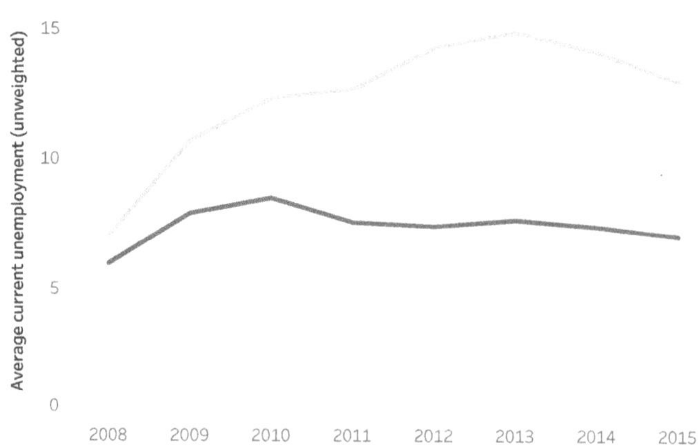


**Source**: Author's calculations based on Eurostat data.

**Note**: Darker line depicts the “Northern” group and lighter one the “Southern” group.

The Eurozone is currently much better equipped to manage contagion of any partial disintegration since the reforms implemented to date have reduced the incompleteness of its institutional architecture. The ESM, as well as the banking union, provide tools that were not available in 2012. Moreover, the private, as well as public sector actors, made an effort to understand the first-round effects of Grexit and similar scenarios and devised strategies to mitigate economic impact. In addition, much of the economic damage of Grexit has already been done. Its sovereign debt has been partially restructured and largely transferred to public institutions (ECB, IMF, ESM) so hardly any holder of these bonds could be surprised by default and/or further restructuring. Similarly, the Greek banking sector has already experienced capital flight and currently relies on public support from the ECB/IMF/ESM, while being sheltered by capital controls. Hence, the key deterrents to redenomination noted by Eichengreen (2007) - the fall-out from sovereign default and banking sector collapse - are somewhat reduced (and seemed even less relevant as the crisis flared in Summer of 2012 and 2015).[4]

Even if the economic conditions might be more manageable under current circumstances than at the earlier stages of the Euro crisis, the legal, procedural and political obstacles remain unpredictable. The Maastricht Treaty designed the single currency as irrevocable, therefore there is no legal procedure for the exit. Moreover, it seems that the only legal way to exit Eurozone is to exit the EU at the same time (Athanassiou 2009), which implies leaving the customs union, single market, and all other EU-related benefits. Such a legal set up only increases the potential economic damage and uncertainty.[5] However, Bootle et al. (2012) argue that economic, legal and technical obstacles could be overcome by a negotiated multilateral procedure for the Euro exit. They review the most likely economic consequences of the negotiated withdrawal and propose a series of measures that can mitigate their effects. While such scenarios might seem plausible on paper, they overestimate the political capacity of the EU to adopt and execute decisions with momentous and irreversible economic impact. The EU decision-making provides numerous checks and balances that practically prevent the swift adoption of a procedure for orderly exit or any secret pre-negotiations that essential for Bootle et al. (2012) and similar scenarios.

---

[4] Additional deterrent for exit might be the need of national central bank to settle the debt within the TARGET2 payment system of the Eurosystem.

[5] The Brexit procedure might clarify numerous aspects of the departure from the EU and thus improve our understanding of political and legal risks.

While the Eurozone increased its capacity to contain contagion of a single-country exit, the legal and political uncertainty remains as extreme as at the onset of the Euro crisis. Even if all important actors were able to prepare plausible exit scenarios, there is no way to secure legal and political commitment to them. Any such arrangements are exposed to unilateral defections as well as unpredictable legal challenges in courts. Hence, any decisive rejection of the single currency by voters in any Eurozone member states guarantees political and economic disruption not seen in Europe in decades. At the same time, this implication also serves as a potent deterrent for voters and/or possible populist governments that might be inclined to pursue break-up strategy.

### 10.6. Swans: Black, White and Grey

The three scenarios outlined above can be enhanced or hampered by various low-probability-high-impact events, referred to as black swans. The traditional expectation is that such "known and unknown unknowns" are likely to generate adverse outcomes. However, not all such events are necessarily bad for Eurozone reform and sustainability. There are also various white swans that can generate more cohesion that is conducive to policy changes. Moreover, some of the black swans may generate spill-over effects increase solidarity within the Eurozone and thus reduce political constraints on reforms necessary for its long-term sustainability. Since many of these events are non-economic in nature, it is difficult to judge ex-ante whether they might be black, white or grey.

The most obvious and relevant known-unknown is the development of the European and global economy. Low energy prices, expansionary monetary policies, lower Euro exchange rate and the return of global growth have already contributed to the stabilization of the Eurozone. Sustained recovery supports demand for European goods and services, thus supporting export-led recovery. In turn, growth makes adopting and implementing reforms easier and helps to contain political shocks. At the same time, the US elections have introduced a new level of uncertainty with regards to the free trade with the US and globally. The new US administration does not seem supportive of European integration and free trade. Its representatives have even accused Germany of unfairly exploiting undervalued Euro to the disadvantage of the US and other trading partners (Donnan 2017).

While the Grexit remains the likeliest case of Eurozone disintegration, the related known-unknown might be called “Grexident”. The Greek stabilization program requires regular rounds of reviews prior to releasing each tranche from the support package. At the same time, the domestic political logic compels any Greek government to contest the requests of the Troika institutions, in order to demonstrate an effort to protect interests of their voters. This regularly leads to tense negotiations running up to the latest possible deadline for the next bond repayment or another event. While the uncertainty related to the Greek referendum in June 2016 was an extreme example of this mechanism, it is likely to be repeated at every evaluation round. Consequently, there is a risk of a miscommunication during such negotiations that can trigger irreversible financial market overreaction damaging Greek and/or other Southern European sovereigns and financial institutions.

Brexit should also figure on the list of known unknowns relevant for the short-term future of the Eurozone. Although the UK is not part of the single currency, it is its most important financial center. The so-called hard Brexit implies that the city of London will not be part of the single market for financial services. While this provides an opportunity to repatriate Euro denominated trading back to the continent, it may also create risks to the financial stability as the EU27 financial institutions lose access to the deepest and most sophisticated financial markets in Europe. At the same time, the Brexit negotiations may also inspire closer political collaboration among Eurozone members, who need to complete the banking union and make progress on capital markets union as they substitute for City's services. Moreover, the Brexit debate has also increased the probability of another referendum on Scottish independence, which only highlights the risks of major disruptions originating from state dissolution. It is not entirely unthinkable in the UK, Spain and perhaps Belgium. Any dissolution inevitably presents a risk to the integrity of the Eurozone (and the sovereign bond markets), as there is no procedure for the successor states to maintain their EU membership.

The crisis-induced reforms such as the fiscal compact or banking union have increased the internal differentiation among the EU members. Moreover, there was a discernible increase in the political calls for multi-speed Europe during the run-up to the 60th anniversary of the Treaty of Rome (Wintour 2017). The representatives of the EU founding member states have suggested that the EU grew too large and too diverse for achieving a quick agreement on necessary reforms and implied that the core group of willing reformers should move ahead. While none of these calls suggested differentiation within the Eurozone, it is one of the options for moving ahead without Eurozone-wide consensus. The proposal for the financial transaction tax is currently testing the willingness of governments to pursue differentiated integration that does not cover all Eurozone members.

The Eurozone crisis is taking place in the context of other crises. The EU is facing a major wave of migration from its neighborhood, which in turn triggered strong political reactions in all member states. One of its consequences was a reintroduction of border controls within the Schengen area. Although controls are temporary and only minor nuisance for the free movement of goods and people, they could be escalated as the internal disputes about the refugee quotas continue. While the migration crisis adds to the overall uncertainty, it creates some silver-lining. Given the dramatic inflows to some "Northern" countries such as Germany, Austria or Sweden, the spending on maintenance, housing, and integration of refugees induces unplanned fiscal expansion.

The EU is also in the midst of a security crisis as it faced a series of terrorist attacks during the past two years. Moreover, the EU needs to respond to the Russian policy in its neighborhood, which includes invasion to Ukraine and Cold War-style military provocations. In addition, the new US administration is keen to stress that the European NATO members should comply with their military spending commitment of 2 percent of GDP. The policy response to such security challenges will require increased spending on security and defense, thus providing additional fiscal stimulus.

Given the definitional unpredictability of events that are behind the veil of uncertainty, this list of known unknowns remains speculative and cannot be systematic or complete in any way. There might be other factors derailing or enhancing the progress of Eurozone reforms then we can imagine. At the same time, the uncertainty does not imply that there are only adverse events in store.

## 10.7. Conclusion

The Eurozone has achieved economic stability and modest growth, yet it remains fragile as this stability relies excessively on the unorthodox monetary policies of the ECB. While reforms of its institutional architecture increased its capacity to manage crises, they are far from complete. The single currency needs to be underpinned by additional elements of economic, financial, fiscal and political unions. Reforms to date were achieved primarily by muddling through, which consisted of gradual and incomplete measures that were implemented at the latest possible moment at the peaks of the crisis. Over time, this reform strategy cumulatively achieved breakthroughs such as the ESM or banking union that would not have been possible before the Euro crisis, but it lost momentum as the immediate threat of disintegration subsided.

The muddling through is likely to continue, unless more systematic reform strategy is permitted by the shift in political consensus. This would require the "Northern" countries to accept more fiscal solidarity in exchange for more supranational control over national economies. At the same time, the muddling through can be disrupted either by voters in countries such as Greece, France or Italy or by any low-probability-high-impact event that is looming on and behind the horizon. The future of Eurozone reforms thus remains at a fragile impasse, awaiting political shock that would propel it either to further integration or disintegration. The Euro remains at the mercy of politics and uncertainty.

## 10.8. References

Allard, C., P. Koeva Brooks, J. C. Bluedorn et al. (2013). Toward a Fiscal Union for the Euro Area; IMF Staff Discussion Note SDN 13/09, 1–29.

Andor, L (2014) Basic European Unemployment Insurance – The Best Way Forward in Strengthening the EMU's Resilience and Europe's Recovery. Intereconomics 49 (4), 184-203.

Athanassiou, P. (2009). Withdrawal and expulsion from the EU and EMU: Some reflections. ECB Legal Working Paper Series, 1–50.

Bauer, M. W., and Becker, S. (2014). The Unexpected Winner of the Crisis: The European Commission's Strengthened Role in Economic Governance. Journal of European Integration, 36(3), 213-229.

Beblavy, M. and Maselli, I. (2014). An Unemployment Insurance Scheme for the Euro Area: A simulation exercise of two options. CEPS Special Report no. 98. Brussels: Centre for European Policy Studies.

Bootle, R. (2012). Leaving the Euro: A Practical Guide. Wolfson Economics Prize Paper.

Commission (2011). Green paper on the feasibility of introducing Stability Bonds. Brussels: European Commission.

Commission (2012). Blueprint for a Deep and Genuine EMU. Brussels: European Commission.

De Rynck, S. (2015). Banking on a union: the politics of changing Eurozone banking supervision. Journal of European Public Policy, 23(1), 119–135.

Donnan, S. (2017) Trump's top trade adviser accuses Germany of currency exploitation. Financial Times, Jan 31.

Draghi, M. (2012) Speech by Mario Draghi, President of the European Central Bank at the Global Investment Conference in London, 26 July. Available at https://www.ecb.europa.eu/press/key/date/2012/html/sp120726.en.html.

Dullien, S. (2014) The Macroeconomic Stabilisation Impact of a European Basic Unemployment Insurance Scheme. Intereconomics 49 (4), 184-203.

Eichengreen, B. (2007). The Breakup of the Euro Area. NBER Working Paper 13393, 11–56.

Enderlein, H., and Haas, J. (2015). What Would a European Finance Minister Do? A Proposal. Jacques Delors Institut Berlin, Policy Paper 145.

Enderlein, H., Vitorino, A., Sapir, A., Rodrigues, M. J., Pisani-Ferry, J., Piris, J.-C., et al. (2012). Completing the Euro: A road map towards fiscal union in Europe. Report of the Tommaso Padoa-Schioppa Group.

Guttenberg, L., Enderlein, H., and Spiess, J. (2013). Making One Size Fit All: Designing a Cyclical Adjustment Insurance Fund for the Eurozone. Notre Europe Policy Paper 61.

Howarth, D., and Quaglia, L. (2013). Banking Union as Holy Grail: Rebuilding the Single Market in Financial Services, Stabilizing Europe's Banks and 'Completing' Economic and Monetary Union. Journal of Common Market Studies, 51(S1).

Juncker, J. C., Tusk, D., Dijsselbloem, J., and Draghi, M. (2015). Completing Europe's Economic and Monetary Union. Brussels: European Commission.

Kudrna, Z. (2016a) The EU's Capital Markets Union: Unlocking Investment Through Gradual Integration. Washington: Atlantic Council.

Kudrna, Z. (2016b). Financial market regulation: crisis-induced supranationalization. Journal of European Integration, 38(3), 251–264.

Lindblom, C. E. (1959). The science of "Muddling through." Public Administration Review, 19(2), 79-88.

Schimmelfennig, F. (2014). European Integration in the Euro Crisis: The Limits of Post-functionalism. Journal of European Integration, 36(3).

Steinhauser, G. (2015). German Document Floats Five-Year Greek Exit From Eurozone, Wall Street Journal, July 11.

Stiglitz, J. (2016). The Euro: How a Common Currency Threatens the Future of Europe. W. W. Norton and Company.

Tsebelis, G., and Hahm, H. (2014). Suspending vetoes: how the Euro countries achieved unanimity in the fiscal compact. Journal of European Public Policy, 21(10), 1388-1411.

Tumpel-Gugerell, G., Benassy-Quere, A., Bento, V., Hoogduin, L., Mazak, J., Romana, B., et al. (2014). Expert group on Debt Redemption Fund and Eurobills. Brussels: European Commission.

Wasserfallen, F. and Lehner, T. (2017), Mapping contestation on fiscal integration: Evidence from new data, paper presented at the SVPW annual conference, St. Gallen, January 12, 2017.

Wintour, P. (2017). Plans for two-speed EU risk split with 'peripheral' members. The Guardian, February 14.

# Conclusion

Europe appears to be on the crossroad. Economic recession morphed into the political stability problem and challenges to both the European project and the European idea itself. To preserve the achievement of the last 60 years, Europe has to reinvent itself and to face both the resurrected spirits of the past and the challenges of the future squarely. The globalization with its bright promises and often misunderstood challenges is here to stay, albeit in the dynamic and somewhat unpredictable form. To face the globalization challenges, Europe has to re-invent itself. EU 2.0 if you wish.

The restoration of economic dynamism is increasingly perceived as the answer for the "European" future – economically, politically and socially. There is a broad consensus that dynamic structural reforms and the restoration of competitiveness on the scale of the global economy are the key answers to current European challenges. However, there are no answers yet to deeper questions: What do mean the structural reforms in particular? What is the role of capital flows? And what constitutes the improvement in global competitiveness?

Moreover, recently an entirely new set of issues came to the forefront. Complex realities which determined the negative vote in the UK referendum in June 2016 appear to have little in common with the economic realities – after all, the UK economic performance in the aftermath of the recession 2009-2010, even if not exemplary, was certainly better than most of other EU countries. Rather, the result of the vote can be attributed to cultural and socio-political factors, from the uncomfortable feelings associated with the increasing presence (both in and out of jobs) of nationals from the other, especially eastern EU member countries, to the resentment triggered by a rising role of a "continental" legal, social, managerial and "lifestyle" practices, often considered "un-british" and being forced on the UK by country's membership in the EU.

The above-described issues are not limited to British Isles. In different "disguises" they afflict many EU countries – developed ones like France, Netherlands, to some degree Italy and Austria, as well as the "new member countries" like Hungary, Poland and Slovakia. Commonly described as "populism" or "neo-nationalism", this wave of political activism by disgruntled groups brings a new dimension to EU political reality and the discussions of the Union's future.

On the European continent, the direct political influence of the neo-nationalism still appears to be limited, except Hungary and to some degree Poland. However, it affects the policy approaches of major parties (Netherlands, Italy, Slovakia) and as a such makes the further integration steps on the EU level both more difficult and more complicated.

Contributions in this volume concentrate on the economic side of the "European" processes. Political contexts and the newly emerging socio-political realities are not at the center of analyses, even if they are not ignored and their influence is recognized by several authors.

Indeed, the actual impact of the "new realities" is still in the future. One may surmise that there will be the latent tension between the economic imperatives of future transnational integration processes and the renewed emphasis on the "national specifics".

The possible (and perhaps even desirable) answer is to proceed in relatively small partial steps, even if some of these may appear as steps backwards. As an example can serve the possibility of the cross-union application of an idea contemplated in Germany – specifically the requirement of the five years working residency period before any legibility for welfare provisions in any country (except the original country of citizenship). Such a measure would address mounting concerns about "welfare tourism" and could be considered as a step toward a pan-european welfare state.

Another possible step addressing the seemingly contradictory requirements of both further integration and the "need" to recognize the "national specificities" could be to determine the "minimum retirement income", applicable uniformly across the EU and financed from the tax revenues of individual countries. Retirement payments over and above this minimum would be provided by different jurisdictions according to individual's tax contributions in these jurisdictions. Indeed, the system would have to be unified across the EU – hence the element of a "structural convergence". Moreover, such a system would provide a pension portability, and hence it would contribute both to labor mobility and an increased productivity via improved resource allocation.

The discussion by authors in this book indicates that the 60 years of the European integration history can be interpreted as the combined processes of structural reforms and the structural convergence. The effort was largely successful, resulting in the creation of the economic body of almost 450 million people (post-Brexit). And, indeed, it is the biggest voluntary non-military association of countries dedicated to freedom and liberty in the world history.

However, attempts to move beyond the economic aspects of the European integration are much less successful and often trigger resentment. And this reality includes not only immigration (both internal and external) but elements of fiscal policies – both taxation and expenditures – as well. Obviously, the wish is not strong enough to erase 1500 years of history and to form a single European identity. Such an identity should be built gradually, building on and incorporating existing diversities, not only economic but cultural and historical as well.

*Editors* *Selinsgrove and Brno, June, 2017*

*Lubor Lacina*

*Antonín Rusek*

# Index

www.ingramcontent.com/pod-product-compliance
Lightning Source LLC
LaVergne TN
LVHW010721210926
848485LV00007B/1411/J
* 9 7 8 1 6 2 2 7 3 2 6 3 0 *